O

Operation Squarepeg

*The Allied Invasion
of the Green Islands,
February 1944*

REG NEWELL

McFarland & Company, Inc., Publishers
Jefferson, North Carolina

LIBRARY OF CONGRESS CATALOGUING-IN-PUBLICATION DATA

Names: Newell, Reg, 1954– author.
Title: Operation Squarepeg : the allied invasion of the Green Islands, February 1944 / Reg Newell.
Description: Jefferson, North Carolina : McFarland & Company, Inc., Publishers, 2017. | Includes bibliographical references and index.
Identifiers: LCCN 2017041547 | ISBN 9780786478385 (softcover : acid free paper) ∞
Subjects: LCSH: World War, 1939–1945—Campaigns—Papua New Guinea. | New Zealand—Armed Forces—History—World War, 1939–1945. | World War, 1939–1945—Amphibious operations.
Classification: LCC D767.95 .N49 2017 | DDC 940.54/26592—dc23
LC record available at https://lccn.loc.gov/2017041547

BRITISH LIBRARY CATALOGUING DATA ARE AVAILABLE

**ISBN (print) 978-0-7864-7838-5
ISBN (ebook) 978-1-4766-2832-5**

© 2017 Reg Newell. All rights reserved

No part of this book may be reproduced or transmitted in any form or by any means, electronic or mechanical, including photocopying or recording, or by any information storage and retrieval system, without permission in writing from the publisher.

Front cover: Embarking from Pokonian Plantation in Papua New Guinea for reconnaissance of Nissan Island on January 31, 1944 (Archives New Zealand)

Printed in the United States of America

McFarland & Company, Inc., Publishers
 Box 611, Jefferson, North Carolina 28640
 www.mcfarlandpub.com

To all those who fought in the Solomon Islands
for freedom from tyranny, and most especially
Major General H.E. Barrowclough and
Rear Admiral T.S. Wilkinson.

Acknowledgments

I would like to thank all of those people who assisted me with this work. Most especially, I would like to thank the veterans Ross Templeton, John Rose, Harry Bioletti, William Laurence, and Ron Tucker. I would like to acknowledge the pioneering work on the Green Islands done by Milton Bush, a veteran of 93NCB, and the assistance of the USS *St. Louis* website. I would like to acknowledge the research assistance of R. Robert Palmer of Missouri, an American researcher of Operation Squarepeg.

The New Zealand Ministry of Culture and Heritage has kindly granted permission to quote from the New Zealand official war histories. Archives New Zealand kindly granted permission to reproduce photos of Operation Squarepeg.

Thanks are due to Ms. Kirsty Nolan for typing this work.

Above all thanks to my wife Heather and my son Michael, for putting up with my obsession with Operation Squarepeg and in the knowledge that every hour spent on this work was at their expense.

Table of Contents

Acknowledgments	vi
Introduction	1
One. The Strategic Landscape, January 1944	3
Two. The Opposing Forces	10
Three. The "Commando Raid"—A Reconnaissance in Force	18
Four. Planning an Amphibious Invasion	52
Five. Bloody St. Valentine's Day—The Ordeal of USS *St. Louis*	67
Six. Invasion	72
Seven. The Push Inland	103
Eight. Japanese Resistance	107
Nine. Tank and Infantry Action at Tanaheran	110
Ten. Aftermath and Consolidation	121
Eleven. Significance and Legacy	172
Chronology	175
Glossary	180
Appendices	194
I: New Zealand Order of Battle for the "Commando Raid," 30 January 1944	194
II: New Zealand Order of Battle, Operation Squarepeg, 15 February 1944	194

Table of Contents

    III: New Zealand and American Units Involved in Operation Squarepeg, 15 February 1944 — 195
    IV: U.S. Naval Forces Involved with Operation Squarepeg, 15 February 1944 — 196
    V: U.S. Navy Task Organization for Squarepeg — 197
    VI: Specifications of the Valentine Tanks of 3NZ Division Tank Squadron — 197
    VII: Echelons to the Green Islands — 197

Chapter Notes — 198
Bibliography — 207
Index — 211

Introduction

In late January 1944, a small force of American and New Zealand soldiers and specialists carried out a hazardous reconnaissance of the Japanese-held Green Islands. Two weeks later the Allied invasion of the Green Islands, codenamed Operation Squarepeg,[1] took place. The invasion faced significant risks and involved a thrust into strategically important Japanese territory. The Japanese defenders were rapidly overwhelmed, and the invasion came to be considered as an example of how a World War II amphibious operation should be carried out.

Operation Squarepeg required rigorous cooperation between the various arms of the American and New Zealand forces. It would prove to be the last operation carried out by 3NZ Division before its disbandment.

Nonetheless, the initial reconnaissance and subsequent invasion remain obscure and are known only to the surviving veterans, their families, the inhabitants of the Green Islands, and specialists in the war in the South Pacific. It is the purpose of this work to illuminate what occurred and to pay tribute to those Allied personnel who made Squarepeg such a resounding success.

One

The Strategic Landscape, January 1944

On 7 December 1941, the Great Pacific War began with a Japanese air raid on Pearl Harbor, Hawaii, which devastated the battleships of the U.S. Navy's Pacific Fleet. The Japanese invaded and overran Malaya, the Philippines, Hong Kong, Burma and the Dutch East Indies. For a period of six months the forces of the Empire of Japan seemed unstoppable. Japanese soldiers earned a grim reputation as skilled, brutal adversaries who fought to the death.

The Japanese juggernaut was halted at two previously obscure but strategic islands. At Midway in June 1942 the Japanese main aircraft carrier force, the Kido Butai, was eviscerated. Between August 1942 and January 1943, a seesaw battle between American and Japanese air, land and sea forces took place for control of the island of Guadalcanal. This resulted in a Japanese defeat and withdrawal.

The year 1943 saw Japanese forces in the Pacific on the defensive. As American military might began to flow into the Pacific, the Allies began the slow pushback of the Japanese. Amphibious warfare expertise allowed the Allies to develop "island-hopping" techniques, using sea power to bypass Japanese strongpoints and to land in areas where the Japanese were weak. The establishment of naval and air bases enabled the Allies to cut Japanese supply lines and render Japanese garrisons ineffective.

As 1944 began, it was clear that the Allies were on the road to victory. However, bitter experience had shown that Japanese soldiers were tough adversaries that had to be burned or blown out of their fortifications. Although the quality of Japanese pilots had markedly deteriorated, Japanese air power remained potent. The nimble Zero fighter plane continued to be respected by Allied pilots. The Imperial Japanese Navy was determined to fight a decisive Trafalgar-like battle which it hoped would tip the Pacific war in Japan's favor. Above all there was an element of desperation on the part of the Japanese military as Allied forces began to advance closer to the Japanese home islands.

Rabaul, Operation Cartwheel and the Genesis of Operation Squarepeg

The main Japanese base in the South Pacific was located at Rabaul, New Britain, and it dominated the strategy of both the Allies and the Japanese. With its airfields and naval base it posed a major threat to any Allied advance up the Solomons chain or into the Philippines. For the Japanese it was a key part of their interlocking defensive system. Allied planners in 1943 developed Operation Cartwheel, a series of complex amphibious operations, with General Douglas MacArthur's forces thrusting northwards along the coast of Papua New Guinea and Admiral William Halsey's

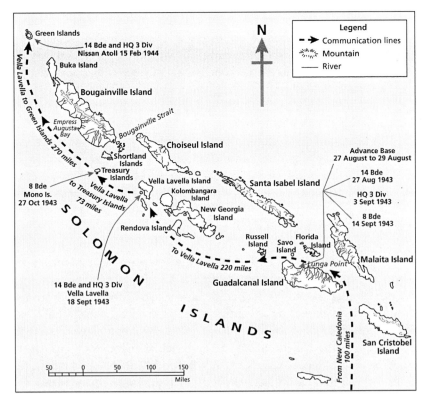

Map one, 3NZ Division in South Pacific (Fran Whild).

One. The Strategic Landscape, January 1944

forces in the Solomon Islands attacking northwards. The two axes of advance were designed to be mutually supporting and to use land-based air power. The original intent had been to invade New Britain and capture Rabaul, but the United States Joint Chiefs of Staff wisely decided instead to isolate Rabaul by air and sea and thereby neutralize it.

As always in the Pacific War, the ability to establish an airfield and project air power was the key to victory. Admiral William "Bull" Halsey, the American commander in the South Pacific (COMSOPAC), considered that taking Kavieng should be the next step in encircling Rabaul. However, the problem was that the seizure of Kavieng could not take place for some time, leaving a hiatus in major operations that he feared "would kill the momentum of the South Pacific Drive." His boss, Admiral Chester Nimitz, wanted "some intermediate operation undertaken in order to retain the initiative and to provoke enemy reactions which would enable us to engage his forces." The Green Islands, a part of Papua New Guinea, at the northern end of the Solomon Islands chain, fitted "the geometric requirements" in that they were close enough to Kavieng for fighter operations to be launched against it, but also within fighter coverage of the Allied airfields at Torokina, Bougainville. The seizure of Emirau was considered as an alternative to Kavieng and it was thought the Green Islands operation would assist this as well.[1] Furthermore, the establishment of a PT boat base on the Green Islands would enable the interdiction of Japanese supply barges traveling between New Ireland and Bougainville. The important thing, however, is that by seizing the Green Islands, it virtually halved the distance from the Allied airfield at Torokina to the main Japanese base at Rabaul.[2] With the seizure of the Green Islands, the encirclement of Japanese forces on Bougainville and Buka would be complete, and a further link would be forged in the iron chain around Rabaul. As Halsey later described it, "Commanding the eastern approach to Rabaul was Green Island." Halsey considered that once the Green Islands, Emirau and Manus Island fell into Allied hands, "Japan's South Pacific Campaign would fall with them."[3]

Halsey still had to convince his superiors Admiral Ernest King, Commander in Chief of the U.S. Navy, and his immediate superior Admiral Chester Nimitz that the best option was to seize the Green Islands. Meetings between King and Nimitz took place in early January 1944 and Halsey's plan for taking the Green Islands was thoroughly examined. King's main objection was that the Green Islands were not suitable for a naval base, but Nimitz countered by pointing out that the alternative, Kavieng, was not suitable either. The clincher was that the Green Islands had the potential to dominate the approaches to Rabaul.[4] Halsey got his green light to proceed.

What made the Green Islands attractive to American planners also made the operation risky. With the main Japanese base at Rabaul only one hundred and seventeen miles away, and Japanese-held Buka thirty-six miles to the southeast, a vigorous Japanese response was likely, especially as the Green Islands were an important link in the Japanese supply system from Rabaul to Buka. As with operations that units of 3NZ Division had undertaken at Vella Lavella and the Treasury Islands, there was substantial risk. Time was allowed for the "partial neutralisation of the powerful enemy air base at Rabaul." Although the seizure of the Green Islands could have been undertaken by 15 January 1944, it was thought expedient to degrade Japanese air capabilities, and the invasion target date was set for 15 February.[5] The codename "Squarepeg" was allocated to the invasion. On 24 January, Admiral Halsey confirmed 15 February as D–Day and gave 3NZ Division (less 8 Brigade, deployed on the Treasury Islands) the task.[6] Admiral Theodore Stark Wilkinson, USN, as Commander of Task Force 31, became the overall commander, with the New Zealand commander, Major General Harold Barrowclough, taking tactical command of the landing.[7] Consequently, the headquarters of 3NZ Division shifted from Vella Lavella to Guadalcanal on 5 January.

The New Zealand unit chosen for the assault on the Green Islands, 14 Brigade, had been involved in stiff fighting while clearing Japanese forces from Vella Lavella. Afterward, 14 Brigade had continued regular patrols around Vella Lavella. In addition, 30 Battalion was selected for further amphibious training on Barga Island on 1–3 December 1943. For the rest of the brigade, further specialist jungle training took place, involving fire and movement exercises. The brigade was ready for further combat operations by December 1943.[8]

There were risks involved in the operation due to Japanese forces on New Ireland, New Britain, Bougainville and Buka. Barrowclough decided that "my force should be strengthened by the inclusion of the 144 Ind Bty [Independent Battery] and the Tank Squadron, though it might not be possible to get the latter organisation into the island until the second or third echelon."[9]

The seizure of the Green Islands was, however, only one aspect. The second was that the islands had then to be turned into an operational base, and that entailed constructing airfields, a naval base and complex logistic infrastructure. Bombs, aviation and naval fuel, and mountains of supplies had to be landed, sorted and safely stored in an organized fashion. The New Zealanders were no strangers to this procedure, having experienced this on Vella Lavella and the Treasury Islands.

The Target—The Green Islands

The Green Islands, part of the Bismarck Archipelago, are located four degrees south of the equator and are situated to the northwest of Bougainville, where by November 1943 the Allies held an enclave at Empress Augusta Bay, and one hundred and seventeen miles from the main Japanese base on Rabaul to the west. The Green Islands are often referred to as "Nissan."[10] The confusion arises because Nissan Island makes up ninety per cent of the land area.

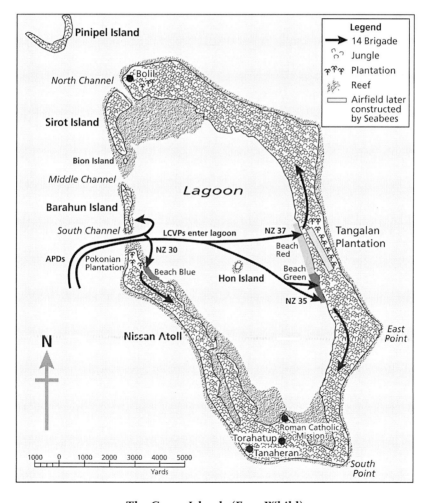

The Green Islands (Fran Whild).

Nissan, the main coral atoll of the group, is thirty-seven miles north-norwest of Bougainville and fifty-five miles from the southeastern end of New Britain. An almost complete oval of solid coral, it is nine miles north to south and five miles east to west. There are three access channels into the inner deep lagoon—north, middle and south. The southern channel was the best, although only sixteen feet deep and up to fifty feet wide. Coral reefs ring the atoll except on the lagoon's eastern shore. The geography of Nissan would later pose problems for unloading cargo. Except for coconut plantations and native clearings, the whole island was swathed in thick jungle. There are two small islands, Barahun and Sirot, just above sea level and covered in thick vegetation and coconut plantations, and these are at the entranceways to the lagoon. There is a very small island called Hon, located in the middle of the lagoon. Although aerial photos indicated the practicability of building an airfield, there was no certainty that this could be done. Nor was it certain that large landing craft could be beached.[11] The main channel between Nissan and Barahun is only fifteen feet deep, restricting its use to shallow draft vessels.

Pinipel Island, located about a mile to the northwest of Nissan, is shaped rather like a horseshoe. It is about three hundred and thirty-three feet high and has prominent cliffs about six miles in length. A New Zealand report commented, "A common feature of The Green Islands is that they are thickly wooded and present to the sea, for the most part, steep cliff faces."[12]

The character of Nissan was captured by a sailor, Alan J. Villiers, who had sailed his sailing ship *Joseph Conrad* there in the prewar period: "A small atoll it is hit by the heavy surf which hit against the low undercut coral cliffs to send plumes of water feathering high in the air in a series of continuous fountains which are visible for miles."[13] The climate is tropical with rainy seasons from December to March and May to October. Rainfall varies from 120 to 140 inches per year. The abundant rainfall meant that vegetation tended to be thick. Nissan is only four degrees from the Equator, so most days are warm and humid. The average daily temperature is in the twenties centigrade. Seasonal and trade winds ensure plentiful rain.

In the prewar period a Roman Catholic mission had been established on Nissan. It had a dwelling built of local materials, a large church, a storeroom and quarters for the islanders. Water supply was by catchment into four tanks.[14]

In 1944, there was a population of some one thousand one hundred and forty-seven Melanesians. They were mainly located on Nissan, with some living on Pinipel Island. The islanders were able to grow some crops in the light volcanic soil, and taro was the main crop. They also subsisted on pigs, goats and chickens. This was supplemented by fish and other seafood. The islanders speak a non–Austronesian language of which there are two dialects, one for Nissan and one for Pinipel. They also speak Melanesian Pidgin.

The health of the islanders varied. Sirot Village had a population of eighteen people, a fifth of whom were afflicted with leprosy. Barahun Island had been inhabited, but the population fled to Yotchibol Village because about 40 percent of them suffered from elephantitis, which they attributed to "evil spirits" on Barahun. A hospital had been built near Periwon. Its facilities consisted of two wards and a native orderly's quarters. A paramount medical orderly named Balus, who had been employed by the Department of Public Health for some seventeen years, was in charge of the medical work and was considered "a splendid type of native."[15]

A copra plantation had been established at Tangalan. A plantation manager had, prior to the Japanese entry into the war, lived in a five-room house made of local materials. Because the plantation area had been developed, it had good roads. There were also good tracks from Tangalan to Balil. A rough track connected the mission with Yotchibol Village.

Water was a critical problem. Wells had been dug, but these yielded only brackish water unfit for human consumption. Capturing rainwater was essential to the population's survival.

There were two good anchorages, one just opposite Yotchibol Village and the second opposite the Mission. An Australian, Flight Lieutenant Robson, was familiar with the area from the prewar period. He recalled that his vessel had experienced difficulty in anchoring at the plantation wharf due to the deep water.

The Japanese had captured the Green Islands on 23 January 1942, and seized Mr. C.C. Jervis, a plantation manager and coastwatcher. (He died when the *Montevideo Maru* was sunk on 1 July 1942, en route to Japan. The number of Australian P.O.W.s drowned make this Australia's greatest maritime disaster.)

The Japanese made use of Nissan as part of their network of barging stations linking their main base at Rabaul with their forces on Buka and Bougainville. The Japanese crews would take advantage of the close vegetation to hide their barges during the day and move during the night to escape air and naval attack. Allied aerial reconnaissance indicated that the Japanese had garrisoned the area lightly and that the numbers of Japanese defenders would fluctuate as barges visited the islands.

Two

The Opposing Forces

The Americans—William Halsey's men

The Americans would contribute three elements to Operation Squarepeg. Firstly, they would provide the shipping to transport troops and supply those troops, plus the naval gunfire to protect the vulnerable transports and pound the invasion beaches and fend off predatory Japanese aircraft. Secondly, they would provide air power to protect Allied forces. Thirdly, they would provide specialist support troops which would enable the full benefits of the seizure of the Green Islands to be obtained. These specialist troops would include Argus Unit 7 to operate radar facilities and the famed Seabees, the Naval Construction Battalions, which would construct airfields and naval facilities.

THE SEABEES (NAVAL CONSTRUCTION BATTALIONS—C.B.s)

The men of the Naval Construction Battalions, also known as the "Seabees," were one of America's war-winning secret weapons. Admiral Moreel, USN, had persuaded the U.S. Navy to recruit construction workers to do heavy construction work for it. The Seabees were used to construct airfields, roads, jetties, buildings, and all manner of infrastructure. They performed prodigies of engineering work in rapid time and enabled the momentum of the Allied island-hopping campaign across the Pacific to be maintained.

The motto of the Seabees was "We build, we fight," and throughout the Pacific War they proudly lived up to this motto. Their primary purpose was to build infrastructure, but inevitably they came under enemy fire. On the Treasury Islands in October 1943, a mixed force of New Zealanders and Seabees had fought side-by-side at Soantalu. There was immense mutual admiration between the two groups.

The Seabees were generally older, mature men who had been involved in the heavy engineering projects of the Great Depression, including Boulder Dam. Because of their age, it was a common jibe amongst the U.S. Marines: "You should never be rude to a Seabee—he could be your father!"

The Seabees received basic military and specialized training in the continental United States and were then deployed in units to where they were needed, including Europe, the Mediterranean and especially the Pacific.

Acorn Units

Acorn units were designed "to accomplish the rapid construction and operation of a land plane and seaplane airbase, or in conjunction with amphibious operations, the quick repair and operation of a captured enemy airfield."[1] The Green Islands were devoid of Japanese airstrips. The Allies would have to create their own. Usually an Acorn unit would be paired up with a CASU, a Carrier Air Servicing Unit, and or a PATSU, a seaplane servicing unit. Argus units were also sometimes attached.

Argus Units

Argus units operated and coordinated various types of air and surface radars. They were essential to effective fighter defense.

The U.S. Marine Corps

The U.S. Marines had developed amphibious warfare doctrine in the interwar period. The *Tentative Manual of Amphibious Operations* provided the blueprint for how amphibious operations in the Pacific were to be carried out. Although no USMC personnel would be deployed on the Green Islands, the imprint of the Corps was to be found in the planning of the invasion.

The U.S. Navy

Various ships of the U.S. Navy were deployed for Operation Squarepeg to provide naval gunfire support if required, to provide AA gunfire, and less glamorously to transport the invading troops.

By January 1944 the USN had achieved dominance over their Japanese counterparts in the Solomons. Nonetheless, the battleships of the

Major General Harold E. Barrowclough (left) and his GSO1 Colonel John Brooke soon after the landing on Nissan. Nissan Green Island 1944. [Archives Reference ADQZ 18905, WA117, 3/16 E11], Archives New Zealand, The Department of Internal Affairs, Te Tari Taiwhenua.

Imperial Japanese Navy still remained a formidable threat until their destruction in the Battle of Leyte Gulf in June 1944.

The Kiwis—Barrowclough's men

The New Zealanders of 3NZ Division, or "Kiwis" (after the national flightless bird) were New Zealand's contribution to the land war in the South Pacific. 3NZ Division had been formed from the cadre of troops sent to garrison Fiji in 1940–41. The men of 3NZ Division were essentially "citizen soldiers" who had enlisted or been conscripted for the duration of the war. Very few of them had been in the Army in the prewar period. The soldiers represented a cross section of New Zealand society. A New Zealand officer, John Rose, found in his first command in 1941 that he was the youngest in his platoon of thirty-five men. He considered that the older age of his men had a stabilizing effect. "There were a lot of farmers, self sufficient and self reliant people. There was a mixture of school teachers, carpenters, all sorts of people."[2] Under the dynamic leadership of Major General Harold Eric Barrowclough, the division had been formed in 1943 and deployed to the Solomon Islands. Due to acute manpower shortages, the division was an understrength two-brigade formation. The New Zealand soldiers had been successfully employed with 14 Brigade clearing Vella Lavella of Japanese troops and 8 Brigade amphibiously assaulting the Treasury Islands (Operation Goodtime). The New Zealand troops were well trained and well supplied and enjoyed high morale. They, with the help of the U.S. Navy, had mastered the techniques of tropical warfare and amphibious assaults.

For Operation Squarepeg, the New Zealand force would consist of 14 Brigade, 3NZ Divisional Headquarters, and supporting elements. Unlike prior engagements undertaken by units of 3NZ Division, the troops on the Green Islands would be under the direct command of Major Gen-

Brigadier Potter circa 1944. Nissan Green Island 1944 [Archives Reference ADQZ 18905, WA117, 3/16 E11], Archives New Zealand, The Department of Internal Affairs, Te Tari Taiwhenua.

eral H.E. Barrowclough. A lawyer in his civilian life, the much-decorated Barrowclough was a battle-hardened veteran of the Western Front in World War I. In World War II he had been in command of 6 Infantry Brigade, 2NZ Division, and had taken part in the grueling Greek and Western Desert campaigns. Barrowclough had been recalled to New Zealand to develop 3NZ Division and had used his superb administrative skills to create a cohesive, well-trained, well-equipped formation. The division had been involved in brigade-sized actions on Vella Lavella and the Treasury Islands, but Barrowclough had not been able to have full involvement in the planning and fighting. Squarepeg, however, was his chance, and Squarepeg was to be Barrowclough's show. He would finally be given an opportunity to use his skills as a divisional commander.

Brigadier Leslie Potter, the commander of 14 Brigade, in contrast, was a professional soldier. He had also served as a junior officer on the Western Front in World War I, but in the interwar period had undertaken various staff and administrative military positions. He was appointed to command 14 Brigade in 1943 and executed the attacks on Japanese forces on Vella Lavella in September 1943, which expelled the enemy from the island.

For Squarepeg, the Kiwis would utilize the Valentine Mark III infantry tanks of 3NZ Tank Squadron. By 1944 the Valentine was obsolete, but its close support gun was still potent. The effort of involving tanks in the Green Islands operation was thought to be justified because the tanks were a force multiplier to make up for the lack of infantry. The Japanese were likely to have pillboxes, which tanks could eliminate, and it was also thought that the experience of transporting the tanks and using them in combat operations in jungle conditions would be beneficial in later combat operations.

Although the soldiers of 8 Brigade had received training in infantry-tank cooperation, their compatriots in 14 Brigade had not. This would bear bitter fruit later as coordination of infantry and tank elements proved problematic.

The proposed use of tanks was not, however, without its teething problems. On Guadalcanal a demonstration of the capabilities of the tanks was organized at Mt. Stewart. It was intended to show to Barrowclough and other members of the brass just what the tanks could do in a close support role. The brass were duly impressed, but not in the way intended. Because of the close vegetation, it was difficult to observe where the tank shells were landing. The tank crew were supposed to clear the breech of the tank barrel before firing, but on this occasion they failed to do so. A shell plummeted into the hill behind the assembled brass and matters came to an abrupt close.[3]

Although 14 Brigade had been involved in coastal operations around Vella Lavella in September 1943, the invasion of the Green Islands would be the first full-blown amphibious assault undertaken by 14 Brigade. It had, however, had the benefit of amphibious warfare training and was in the good hands of the U.S. Navy, experienced practitioners of the art of amphibious assault.

The New Zealanders were equipped with British-style weaponry, and their logistics supply line traced all the way back to New Zealand. Generally, their weaponry was incompatible with American weaponry, so the New Zealanders were in some ways an American quartermaster's nightmare. The New Zealanders were on American rations. Although some rations were welcomed, novelties such as Spam, Chili Con Carne and Vienna sausage were much-loathed items for New Zealand soldiers raised on a diet of beef and sheep meat.

The New Zealand troops deployed for Squarepeg were an interesting mixture of infantry, artillery, signals, ordnance, supply, medical, engineers, and other supporting units. This reflected the need not only to take the Green Islands but to hold them.

The Japanese–SNLF

The Japanese soldiers on the Green Islands were members of the Imperial Japanese Special Naval Landing Force (SNLF). A New Zealand analysis described them as "husky, square built fighters with a reputation similar to that of the U.S. Marines."[4] The Special Naval Landing Force (Tokubetsu Rikusantai) was created by the Imperial Japanese Navy as naval infantry to handle a wide range of tasks from garrison duty through to combat operations. By the start of the Pacific War, the SNLF had evolved into "an elite organization whose units were tasked to handle difficult assignments."[5] Their role in the Pacific War became more prominent due to the interservice rivalry between the Imperial Japanese Navy and the Imperial Japanese Army. Put simply, the Army remained fixated on the war in China and the threat from Soviet Russia. The Navy was focused on the "Strike South," and SNLF units took part in the invasion of the Philippines, Wake Island, the Dutch East Indies, the Solomon Islands, and New Guinea. At Tarawa in November 1943 the troops of the SNLF cemented their fearsome reputation by inflicting grievous casualties on the 2nd U.S. Marine Division. As the war progressed, the SNLF found itself committed to garrison roles, and by 1944 "they were no longer elite troops in any sense, due to lack of training, leadership, equipment and morale."[6]

Japanese soldiers were the product of a highly regimented training system and were indoctrinated with very strong nationalistic values of honor, reverence for their Emperor, a belief in their racial superiority, group solidarity and self sacrifice. Training was brutal, with slaps, punches and kicks being frequently applied. Intense discipline was believed to be the cement that held the Japanese armed forces together and which would enable them to overcome any material advantages that an enemy might have.

Japanese soldiers were expected to die rather than surrender. To become a prisoner of war was to bring down intense shame on your family and loss of honor for the individual. Generally, Japanese soldiers would fight to the death. Allied soldiers learned from bitter experience that Japanese soldiers appearing to surrender would all too often be intent on taking a few Allied soldiers with them to the afterlife. Surrenders were treated with great caution. The majority of Japanese troops who were captured had been rendered unconscious by explosions, or were starving, sick and isolated from their comrades. Often Japanese soldiers preferred suicide to capture, sometimes holding grenades to their stomachs to ensure certain death. Very few Japanese were taken prisoner on the Green Islands. It would, however, be a mistake to dismiss the Japanese as mindless automatons who placed no value on their own lives.

The Japanese soldiers were well fed and well armed, and the Green Islands provided them with excellent defensive terrain. The standard of their rifle marksmanship would impress the New Zealanders. The SNLF soldiers were distinguished from their Army counterparts by their dark green uniforms and the anchor symbol on their headgear. They were equipped with the same weapons as Army troops. These included the Ariska bolt-action rifle, Nambu Type 99 light machine gun, the 50mm Type 89 grenade launcher hand grenades, and the long-barreled 20mm Type 97 antitank rifle.

In early 1944, Japanese forces in the South Pacific were full of fight and determined to stubbornly resist the Allied advance towards their homeland. They either refused to acknowledge that Japan was losing the war or could not conceive of this. Either way, they could be counted on to fight skillfully and fiercely.

The Green Islands were an integral part of the Japanese supply network linked together by barges.

The Japanese, in the bitter naval battles around Guadalcanal, had come to appreciate that using their destroyers as supply vessels in "Tokyo Express" operations was not only costly but also uneconomic. As they lost merchant shipping, the Japanese came up with the idea of using cheap, easily built, wooden motorized barges called "Daihatsus." These were shallow-draft barges that operated in very shallow coastal waters, which meant Allied destroyers could not get to them without risk of running aground. The Japanese kitted these out with formidable weaponry, sometimes including antitank guns. The Daihatsus became the favorite target of Allied aircraft and PT boats, fast U.S. Navy motor torpedo boats. As a countermeasure they tended to move at night, when they had a greater chance of escaping Allied attacks, and to lie up camouflaged during the day.

The attitude of the Japanese to the Solomon Islanders varied but was often brutal, with the destruction of gardens, canoes and food sources, the despoliation of churches, and molestation of females. The Japanese believed that as members of the Yamato race they were racially superior beings, and that gave them license to be brutal to their inferiors. The European record of exploitation of native peoples is sometimes an uncomfortable one to modern eyes, but pales in comparison to the overall Japanese treatment of local peoples, particularly if they were perceived as being hostile or uncooperative.

Three

The "Commando Raid"—
A Reconnaissance in Force

The German military philosopher Carl von Clausewitz wrote in his classic work *On War*, "War is the realm of uncertainty."[1] For the Allied planners, the Green Islands abounded in uncertainties.

The Green Islanders—Pro-Japanese or Pro-Allied?

One of the problems faced by the Allies in the Solomons was that there was uncertainty as to the sympathies of the local indigenous population in the Solomon Islands. The war in the Pacific had erupted suddenly for the islanders, and they had no real idea as to the issues between the Allies and the Japanese. As the Japanese advanced southward, the colonial police and administrative structures were destroyed. Anarchy sometimes erupted. The Japanese portrayed themselves as liberators of the oppressed colonial peoples and sought to gain their support. In most cases the Solomon Islanders stayed staunchly loyal to the British Crown.[2] On other places, such as Kieta in Bougainville, a prewar Japanese resident had been able to secure the islanders' support as guides and even trackers for hunting down Europeans. It was simply unknown as to where the sympathies of the Green Islanders lay. In the Operations Order for 30 Battalion it was stated, "It can be expected that natives will be hostile and necessary precautions will have to be taken."[3] An intelligence report prepared by Flight Lieutenant Robson, an Australian coastwatcher, had commented on the islanders of Nissan: "Most of the natives are lazy troublemakers. They take quite an interest in the Mission, but only to the extent that the interest does not entail personal exertion in Mission gardens or buildings."[4]

The Mosquito Fleet Makes a Reconnaissance

Admiral Wilkinson faced an acute problem. Little was known of the tidal and hydrographic features of the Green Islands. The critical importance of accurate hydrographic information had been rammed home at Tarawa in November 1943. It seemed that inordinate casualties had been suffered by 2nd U.S. Marine Division as a result of low tides that meant "no landing boats could cross the reef." As a result, "Thousands of Marines had to wade the six to eight hundred yards to shore and hundreds fell to Japanese gunners."[5]

A lesser example is Operation Dovetail in July 1942. This was a rehearsal for the USMC invasion of Guadalcanal. It occurred on the island of Koro in the Fijian Islands and was distinguished by landing craft at low tide hitting coral outcrops and being damaged.[6]

Wilkinson knew that marine charts relating to the Green Islands were of dubious utility and totally inadequate.[7] The basic information necessary to plan an amphibious operation was lacking. Steps had been taken to find out as much information as possible on the Green Islands, including interviewing prewar visitors, but these efforts had yielded only low-grade information.

Photo reconnaissance aircraft had taken photos of the Green Island Group on 3 November, 26 November, 3 December, and 19 December 1943. The photo reconnaissance work was undertaken by aircrew from the inelegantly named Squadron VD-1. This was a specialist U.S. Navy unit which flew the "navalized" version of the B-24 Liberator bomber, the four-engine PB4Y-1. VD-1 was set up in January 1943.[8] Photo reconnaissance work, generally unescorted, over long expanses of the Pacific, was highly dangerous and taxing work. Commander McIlroy of VD-1 flew several of the photo reconnaissance missions over the Green Islands in Plane No. 74 and took photos at low altitude. Sadly, the photos obtained were described as "partial and poor." An on-the-ground view was needed.[9]

In order to conduct a proper reconnaissance in force, Wilkinson had to find out certain basic facts—were the depths of the lagoon entrances deep enough to allow a landing craft to pass through them? Were there any impediments, such as coral outcroppings or Japanese mines which could block or damage landing craft?

Wilkinson's solution was to send PT boats, small motor torpedo boats, on a mission to find out. PT boats were ideal for the mission—low in the water, fast, and with the potential to be stealthy. PT boats had acquired the nickname the "Mosquito Fleet" because of their ability to sting the enemy with their torpedoes and armament. The PT boats had been used to carry out barge-busting missions, striking at the Japanese Daihatsu and attempting to sever the Japanese supply lines.[10] The shallow draft of the PT boats enabled them to come close inshore where the Japanese barges sought shelter. The PT boats had two major drawbacks. The first is that, having on board high octane fuel and explosives with very little protection against enemy fire, the PT boats were extremely vulnerable to air attack. The second was that at high speed they left a phosphorescent wake that the Japanese could trace back to its source.

The PT boats chosen for the preliminary reconnaissance of Green were PT-176 and PT-184 of Motor Torpedo Squadron Eleven. They were to be accompanied by two seventy-seven-foot PT boats that had been converted to the role of gunboats, PT-59 and PT-61.[11]

The mission was to be carried out under cover of darkness on the night of 10–11 January 1944. The historian Robert J. Bulkley comments:

> The weather was too rough for the seventy-seven-footers, which had seen hard service and now were carrying the extra weight of two 40mm guns, one fore and one aft. Seas tore their radar masts loose, fouled gears on the forward 40mm guns, stripped beading from their chines, and opened seams. The 61's smoke screen generator broke loose and in going overboard carried away an exhaust stack. Water shorted out the 59's radio, starting a small fire in the charthouse. The gunboats could not keep up with the other PTs.
>
> The 176 and 184 arrived at Green Island at 2230, entered the southern channel, took soundings and departed at 0015 with the knowledge that there was seventeen feet of water, ample for landing craft. There was no indication that the enemy had been aware of their presence. Rear Adm. Theodore S. Wilkinson, Commander Third Amphibious Force, said, "This passage of the channel by two PT boats, within close rifle and machine gun range of possible enemy positions on either side, was a bold exploit, consistent with the reputation for courageous accomplishment of difficult and hazardous tasks which the MTB Squadrons have acquired and confirmed by their operations through this area."[12]

The crew of the PT boats used native canoes obtained from the Treasury Islands to accomplish their task of checking the width and depth of the channels.[13] This information was critical to the decision to invade. Barrowclough noted in his war diary that the Naval Recce party had been directed to check out the main entrance channel between Barahun Island and Pokonian plantation "with a view to checking up on its width, depth, and to see if any obstructing niggerheads [coral outcroppings] could easily be removed. We await their report with much interest as, only if this is favourable, will the second part of the operation proceed. We are also anxious to see if there are any signs of Jap activity."[14]

However useful the information obtained by the PT boats was, the reality was that it only scratched the surface of what was needed. Amphibious operations are complex, demanding matters, unforgiving of errors. Small mistakes have potential to result in catastrophic results. More information of a technical nature was needed.

Planning the Commando Raid

As coastwatchers had been unable to operate in the area[15] and the loyalties of the local islanders were thought to lie with the Japanese, it was decided to send a force to discover beach information and the enemy's strength. Dubbed a "Commando Raid," this was more concerned with obtaining information than destroying enemy units. As with the Cowan patrols on the Treasury Islands, there was a risk of alerting the Japanese to the invasion.[16] Despite the success of the Cowan patrols and the existence of a specialist USMC amphibious reconnaissance team, COMSOPAC decided to send a larger force.

Discussions were held at Guadalcanal on 31 December 1943, between Admiral Fort, USN, and Major General Barrowclough. On the subject of the proposed reconnaissance in force, Barrowclough noted in his diary:

> There was considerable discussion as to when this preliminary reconnaissance should be undertaken. The fact that it was made would, of course, advertise our intention to invade this Island. It was felt that the information required to be gained was of such importance that the risk would have to be accepted. I urged that it be undertaken at a time which would leave the shortest possible interval between the reconnaissance and the invasion if the results of the reconnaissance were to be of any use to us in planning the invasion. General Harmon, who was present, promised that he would, during the interval between the reconnaissance and the invasion, intensify the air and naval coverage of that area so as to prevent, or at least forewarn us, of any Japanese attempt to strengthen the garrison on the Island.[17]

Barrowclough reported to Lt. General Puttick, his superior at Army Headquarters in Wellington, New Zealand:

> The Green Island project involved certain reconnaissance work which had hitherto generally been done by sending small parties ashore from a submarine. Green Island, however, is a very small island and has a native population of 1,500, most of whom were thought to be Japanese sympathisers and COMSOPAC decided that it would be impracticable to send a secret reconnaissance party on to the island with any hope of getting the information he requires. He therefore asked me to undertake a reconnaissance in force and I think I can do that satisfactorily by using 400 men of the 30th Battalion which is the only infantry unit in my command which has not yet had battle experience. They are all keen to

undertake it. The plan is to land them on the island at midnight, leave them there for the whole of the following day and evacuate them the following midnight. In order that the information they get can be put to practical use, it is essential that this party should go in some 10 days before the main operation. Naturally, I would have preferred not to give this forewarning of our intention but I agree that it is inevitable. We are calling the operation not a reconnaissance in force but a commando raid. We shall probably contrive to leave behind under as realistic circumstances as possible a bogus order for the operation describing it as a commando raid directing the troops to destroy any equipment used in the barge staging operations which the Japanese are carrying out. I shall instruct them to patrol at length inland with the object of finding and destroying any dumps of oil, fuel, etc. The real object, of course, will be to investigate the ground with a view to ascertaining its suitability for airfield construction and also to undertake certain hydrographic surveys that are requisite if we are to ascertain that we can effect landings at the points we desire.[18]

The New Zealander commander of the raid, Lieutenant Colonel Frederick Charles Cornwall, was unusual in many respects. He was born in England on 1 September 1892, and emigrated to New Zealand. He joined

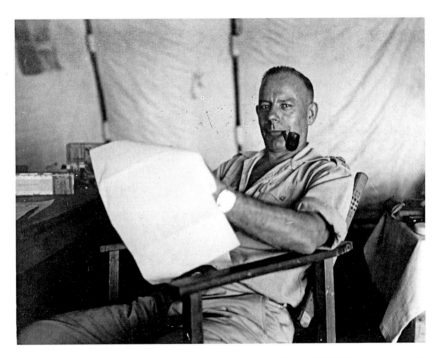

Lt. Colonel F.C. Cornwall, Commander 30 Battalion, 3NZ Division, 3 April 1944. Nissan Green Island 1944 [Archives Reference ADQZ 18905, WA117, 3/16 E11], Archives New Zealand, The Department of Internal Affairs, Te Tari Taiwhenua.

the Territorials [NZ Militia], prior to World War I and was appointed as an NCO with the NZ Expeditionary Force. He was wounded on Gallipoli. Once he recovered, he rejoined the New Zealand forces on the Western Front. His defining moment was in 1917, when he led an attack on a German pillbox and captured twenty-five Germans. In the attack, he was wounded in the shoulder. He was awarded the Military Cross and commissioned as a 2nd lieutenant because of gallantry and distinguished service in the field. Because of his wound, he was returned to New Zealand and was hospitalized. The war ended before he was able to return. In the postwar years he was placed on the reserve of officers, and initially he had an involvement with the Territorials. This proved difficult to maintain because he failed to attend Territorial camps and parades due to transport difficulties. On the outbreak of World War II he was considered too old to be sent overseas. However, the NZ Army was desperately short of trained men, and he was commissioned as a captain with 35th Battalion. He served in Fiji and gained the rank of major. He was appointed as the commandant of the Base Training Depot and seemed destined for a non-combat role. That changed with his appointment as a lieutenant colonel to command 30 Battalion on 11 September 1943.[19] At the age of 52 he was comparatively old to lead the Raiders. 30th Battalion had been held in reserve on the struggle for Vella Lavella, so Cornwall's last combat experience had been in 1917, and his last contested amphibious operation had been the ill-fated Gallipoli campaign.

The "Commando" unit, totaling 360 personnel, was simply 300 ordinary soldiers[20] selected from 30 Battalion.[21] The New Zealand soldiers consisted of A, D and C Companies, 1 Platoon from B Company, and mortar sections, supplemented by a reconnaissance section, intelligence personnel, signals personnel, a medical officer and orderlies, and the padre of 30 Battalion.[22] However, the use of the word "commando" cast the operation in a glamorous light, and the men of 30 Battalion readily embraced the term.[23] Regardless of what it was called, the raid provided the raiders with the possibility of medals and promotion. Attached to the unit were thirty USN intelligence, communication, airfield, landing craft and beach specialists, mainly from Admiral Wilkinson's HQ, but including New Zealand Artillery, Engineer and ASC officers. An Australian member of ANGAU, a prewar plantation owner, Lt. F.P. Archer, attached to the British Solomon Islands Administration, provided expertise in pidgin.[24] He also knew the Green Islands well. The primary role of the New Zealand troops was to protect these specialists.[25]

One group of specialists were led by Captain Junius T. Jarman of the

United States Coast and Geodetic Survey. Jarman was an expert in marine chart compilation and hydrographic surveys and was the captain of USS *Pathfinder*, a survey ship. He recalled, "I was detached [from USS *Pathfinder*] on January 15, 1944 to lead an Advanced Survey Party composed of 4 officers and 17 men. This group proceeded to Guadalcanal from Noumea, New Caledonia. Upon arrival we were attached to Naval Advance Base Unit 11. This was something new and the name was abbreviated thus 'NABU-11.' It was a group of men and officers trained and organized to land with combat troops and immediately begin functioning as a Naval Base."[26] Specialist equipment for taking soundings had to be removed from *Pathfinder* and installed on one of the raider's landing craft.

The raid illustrates the complex multinational nature of amphibious operations. The force was under the overall command of Captain Ralph Earle, USN; the New Zealand troops were commanded by a New Zealander, Lt. Col. Frederick Cornwall; and the naval unit was commanded by an American commander, J. MacDonald Smith, USN.

The plan was for the troops to be transported to the target by auxiliary personnel destroyers (APDs). These were specially modified destroyers used to transport troops, particularly raiders. The APDs were fast but had the drawback that they lacked the full armament of a normal destroyer. Consequently, they would have to be protected by normal destroyers.

Speed was of the essence. It was intended that the APDs would arrive at their destination and lower the landing craft carried on derricks.[27] The troops would clamber down cargo nets into the waiting landing craft. The APDs would then withdraw at speed and return at midnight the following night.

The information on the Japanese defenders was "sketchy"! There were "positive signs of enemy occupation and Force must expect opposition at all points. NISSAN I. is used mainly at night for a temporary staging point between BUKA—NEW BRITAIN or NEW IRELAND." Japanese activity was thought to be evidenced "by new clearings, track activity at key beach defense points, gutted barge in lagoon, and beached barges on outside coast." Most puzzling and concerning for the invaders were a series of new clearings revealed by photo reconnaissance aircraft at Tanaheran, Pinipel, south of Pokonian Plantation, Perinon, Sior, the northeast tip of Nissan, southeast of Tangalan, and on the west side of Barahun Island.[28] What unpleasant surprises were the wily Japanese defenders preparing?

The intention of the invaders was threefold—carry out a reconnaissance with a view to establishing an air and P.T. boat base; reconnoiter for landing facilities for landing craft and ships; and make as "general terrain and hydrological recce as may be practicable under the circumstances."[29] Two alternative plans were developed. Which one would be utilized was dependent on how favorable the weather conditions were on the outside coast.

Both plans involved securing Barahun Island so that the channel could safely be used by the follow-up invading force. The plans differed in the selection of landing beaches. Both plans contemplated a withdrawal and re-embarkation to the waiting APDs at about midnight on 31 January/1 February 1944.

Emphasis was placed in planning on the information gathering aspects. The raiders were instructed: "The *primary object* of the mission is recce. Where possible enemy defended localities will be by-passed, but holding detachments may be detailed to pin the enemy while the remainder of the party proceeds on recce."[30]

Although wireless sets were provided to the soldiers, orders were given to maintain wireless silence until zero hour, or up until the element of surprise was lost. Regardless, it was expected that wireless communication would only be used in an extreme situation and a listening watch was maintained during the raid by a post on Vella Lavella.

In line with the reconnaissance nature of their mission, the soldiers were lightly armed—Lee Enfield rifles (100 rounds per man), Bren guns (525 rounds distributed among the section), Thompson submachine guns (300 per gun, with a further 200 distributed among the section), pistols (36 rounds), grenades (31), and 3-inch mortars (80 rounds of high explosive and 10 of smoke) and various colored flares. Rations were similarly light—48 hours worth of K rations, one emergency ration, and one D ration. An emergency reserve of C rations was to be retained on board the landing craft. Water was a critical consideration—full water bottles were to be carried by each man, with an additional 2 gallons of water in tins per section. No doubt to the relief of the troops, gas masks and steel helmets were not to be worn. Signals equipment consisted of three No. 48 wireless sets, three DSSR wireless sets, and coils of combat wire. That equipment would not be operational in the initial phase of landing, so signaling was to be carried out by means of short flashes from flashlights.

A scale model of Nissan was built by 38th Field Park Company based on aerial photographs. The model proved particularly useful in planning the operation.[31] Since the initial landing was to be carried out in darkness, the infantry were given intensive training: "Practice in forming perimeters both by day and night was carried out at the Mumia and Juno beaches [on the Island of Vella Lavella]. Every man learned his position in the assault boat, his companions on his right and left flanks in the perimeter, the ammunition carried by his section mates and where it was carried; every man learned, too, the number of paces to take in from the bush line, the whereabouts of his platoon commander, and finally once having dug in, not to move one's fox-hole in any circumstances."[32]

The New Zealand troops were briefed by Lt. Colonel Cornwall on 25 January 1944: "Briefly, your task is this—to disembark from destroyers at midnight into assault boats, land on a certain island which the Japs are using as a staging point for barges, dig in and wait for daylight. You will then, all going well, be split into small groups and go as protecting parties to men having specialist reconnaissance duties. At midnight we will rendezvous with the destroyers and come home."[33]

The Raiders Gather

Amphibious operations are incredibly complex logistically and the Raid was no exception. At 1500 hours on 28 January 1944, a transport unit made up of the special troop carrying destroyers, the APDs *Talbot*, *Waters* and *Dickerson*, took on board a group of thirty U.S. naval personnel. At 1800 hours, screened by the destroyers *Fullam*, *Bennett*, *Guest* and *Hudson*, the transport unit sailed for Hathorn Sound, New Georgia, where the APDs took on fuel. Then it proceeded through the Blackett Strait to Juno River, Vella Lavella, where it arrived at noon on 29 January.[34]

However, preparations did not all go smoothly and did not augur well for the success of the raid. Commander J.D. Sweeney, USN, of Transport Division Twelve later reported:

> D minus one day was 29 January, when the troops assembled at Juno beach [Vella Lavella] and were taken by LCPs [Landing Craft, Personnel] to the destroyers. The APDs (army [*sic*] personnel destroyers) which transported the men were the USS *Talbot*, *Waters* and *Dickerson*.
>
> A conference was held aboard the *Talbot* in the afternoon when executive navy and army officers assembled in the ward room to discuss and confirm details of the raid. That night a practice landing was carried out. It was intended to land on Juno beach but this plan was abandoned, for after milling around for some time no one could decide just which part of the coast was Juno. Eventually, a landing was made on the more easily discernible Mumia beach, after which the craft returned to their destroyers. Many of the men slept on their life-belts on deck rather than in the crowded quarters below.[35]

The failure of the ships' captains to find Juno Beach is understandable given the wartime conditions. The coastline was in darkness,[36] charts were

Three. The "Commando Raid"   27

NZ soldiers of 30 Bn board USS *Talbot* off Mumia, Vella Lavella (photograph by Combat Photo Unit 9, HQ Comthirdphib, SOPAC). Nissan Green Island 1944 [Archives Reference ADQZ 18905, WA117, 3/16 E11], Archives New Zealand, The Department of Internal Affairs, Te Tari Taiwhenua.

of dubious reliability, navigational aids were relatively primitive, and ship-to-shore communication was problematic. It was not the first time in the South Pacific War that landing beaches could not be found, nor would it be the last.[37] The most important thing, however, is that the troops were successfully landed on Mumia Beach and were re-embarked.

The force sailed from Vella Lavella at 0600 hours, first light on 30 January 1944, in three Auxiliary Personnel Destroyers (APD[38]) with four destroyer escorts. At 1600 hours two PT boats, PT-176 and PT-178, joined the convoy off Torokina, Bougainville.

The soldiers whiled away the time talking, smoking cigarettes, playing bridge or checking their weapons and equipment. Food was provided by the ship's mess and the decks were crowded with men finding places to eat their food from the trays provided.

As the time for the raid grew closer, the troops took turns applying camouflage paint to each other. "It's make-up time and mates in turn smother each other's face, neck and hands with green combat paint."[39]

NZ soldiers of 30 Bn board USS *Talbot* off Mumia, Vella Lavella (photograph by Combat Photo Unit 9, HQ Comthirdphib, SOPAC). Nissan Green Island 1944 [Archives Reference ADQZ 18905, WA117, 3/16 E11], Archives New Zealand, The Department of Internal Affairs, Te Tari Taiwhenua.

Commander J.D. Sweeney on *Talbot* later reported:

> At 0000 [midnight], January 31 the transport unit approached Green Islands on an easterly course and were guided to the transport area by the *FULLAM*. Visibility was good and the *TALBOT*, the leading APD, stopped about one thousand yards off the entrance, between Barahun and Nissan Islands with the other two APDs close astern. The PT boats came up on the *TALBOT's* starboard bow and the boats from the *TALBOT* and *WATERS* formed astern of them. The *DICKERSON's* boats were slow in forming up so the PT boats, along with the *TALBOT* and *WATERS* boats, proceeded through the inlet. One PT boat then came out and guided the *DICKERSON's* boats through the inlet.[40]

Because of their experience of the Green Islands, two of the PT boats that had taken part in the initial reconnaissance in January 1944 led the way.[41] PT-176 and PT-178 led the landing craft into the lagoon. The destroyers remained outside the lagoon entrance, leaving the PT boats as the only covering force.[42]

The invasion force arrived off Nissan at 2350 hours, 30 January 1944. The personnel were offloaded down cargo nets—with some difficulty due

The raiders disembark at Pokonian Plantation, 31 Jan 1944 (photographs by Combat Photo Unit 9, HQ Comthirdphib, SOPAC). Nissan Green Island 1944 [Archives Reference ADQZ 18905, WA117, 3/16 E11], Archives New Zealand, The Department of Internal Affairs, Te Tari Taiwhenua.

to rough sea conditions—into LCVPs, which were then escorted by two PT boats from Bougainville. Seasickness was rife.[43] One PT boat led a column of 12 landing craft through the gap between Barahun and Nissan and into the lagoon when tidal conditions were right. A New Zealand officer, Lieutenant Frank Rennie, later commented, "It would have been disastrous if we had been fired upon from high ground as the 12 barges went through the gap."[44] The Allied personnel landed on the lagoon side of Pokonian Plantation, Nissan. No doubt to Sweeney's immense relief, at 0300 hours a radio signal was received from a PT boat advising that the troops had been landed without opposition.

As Sweeney had observed, *Dickerson* was slow in disembarking her raiders and the survey party.

One casualty was suffered while manning the boats—Private E.L. Hosking of 30 Battalion. He was kept on board *Dickerson*.[45]

Dickerson's boats had cleared the ship by 0005 hours and proceeded slowly to their rendezvous area on the starboard bow of *Talbot*. No doubt to the consternation of the crew, on arriving at their rendezvous area five minutes later there was no sign of any other boats. They then made a wide circle to the left of the proposed entrance. Ten minutes later a TBY message was received and the boats entered the channel. A further message was received five minutes later to proceed immediately and speed was increased. A PT boat then directed the boats into the lagoon and they arrived at 0035 hours. *Dickerson*'s commanding officer, Captain J.R. Cain Jr., reported, "After clearing foul water a turn to the right was executed.

U.S. soldiers and 30 Battalion personnel land at Pokonian Plantation (photographs by Combat Photo Unit 9, HQ Comthirdphib, SOPAC). Nissan Green Island 1944 [Archives Reference ADQZ 18905, WA117, 3/16 E11], Archives New Zealand, The Department of Internal Affairs, Te Tari Taiwhenua.

At 0040, the other PT boat approached and led the way to the beach vicinity, where boat APD 7–1 led the rest of the way to Red Beach, landing there between 0045 and 0050. All troops disembarked and a watch was established in the boats, the condition of which was reported hourly to Commander Smith."[46]

The APDs then proceeded to take position off the Green Islands until 0120 hours, and then proceeded at 19 knots to the vicinity of the Treasury Islands in order to get under the protective umbrella of Allied fighter cover before daylight. The invaders were on their own.[47]

In *Pacific Kiwis*, a 3NZ Division unofficial history, a participant recalled his experiences:

> The hours pass and at 11:30 p.m. comes the call the troops have been waiting for.
> "Gear On!"
> "Set condition one able," comes over the speaker system from the bridge. These are code words to move to the decks. The troops feel their way to their boat stations, hanging onto the man in front.
> "Lower all boats to the rail." The coxswains get in and the boats sink with them to the water. The troops clamber over the ship's side into the assault boats.
> "Cast off," and the boats move away from the mother ship.
> "Go on in—I order you to go through," shouts Commander J. Macdonald Smith, USN, from the first LCP to the patrol torpedo boat commander. Twelve assault boats follow the wake of the boat in front. In the first assault boat the troops crouch, huddled on the floor. The coxswain curses a section corporal who is sick over his legs. You know you are through the lagoon entrance for it is calmer now.
> "Quarter right," orders the commander to the coxswain.
> "Quarter right it is sir," replies the coxswain.
> "Fifty yards to go," says the commander.
> The keel of the boat grates on the bottom like sandpaper on wood. The ramp drops with a clatter. The colonel jumps off, stumbles, calls out, "It's deep." The commander follows and then the platoon runs up the beach into the bushes. Soon all you can hear are shovels slipping through the sandy soil with a sound like ripping silk. A coconut falls among the fox-holes and somebody sniggers.[48]

Harry Bioletti, an officer with 30th Battalion, took part in the Commando Raid and later recalled:

> We travelled up in APD's and then climbed down the rope ladders onto landing craft. We went through the atoll entrance in line ahead. Commander Smith, USN was in charge of our craft and when the Coxswain was reluctant to enter the lagoon he said "I order you to go in." The entrance was 50 foot wide. Our craft had sufficient depth and we turned right and right again and began exploring. I was not aware of any potential danger till our landing craft nosed into an inlet and we heard the bolt of a rifle being closed. We decided to get the hell out of it. Middleton came through the same area later and the defenders opened fire and killed him.

Recce party lands near entrance to Tapangat Inlet, 31 January 1944 (photographs by Combat Photo Unit 9, HQ Comthirdphib, SOPAC). Nissan Green Island 1944 [Archives Reference ADQZ 18905, WA117, 3/16 E11], Archives New Zealand, The Department of Internal Affairs, Te Tari Taiwhenua.

> There was no communication between the units and it was as black as Egypt's night. I was down front of the landing craft. When the ramp went down we got off and began digging foxholes in the sand. Then dawn came and we found ourselves surrounded by natives. We asked them if there were any Japs around. The trouble is that they did not understand numbers and the conversation had to be in Pidgin English. They were friendly and we gave them food.[49]

The following day a patrol examined Barahun. Two companies were sent across the lagoon to Tangalan Plantation on the eastern side. As their landing craft surged across the lagoon, an RNZAF Ventura bomber came in low and attempted to communicate by Aldis signal lamp, eventually dropping a roll of toilet paper on the beach. Lt. Frank Rennie recovered it and then shook his fist at the fast disappearing plane. Rennie thought it was simply "a raw joke" on the part of the RNZAF. The message contained in it was, unfortunately, not recovered. The pilot was attempting to warn the troops that a large Japanese barge had landed on the seaward side of the atoll.⁵⁰

The sequel occurred some five days later when the aircrew met some of the raiders. The airmen said, "Did you get our message?" "No.... What message?" "Didn't you pick up that roll of toilet paper?" "Yes, of course we did. And a raw joke that was too." "That wasn't a joke, it had a message rolled up in the centre, telling you to look out for Japs from five barges on the South Coast. We felt sorry for you chaps down there and thought we would put you wise."⁵¹

Embarking from Pokonian Plantation for recce of Nissan, 31 January 1944 (photographs by Combat Photo Unit 9, HQ Comthirdphib, SOPAC). Nissan Green Island 1944 [Archives Reference ADQZ 18905, WA117, 3/16 E11], Archives New Zealand, The Department of Internal Affairs, Te Tari Taiwhenua.

The specialist hydrographic team began their work. Captain Jarman recorded, "My group investigated Middle and South Channels into the lagoon for least depth, ran a few exploratory lines in an east-west direction across the lagoon, and ran several sounding lines, north-south direction, along the shoreline to assist in locating LST landing sites. We also obtained 24 hours of tidal data to assist in estimating the tidal stage on 'D' day."[52]

Three other parties in barges explored the beaches around the lagoon and the mission station to the south. Newly cut tracks in the vicinity of the mission indicated the probable presence of the Japanese, but no contact was made. Lt. Archer made contact with friendly locals who provided information on the Japanese. While returning, he carried out an examination of the lagoon beaches. About a mile south of the Allied beachhead at Pokonian Plantation, a Japanese barge was discovered moored in a small bay under trees. Friendly islanders had said that there were no Japanese in the area. The U.S. Naval Officer, Commander J. MacDonald Smith, ComLCIFlot Five, in charge of the naval units, using his binoculars could not detect any sign of life and decided to investigate. The barge could have been derelict. Smith decided to take a closer look.

Lieutenant Robert T. Hartman, the USN public relations officer who took part in the raid, described what happened next:

> In we went again crouching low. It's a good thing we were, for the moment our bow hit that quiet little strip of sand all hell broke loose. In considerably less time than it takes to tell, the air filled with lead. Over the side—not ten feet away—was an expertly camouflaged Jap barge. Alongside was another. The Japs—two of those barges would carry about one hundred—had dug themselves pill-boxes in the coral cliffs that rose steeply from the beach behind the hideout. They were in the overhanging trees also. On their first burst of heavy machine gun fire they killed the coxswain. They knocked out both of our bow gunners before they got off a shot. In fact, they hit everybody forward of the motor, except Commander Smith—who was standing without a helmet up by the ramp. He was the only one left who knew how to run the boat! I was crouched just behind one of the natives, just at the centre of the boat. All the time the Japs were pouring machine gun and rifle crossfire into us from all directions, including above. Our boat was stuck on the beach and the occupants were dropping like flies. The New Zealand officer (Lieutenant O'Dowd) fell wounded. Another murderous burst from the machine gun not ten yards away cut down one of the overhanging branches and covered the stern half of the boat. Through this two of the New Zealanders, with as much guts as I ever hope to see, were pouring fire from their tommy guns back into the inferno. One Jap dropped from a tree but there was no noticeable let-up in the deafening fire we were taking.
>
> Commander Smith had ducked down at the first burst but he had his back to the coxswain and didn't know he was dead. He kept shouting, "Back 'er off—back 'er off! and he finally looked round at the shambles and saw that nobody was left to back 'er off but himself. Cool as a cucumber he crawled back to the wheel,

The raiders carry out their recce of Nissan, 31 January 1944 (photographs by Combat Photo Unit 9, HQ Comthirdphib, SOPAC). Nissan Green Island 1944 [Archives Reference ADQZ 18905, WA117, 3/16 E11], Archives New Zealand, The Department of Internal Affairs, Te Tari Taiwhenua.

keeping below the gunwales. He got the thing in reverse after anguished seconds that seemed eternities. The wounded gunner summoned his last strength and tried to help. The Japs were still pouring it into us and no one will ever shake my belief that it was pure miracle that prevented them from killing every soul in that boat. After a couple of agonizing tries the boat slipped off the sand and floated. Up to that moment I was quite sure that we would all be killed and was praying only that God would receive us properly. Now I began to pray that God would get us out of here—but it wasn't over yet. Commander Smith was backing off blind and taking a quick peep over the side now and then. Any minute we were likely to hit one of the innumerable coral heads and be stuck again, but we missed them somehow. The enraged Japs kept on firing until we were a couple of hundred yards off shore but after we got out of point blank range they didn't hit anything.

We heaved the branch over the side and patched up our wounded as best we could. The boat looked like a slaughter house. Our boat suffered more than 50 per cent casualties and everyone forward of me had been hit.[53]

The lagoon shore, Pokonian Plantation, 31 January 1944 (photographs by Combat Photo Unit 9, HQ Comthirdphib, SOPAC). Nissan Green Island 1944 [Archives Reference ADQZ 18905, WA117, 3/16 E11], Archives New Zealand, The Department of Internal Affairs, Te Tari Taiwhenua.

Another person who was in the same landing craft was an American war correspondent called Vern Haughland. Vern Haughland (1908–1984) had previously been in the front line in the South Pacific and faced Japanese fire. At one point in his career as a war correspondent he had to bail out of a crippled B-26 Marauder bomber over Papua New Guinea and spent forty-seven days lost in the jungle. He had the rare distinction of having the Silver Star medal pinned on him by General Douglas MacArthur for his heroism. He was the first civilian to receive this award.[54]

Haughland marveled at his luck on the Commando Raid, believing that "the Japanese should have been able to kill every one of us!" As the landing craft approached the Japanese barges, they appeared to be abandoned. The two .30 caliber machine guns on the landing craft were manned and "every rifle and tommy gun aboard was in readiness." The Japanese waited till the Allied craft "scraped to a stop on the sandy beach directly beneath the twenty foot bank of coral and earth behind which they waited." The Allied craft had unwittingly entered a killing zone.

When the Japanese opened fire they caught the Allied crew by surprise. "Craftily, the Japanese had drawn their bead on our gunners and boat crew. Their first volley killed the coxswain and quickly they picked off the port and starboard machine gunners silencing our primary defense weapons and within two minutes all four men in the boat crew were down!" The survivors were now at the mercy of the Japanese and the situation seemed totally hopeless.

Sometimes in war, leadership can be a decisive factor in survival or death. Commander Smith had been standing in the bow of the landing craft and by rights he should have been one of the first killed. Miraculously, he had the presence of mind to direct the landing craft off the beach. Haughland later described how Smith had gotten the landing craft "into the lagoon while death rained all around him. Smith estimated later that the Japanese opened up with one .50 caliber machine gun, numerous rifles and possibly grenades."

Haughland's survival was nothing short of miraculous:

> "I was in the boat's stern, but we were so far up on the beach that the gunfire ripped a five inch bough off a tree over my head. It plunged down on top of me. I heard bullets thudding into the bough across my shoulders and into the hull at my back, sending splinters stinging against my cheek and forehead." Haughland glanced down at his feet and saw a pool of blood and thought that he had been hit. However, it was one of the Islanders who was bleeding profusely.
>
> The soldiers on the landing craft still had some fight in them. One New Zealand soldier yelled out, "I got two of the blawsted bums. Saw them toss up their guns and fall." [I strongly suspect Haughland sanitized this for his readership! I feel sure the language would have been much more colorful.][55]

The cost had been high. Lt. Peter O'Dowd, a New Zealand officer who commanded the 30 Battalion Carrier Platoon and the 30 Battalion reconnaissance section, later died of his wounds. The coxswain from *Talbot*, H.P. Van Deusen, was killed, as was Fireman Second Class A.E. Bryant, also from *Talbot*. The wounded included Ensign R.M. Greenlees, a boat officer from *Talbot* (serious); Seaman First Class E.E. Miller, from *Talbot* (moderately serious); two native guides from the Solomon Islands Constabulary, Maita (slight) and Konam (moderately serious); and Private L.J. Bishop, a New Zealand artilleryman.[56]

Commander Smith returned in his bullet-riddled landing craft to the headquarters the invaders had set up at Pokonian. Itching for revenge, he wanted to return to destroy the Japanese, but Colonel Cornwall, the New Zealand commander, insisted that the reconnaissance missions be finished first. The Allies had to content themselves for the moment with lobbing about a hundred mortar rounds into the area around the barges. The

Pokonian Plantation, 31 January 1944 (photographs by Combat Photo Unit 9, HQ Comthirdphib, SOPAC). Nissan Green Island 1944 [Archives Reference ADQZ 18905, WA117, 3/16 E11], Archives New Zealand, The Department of Internal Affairs, Te Tari Taiwhenua.

mortars, which had previously been firing at a distance of 1400 yards, moved to within 600 yards of the Japanese defenders and resumed firing. In the late afternoon, once the reconnaissance missions were complete, an assault was launched on the Japanese positions. Major A. Bullen was ordered to take two platoons and to finish the Japanese off. The platoons set off in separate landing craft. The intention was that the two platoons would land 100 yards to the left and right of the Japanese. Four other landing craft would then provide covering fire with their machine guns and rifles, and then an assault would be made. A frontal assault was intended. One infantry platoon in a landing craft landed on either side of the Japanese barges. The troops were equipped with gelignite and were intending to blow the barges up. Hardly had the two platoons landed when suddenly six Zero fighters[57] appeared and began bombing and strafing the Allied landing craft.

> The coxswains revved their engines and zigzagged in all directions as six Jap fighter planes peeled off, the loading edge of their wings spitting red tracer bul-

lets, spattering the water into miniature geysers and clipping through the flimsy sides of the craft like a ripsaw.

Back on Pokonian the alarm was given—"Take cover—take cover—air raid." You could hear the drone of low flying aircraft coming closer and closer. "Get the hell off the beach with those barges," roared an American officer to the coxswains of the remaining boats and they had the unenviable task of reversing their craft into the lagoon and taking evasive action. You could see the small 50 pound bombs leave the Zeros and fall in a diagonal flight towards the water. Small cascades of water flicked around the barges as the strafing planes passed overhead. You could see the Nip pilots turn their heads to look down on the beach as they roared by. Two platoons found themselves with Japanese troops in front and strafing Zeros to their rear.[58]

The scene is described in *Pacific Kiwis*:

"It will be our turn soon," everybody thought as they lay in fox holes in the plantations. Some in their eagerness scooped sand out of their trenches with their hands, others with arms like flails shovelled deeper into their slit trenches to get more protection. The barges were still being strafed while one badly aimed bomb fell somewhere on the seaward side of the coast.

Why the Zeros failed to make another run and strafe the beaches is a mystery, for had they done so, casualties would have been certain.[59]

Harry Bioletti recalled, "I saw a Japanese fighter plane come over. As I looked up I could see the Japanese pilot looking down at us."[60]

Frank Rennie observed, "The combined fire power of the barges must have kept the Japanese from coming too low, but with the advantage they had, why they didn't press this home will always be a mystery. Our barges were peppered with holes including the one carrying the explosives. We would have been very badly placed had the Japanese concentrated on the barges—and on us."[61]

The Japanese may have suffered a casualty from ground fire. Captain Cain reported, "One plane was apparently hit by fire from the boats after making his dive. The engine started missing and smoking and the Zero jettisoned its bombs on the north side of the small island in the lagoon. When last seen, the plane was losing altitude."[62]

Perhaps deterred by the ground fire, or simply because they had expended their ammunition and fuel, the Japanese fighters withdrew. Mercifully, the casualties from the air raid were light. An American sailor, Arthur Rolland Jensen, USNR, was killed, and two American sailors—Vernon Michael Cunningham, USN, and James Clement Bruton, USN—had been wounded.

A measure of how serious the situation was is that an uncoded signal was sent from Nissan: "Request air cover—being heavily strafed."[63] This

RNZAF Ventura bomber overflies the raiders (photographs by Combat Photo Unit 9, HQ Comthirdphib, SOPAC). Nissan Green Island 1944 [Archives Reference ADQZ 18905, WA117, 3/16 E11], Archives New Zealand, The Department of Internal Affairs, Te Tari Taiwhenua.

message in plain language and another one in code were picked up by a New Zealand listening post on Vella Lavella.[64]

The Withdrawal of the Commando Raid

Commander Smith thought that the islands could have been secured[65] and the idea of remaining was very tempting. However, as against that, there were no plans in place for reinforcing the raiding force, and there was the ever-present threat of further air strikes from Rabaul. The raiders had been lucky that the initial air raid had been so ineffectual. In addition, there was the possibility of further Japanese reinforcements arriving, or indeed of further hidden Japanese troops being encountered. There were also the wounded to be considered.

The decision was made to withdraw. As darkness began to fall, the two platoons reboarded their landing craft, checked that everyone was accounted for, and headed for the shelter of Barahun. There they waited until midnight for the return of the APDs. Whilst the initial invasion had been difficult, the withdrawal of the raiders presented a whole new set of problems. A receding tide and darkness hampered the withdrawal. At one

Private J. E. Hickey returns from recce. Note the No. 48 Radio used for communication, 31 January 1944 (photographs by Combat Photo Unit 9, HQ Comthirdphib, SOPAC). Nissan Green Island 1944 [Archives Reference ADQZ 18905, WA117, 3/16 E11], Archives New Zealand, The Department of Internal Affairs, Te Tari Taiwhenua.

point a landing craft became grounded and had to be manhandled into deeper water.[66] Sea conditions outside the lagoon were rough, with a ten-foot swell "tossing the small landing craft about precariously on the crest of waves and against the sides of the ships."[67] This made the transfer from the landing craft to the waiting APDs immensely difficult and fraught with danger, a process made more difficult by the inky blackness. *Dickerson* began taking landing craft aboard at 0020 hours in "rough water." Her War Diary records that oil was pumped overboard to quiet the waves. The after davit hoisting pad of boat #4 failed, necessitating a jury rig. Wounded in boat #4 were hoisted aboard with lines.[68] But the troops were able to re-embark, albeit perilously and after some hours.[69] An American officer was crushed between the landing craft and APD.[70] Eventually the raiders were able to return to Vella Lavella.[71]

For Harry Bioletti the withdrawal was nightmarish:

> We had problems getting back to the waiting APD's. The withdrawal took place at night and it was pitch black. The landing craft went out in single file and we had to steer by following a red light on the back of the craft in front. At one point we momentarily lost contact with the craft in front.
>
> When we reached the APD's there was shouting, "Come on up!" One of the men got crushed between the APD and the landing craft as he attempted to climb the ropes.[72]

During the raid, Brigadier Potter anxiously awaited news on the destroyer USS *Fullam* positioned off Empress Augusta Bay, Bougainville. The wounded were triaged on board ship, and on reaching base, several were evacuated on SCAT flights. Others were treated at U.S. Mobile Base Hospital #8.

There were some unexpected beneficiaries of the raid. As the naval force withdrew, the American destroyer USS *Waters* encountered a barge containing forty-two men whose craft had developed engine trouble and were adrift between the Russell and Savo Islands. A line was secured and the barge towed into Kukum.[73]

Aftermath

The casualty list was one New Zealander and three Americans killed and two New Zealanders, three Americans and two native guides wounded.[74] Not included in the official casualty list were one U.S. Naval officer and two New Zealand soldiers who suffered leg and ankle injuries incurred in getting in and out of the landing boats. There was also a

Three. The "Commando Raid" 43

The raiders mortar Japanese barges south of Pokonian Plantation (photographs by Combat Photo Unit 9, HQ Comthirdphib, SOPAC).

machine gunner who suffered second-degree burns on one hand whilst firing at the attacking Zeros.[75] All things considered, the raiders had escaped lightly.[76] Japanese casualties are unknown, but *The Pacific* suggests seventeen Japanese were killed by mortar fire.[77]

Much valuable information was obtained, including details of the lagoon water depths, suitability of landing beaches, the effects of tides, and a suitable site for the airfield. The New Zealand engineers were in their element:

> Cross section profiles of each landing place were plotted, onto which scale models of LSTs were placed. These indicated just how close to the shore and in what depth of water the landing ramps would be dropped. From this we were able to advise the American naval authorities that trestle bridging would be required and to tell our GOC just where the vessels could be placed for the loading of essential equipment. Also from the surveys of the sapper personnel it was possible for our HQ to estimate the amount of work required at each landing place. Units participating were thus detailed to provide the personnel, tools, materials and equipment required in the first assault waves of landing troops. Preliminary works to be done ashore and to facilitate the beaching and unloading of the all important LSTs were also made plain.[78]

However, not all of the engineers' advice was accepted by the U.S. Navy. On one of the Blue beaches (the landing beaches were color coded) the engineers' advice was ignored. No doubt to the immense satisfaction of the engineers, on the day of the invasion one of the navy commanders in the heat of the moment decided to ignore his orders and to land on an adjacent beach, coincidentally the very beach originally chosen by HQ Divisional Engineers.[79]

The best landing beaches for the artillery were identified and positions marked out for the placement of the guns. For example, a detailed report on Blue Beach near the Pokonian Plantation, which noted the existence of a small cemetery, highlighted where trees would need to be felled to create fields of fire, and it also set out the work necessary to create beach exits.[80]

The islanders advised that there were roughly a hundred Japanese

The raiders fire mortar bombs at the Japanese barge and its defenders. Note the soldier holding the next mortar bomb to be fired and the people with binoculars observing the results (photographs by Combat Photo Unit 9, HQ Comthirdphib, SOPAC). Nissan Green Island 1944 [Archives Reference ADQZ 18905, WA117, 3/16 E11], Archives New Zealand, The Department of Internal Affairs, Te Tari Taiwhenua.

located to the south of Nissan, although that number tended to fluctuate. The reconnaissance also established that the tracks on the island corresponded with what was on the maps.

A mystery was also resolved. Aerial photographs had shown small clearings and stone-enclosed spaces at regular intervals around the coast, apparently made by the Japanese and thought to be "probable beach defences" or enemy preparations "suspicious because of size location and intense activity evident."[81] However, it was soon established that the work had been done by a local cargo cult.[82] The intelligence officer who questioned islanders on the Commando Raid on the existence of these enclosures had been a planter in Bougainville prior to the war. The Islanders told him, "A fanatical native, apparently with very persuasive powers, had convinced his fellow tribesmen that at some time propitious to the gods, food and stores would be delivered to them by a phantom ship. Sheds and enclosed spaces had been constructed on prominent features so that the ship would not miss any at night."[83]

The lack of air cover had almost proved catastrophic.[84] Allied fighter aircraft would have been near the limit of their operational range, but missions against Rabaul, which was much further away, were being routinely undertaken. P-38 Lightning twin engine fighters had long-range capability, especially if equipped with long-range drop tanks. There were airfields on Bougainville, including the RNZAF base at Torokina.[85] U.S. night fighters may actually have been in the vicinity,[86] as aero engines were heard in the distance as the troops awaited evacuation at midnight. So why wasn't fighter cover provided for the Raiders? There are two likely reasons. Firstly, the ability of fighters to linger over the Green Islands would have been limited, and as the actual invasion would later show, any combat air patrol would have been porous. Secondly, any fighter planes over the Green Islands would have been detected by the Japanese and excited their interest. The lack of immediate air cover was a gamble, but a reasonable one in the circumstances.

At first sight the composition of the raiding force seems odd—not small enough to be stealthy, nor big enough to deal with substantial opposition. The official New Zealand history, *The Pacific*, provided an explanation: "There were good reasons for the employment of so heavy a force in both the raid and this operation [referring to the later main invasion]. The Green Islands lay some hundreds of miles beyond areas held by the Allies and were close to Rabaul; a large number of specialists, working alone in small separate groups, had to be protected; very little information was available about these islands, as no intelligence parties had been put

The raiders pull out from Pokonian to move into the lee of Barahun Island. The raiders had been strafed by Zeros 45 minutes before this photograph was taken (photographs by Combat Photo Unit 9, HQ Comthirdphib, SOPAC). Nissan Green Island 1944 [Archives Reference ADQZ 18905, WA117, 3/16 E11], Archives New Zealand, The Department of Internal Affairs, Te Tari Taiwhenua.

ashore from submarines to make preliminary investigations; and a desire to avoid any unnecessary waste of life."[87] Yet the basic question remains as to why different methods had not been used. After all the technical information gathering for Operation Goodtime, the invasion of the Treasury Islands had been undertaken by stealth by a small group of specialists.[88] For that matter, the American invasion of Vella Lavella on 15 August 1943 had been preceded by a small group of six specialists delivered to the island by PT boat.[89] Bulkley describes how PT boats were used in March 1944 to land a reconnaissance party on Massau in the St. Mathias Group, where the Japanese had set up a radio station and seaplane base. Having reconnoitered the island and ascertained that the Japanese had gone, a larger party returned to the island on 24 March and destroyed the Japanese facilities.[90] These types of activities became almost commonplace in the menu of PT boat operations.

Three. The "Commando Raid" 47

Conceivably a small stealthy force would have been preferable, with far less risk of unnecessary casualties and less chance of alerting the Japanese as to Allied intentions. Furthermore, it is curious why the U.S. Marine Corps had not used its specialist reconnaissance teams to investigate the Green Islands.[91] The feasibility of a stealthy reconnaissance is further shown by the fact that, as *The Pacific* notes: "The first really accurate information which paved the way for the raid was obtained on the night of 10 January 1944, when a special naval party in two American motor torpedo boats surveyed without detection the two lagoon entrances and found that the southern channel between Barahun and Nissan Islands was 16 ft deep and 40–50 ft wide. It would therefore take the larger landing craft, including heavy LST's."[92] If PT boats could carry out an undetected reconnaissance, they could presumably have landed a specialist team. A PT boat, well camouflaged with netting and laid up during the day in one of the inlets, would have been much less susceptible to discovery than 12

Advanced dressing station at Pokonian Plantation. Wounded NZ soldier and native guide receive treatment (photographs by Combat Photo Unit 9, HQ Comthirdphib, SOPAC). Nissan Green Island 1944 [Archives Reference ADQZ 18905, WA117, 3/16 E11], Archives New Zealand, The Department of Internal Affairs, Te Tari Taiwhenua.

Private F.W. Dement with wounded native guide Konan, 31 January 1944 (photographs by Combat Photo Unit 9, HQ Comthirdphib, SOPAC). Nissan Green Island 1944 [Archives Reference ADQZ 18905, WA117, 3/16 E11], Archives New Zealand, The Department of Internal Affairs, Te Tari Taiwhenua.

LCVPs. The Japanese *Daihatsu* motorized barges routinely sheltered during the day under camouflage netting and generally moved at night to avoid air attack. The Allies could have taken a leaf out of that book and done likewise.

The answer probably lies in the fact that the Americans knew the Green Islands were used as a staging point for barge traffic and the Japanese were "present in light strength."[93] By sending a relatively large force, the Americans were anticipating contact. Yet such a large force could only alert the Japanese to the planned invasion. Indeed, the raid was set for 31 January, which was considered the latest time at which information could be used to assist in the attack without giving the Japanese enough time to reinforce the garrison.

Barrowclough's perspective was that it was the right decision to carry out a reconnaissance in force. He wrote in his War Diary: "The nature of the opposition and the fact that there were two Jap barges in the lagoon demonstrated beyond doubt that a secret reconnaissance could have achieved nothing of any value and that the reconnaissance in force was necessary if we were to obtain the information that was desired."[94] Arguably also, a larger, better protected group would be able to obtain information more effectively by operating openly rather than a small group having to limit its activities by having to remain hidden. There was probably also, by this stage of the war, a certain complacency creeping in. It seemed that the Japanese were on the ropes and therefore not much of a threat.

The Japanese Reaction

When a report from a Japanese lookout was received on 31 January, the commander of the southeast area immediately ordered an aerial reconnaissance and a fighter bomber strike. The attacking pilots reported the presence of six motor torpedo boats. Japanese forces on the Green Islands signaled that they were being attacked, had incurred heavy losses, and were going to destroy their code books. They requested reinforcements. The garrison then fled northwards to the Feni Islands in three landing barges. Their escape was noted by an RNZAF reconnaissance plane.[95]

Reinforcements were dispatched from Rabaul in two Japanese submarines at midday on 1 February 1944. The soldiers were from the Wada Company. There were one hundred and twenty-three soldiers, but on arrival it was found that the rising storm made their disembarkation difficult. Only seventy-seven of the soldiers were able to land on the northeast coast of Nissan at midnight. The rest had to return to Rabaul.[96] Meanwhile, some of the original Japanese garrison who had fled returned on 5 February.[97] The two groups of Japanese soldiers met up and set up a headquarters in caves to the south of Pokonian Plantation, and most of the garrison occupied the area around the mission. Gillespie observes, "At that time the garrison numbered one hundred and two but was increased by a small undetermined reinforcement from Rabaul before the actual seizure of the group."[98]

The net effect of the Commando Raid had been to increase potential

Funeral of Lt. P. O'Dowd on Nissan, 31 January 1944 (photographs by Combat Photo Unit 9, HQ Comthirdphib, SOPAC). Nissan Green Island 1944 [Archives Reference ADQZ 18905, WA117, 3/16 E11], Archives New Zealand, The Department of Internal Affairs, Te Tari Taiwhenua.

opposition. As Harry Bioletti of 30 Battalion wrote, "One question which the boys asked themselves was—Will the Japs be waiting to oppose our landing when we return to Green Island?"[99] Barrowclough echoed the sentiment: "The fact that we are interested in the Island must now be abundantly apparent to the Japanese High Command. What they will wish to do about it and what they will be able to do remains a problem."[100]

The Islanders and Their Attitude Towards the Allies

Ironically, the belief the islanders were pro–Japanese proved to be misconceived. The Green Islanders were pro–Allied and provided useful information to the Allies. The eminent American historian Samuel Eliot Morison comments that the Allied forces "found the Green Islands to be inhabited by some 1,200 Melanesians who were so friendly to us and so hostile to the Japanese that in the operation plan the usual preliminary naval and air bombardment was omitted."[101]

In an attempt to influence the islanders, the raiders had carried with them gifts of colored fabrics, food and tobacco. These gifts certainly made a favorable impression on the islanders. In contrast, the Japanese had alienated the islanders by "killing off the pig population and robbing fruit and vegetable gardens."[102]

Four

Planning an Amphibious Invasion

The planning for Squarepeg was to be unique. The two prior combat operations of 3NZ Division, Vella Lavella and the Treasury Islands, had been carried out at a brigade level, and planning had accordingly been carried out by the brigade staffs of 14 and 8 Brigades respectively. For Squarepeg the planning was primarily carried out by the divisional staff.

The success of Squarepeg and the fact that things went like clockwork, with thousands of troops and tons of equipment offloaded on the first day, was due in no small part to the meticulous planning that preceded the invasion. By 1944 the New Zealanders had experienced several major shifts from New Zealand to New Caledonia to Guadalcanal, and the movement into the forward zones of Vella Lavella and the Treasury Islands. The experience of these shifts provided the New Zealanders with practical knowledge and tables for loading and unloading men and equipment. However, the invasion of the Green Islands dwarfed the prior shifts in terms of the size and complexity.

Most of the planning fell to the "Q" Branch (or Quartermaster Branch) of the division, the part that dealt with supplies and transport. Lieutenant Colonel P.L. Bennett, AAQMG, and his deputy Major G.B. Gibbons were at the center of the planning.[1] Specialists assisted, and Barrowclough commented that these "very efficient planning and movement control staff" helped resolve the loading problems.[2]

Gathering the troops and resources was no mean feat. On 11 January, divisional HQ was still moving from New Caledonia to Guadalcanal. At that time, 14 Brigade and divisional troops were concentrated along the southeast coast of Vella Lavella.[3]

Barrowclough and his senior staff officers set up his divisional headquarters on Guadalcanal on 5 January 1944, and were rapidly joined by the commanders of 14 Brigade's main units. These officers then began planning the invasion with their American colleagues on Admiral Wilkin-

Four. Planning an Amphibious Invasion

LSTs at Kukum Beach, Guadalcanal, take on NZ troops February 1944. Nissan Green Island 1944 [Archives Reference ADQZ 18905, WA117, 3/17 E 2 2], Archives New Zealand, The Department of Internal Affairs, Te Tari Taiwhenua.

son's staff. This planning group formed a combined planning organization which embraced Army, Navy and Air Force.[4] By necessity, the New Zealand Army planners had to work closely with their counterparts from the U.S. Navy, who had the details of the ships and their load-carrying capacity. The planners had to make the maximum use of the shipping available, which varied from the APD destroyers through to the cavernous holds of the giant Landing Ship Tanks. 3NZ Division Operation Order No. 101 was issued on 4 February, followed two days later by air and naval support plans and supplemented by Admiral Wilkinson's Operations Order 2–44 on 5 February.

It did not help that the invasion date was changed a number of times. On 4 January 1944, Barrowclough was told that the invasion date was set for 1 February 1944, only to be told the following day that the invasion date was to be 15 February 1944. This had flow-on effects for the Army, Navy and Air planners, causing them to revise their plans. Compounding matters was uncertainty as to whether Squarepeg would suffer further postponements. This state of uncertainty existed until 24 January 1944, when Halsey confirmed the invasion date.[5]

Planning was not straightforward due to the initial shortage of information. At least three operational plans were produced and the expectation was that the planning had to be sufficiently flexible to accommodate changes. As part of the planning, weather conditions had to be considered. A detailed meteorological report was prepared with input from meteorologists from the RNZAF.[6]

Establishing local air superiority soon after the landing was a key priority. A Seabee regiment, comprising two battalions totaling about two thousand men, was directed to build airfields. It was anticipated that one airfield would be built within thirty days of landing, followed by a second fifteen days later.[7] Once an airfield had been built and fighter and bomber squadrons based there, then the Green Islands would be much more secure against Japanese invasion or air attack.

Usually amphibious shipping was scarce. On this occasion, however, Brigadier Dove commented:

> The shipping side is very satisfactory. We can practically write our own ticket.
> The number of LSTs we can take seems only governed by the availability of landing beaches, possibilities of fighting conflicting with the necessity for quick unloading. Landing beaches are difficult to find in TANGALAN PLTN [Tangalan Plantation].[8]

Available to the planners were 34 landing craft consisting of 8 APDs, 13 LCIs, 7 LSTs and 6 LCTs. The task involved getting onto these craft 5,806 men, plus 4,344 tons of supplies and equipment for D–Day alone.

To complicate matters even further, the stores and equipment were spread over Vella Lavella, Guadalcanal, the Russell Islands and Ondonga.[9] Scheduling the concentration of men and supplies so that they would arrive in good order and at prescribed times in pre-computer days can only be described as a herculean task. Even getting the various groups organized—the assault troops, signalers, supply personnel, artillery and engineers—was a mammoth undertaking.

The heavy equipment had to be loaded onto the specialist amphibious craft—the LSTs and LCTs. This had to be done in such a manner that the supplies and equipment needed first on landing would be loaded last onto the vessels, a process called "combat loading." In addition, a certain amount of redundancy had to be built into the planning so that in the event that one vessel was destroyed, it would not imperil the success of the invasion.[10]

By necessity, not all the men, supplies and equipment could arrive on D–Day. A series of five echelons was planned for every fifth day after D–Day.

It was anticipated that some items of heavy equipment would be vital on D–Day. Bulldozers were allocated to the amphibious vessels so that they would be the first off and able to construct ramps to the landing craft, and clear roadways and supply areas. In the planning, trestle bridges were included to cover the eventuality that the water was too deep for the bulldozers to be landed.[11]

Orders were given that vehicles were to be loaded to capacity and loaded with chains on all wheels. Minimum quantities of field cooking equipment were to be taken.[12] In the planning, provision was made for five days of supply of suitable food for an estimated native population of 1,500. These supplies were in the first echelon.

An example of the detailed level of planning were the LST conferences. On 10 February 1944, a conference was held at LST Headquarters, Lyons Point, Florida Island, by the Commander LST Flotilla Five, Captain G.B. Carter, USN. The purpose was to discuss and make preparations for the first echelon to travel to the Green Islands. Task Unit 31.43 was created and the Commander LST Group Fifteen, Commander V.K. Busck, USN, was placed in command of LSTs 70, 207, 220, 354, 446, 447 and 472. The commanders, medical officers and firefighting representatives from each LST attended. Briefings were held on movement and cruising dispositions, the use of barrage balloons, and communication plans.[13]

This was followed two days later by a similar briefing for the LSTs of the second echelon. Commander R.W. Cutler, USNR, of LST Group Thirteen was placed in command of LSTs 39, 71, 117, 18, 123, 166, 247, 269, 334 and 390. The second echelon was a mixed unit of LSTs and LCIs. The LCIs 65 and 223 were to be accompanied by the tug *Menominee*.[14]

The importance attached to Squarepeg can be gauged by the allocation of significant numbers of the precious LSTs. They were an integral part of any successful amphibious operation in the Pacific because of their load-carrying capacity and ability to land and retract from beaches.

Referring to the first echelon, Captain G.B. Carter, USN, proudly recorded: "This echelon [is the] best equipped of any LST Echelon of the Flotilla in its ten months operating in combat areas of the British Solomon Islands. Each ship had the anti-aircraft guns permanently mounted (seven 40mm and fifteen 20mm) plus additional temporary mounts in the cargo load. Each ship floated one barrage balloon which functioned well throughout the trip. There were twenty-nine trailers in the unit, three LCVPs were equipped with a 500 GPM Chrysler fire pump, pontoon

NZ gun crews man a 40mm antiaircraft gun on the deck of LST en route to the Green Islands, February 1944. Nissan Green Island 1944 [Archives Reference ADQZ 18905, WA117, 3/17 E 2 2], Archives New Zealand, The Department of Internal Affairs, Te Tari Taiwhenua.

bridge sections were carried by all LSTs. Each ship had trained unloading teams and organized medical teams."[15]

Deciding to invade the Green Islands was one thing, but the question was "where?" The geography of the Green Islands shaped the choices of landing sites. The various beaches, in accordance with longstanding amphibious warfare tradition, were given color-coded names to avoid confusion—Red, Blue and Green Beaches. Calculations were undertaken of disembarkation of materiel and how long it would take to complete. Beachmasters were appointed to control each beach to ensure that the operation went smoothly. ASC officers, namely Captains G.N. Somerville, J.F.B. Wilson, J. Sykes, and D.R. Hopkins, were allocated for this task.[16]

In an amphibious operation, small errors can magnify in significance to the point where the whole operation is imperiled. For example, if the troops in the first wave were landed in the incorrect spot, or supplies of ammunition of the right caliber were not readily available, then problems would multiply in a cascade type of effect with consequent loss of life. Planning had to be as thorough as humanly possible.

Colonel Joseph Alexander, a USMC historian, pithily summed up amphibious operations: "The essence of amphibious warfare is an assault launched from the sea against a hostile shore, an operational scenario typified by the mandate to build combat power immediately from ground zero to full striking strength to attain landing force objectives and avoid defeat in detail."[17] Unlike conventional military operations, in which the attacker generally has the advantage of attacking with maximum force, an amphibious attacker starts weak, with piecemeal forces landed on a hostile shore, and has to progressively build up strength. This is what makes amphibious assaults so dicey and which had to be constantly borne in mind by the planners of Squarepeg. Nothing could be taken for granted.

Alexander also makes the point, "There is no such thing as a near miss in amphibious warfare. An assault launched from the sea is so complex, so inherently risky, that defeat—should it occur—becomes catastrophic."[18] Good planning, the right equipment, realistic doctrine, training, flexibility, good leadership and a measure of good luck are essential ingredients to any successful storm landing. *Headquarters*, an unofficial Third Division history, captured the flavor of the preparations by the New Zealand signalers:

> Additional equipment was received by the quartermaster and once again his department became exceptionally busy crating equipment into "two man" loads for shipment and in issuing to personnel pup tents, jungle knives, grenades and jungle rations. The pup tents, as the name implies, were a miniature type of tent constructed in two halves which domed together along the top to form one unit. Each man carried one half of a tent, together with a small collapsible pole, and on bivouacking he linked with a mate to construct a complete shelter for two men. Jungle knives with knuckle duster handles were another new issue. Although nothing pretentious in appearance they offered a light and yet useful weapon for self defence. The enemy's throat slitting tactics with knives had been well reported and practical experience had now proved the stories no myth. To combat and defeat the Jap entailed being one jump ahead of his trickery and treachery, for which he had no limits. Evidence of the New Zealanders' realization of this was borne out in the appearance in the forward areas of ambulances devoid of their familiar red crosses on the circular white background. These had been eliminated to avoid being used as targets by fanatics who respected nothing.[19]

In most amphibious operations in the Pacific War, an intense naval bombardment took place prior to the invaders landing in order to destroy the defenders' fortifications and facilitate the invasion. However, the decision had been made not to undertake this due to the risk of harming the

NZ personnel on the weather deck of an LST bound for the Green Islands. Note the antiaircraft guns and how tightly packed the deck is. Nissan Green Island 1944 [Archives Reference ADQZ 18905, WA117, 3/17 E 2 2], Archives New Zealand, The Department of Internal Affairs, Te Tari Taiwhenua.

local population. Nonetheless, it was intended that if the assault troops encountered resistance, naval gunfire support would be available. Because of the relative shallowness of the lagoon entrances and limited sea room, no battleships were designated. The role was given to destroyers.

One of the primary tasks of the invaders was to organize the assaulting troops and to ensure that they were properly trained. Although 14 Brigade had been in combat on Vella Lavella, they had not carried out an assault landing. They had to prepare for the move to the Green Islands, and this involved weeks of preparation as they boxed up equipment and supplies for transport and prepared their gear to ensure it was properly functional. Some of the soldiers' tents that were wet and heavy simply fell to bits, having rotted in the humid conditions. Fires marked the process as excess items that could not be packed were consigned to the flames. By 13 February the camps on Vella Lavella had been emptied except for small rear area parties.

An Army Board publication, *Guadalcanal to Nissan*, records:

> By 13 February most of the LCIs, LSTs and LCTs had reached Vella Lavella, via their various ports of call, to complete loading. There along the several beaches, landing craft butted in on the sand, two or three at a time, pulling out to the open seas as soon as their complement was aboard. The day was as perfect as the setting. Against a backcloth which was a wall of jungle, piles of boxes, lines of vehicles, and guns and bundles of equipment spread over the sand. Men splashed in the water or lay in the welcome shade of trees and palms beyond the dusty coral road behind the beaches. As each vessel came in, groups of men moved to their particular piles of gear and equipment, clearing it in record time; trucks and jeeps and guns disappeared into the interior of the heavy craft. By evening the beaches were clear and landing craft moved slowly over many leagues of peacock blue and green water which caught the sunset as in a vast mirror, for not a breath of warm wind ruffled its surface. By midnight the convoy was on its way. Next day came the APDs to embark the assault battalions who practiced the landing before they, too, departed north, escorted by five destroyers. Moving slowly ahead, the leading convoy passed the Treasuries at midday, two long files of ships with their destroyer screen far out. The day was cloudless, except for tumbling piles immediately above the larger islands, and a burning sun threw back the heat from a burnished indigo sea. Planes could be seen taking off from Stirling Island as though catapulted into the air over the edge of the cliff, maneuvering into position before disappearing in flights to the north on softening-up missions.[20]

For the New Zealand Signals Corps, the move was a difficult one:

> On the evening of 12 February the sections were ready to move. The now familiar mode of amphibious transport in LSTs and LCTs made their appearance at nightfall off Vella Lavella, and nosed their way on to the beaches to take aboard their complements of vehicles, equipment and troops. Each signal vehicle had been packed with equipment until its springs lay flat, and as each driver drove his overloaded quad or jeep up the ramp of these modern Noah's arks onlookers held their breath lest they shouldn't make it, and then gave a sigh of relief as the vehicles, one by one, disappeared into the interiors of the various ships on which they were to travel. Should any of the vehicles not have "made it," there would have been no alternative but to leave them aside, for the loading and movement of the convoy, which ultimately embraced 34 invasion craft that similarly loaded equipment and troops from Guadalcanal, Russell Islands and Ondonga, was finely timed. So detailed were the plans that the personnel of the entire force consisting of divisional headquarters, the 14th Infantry Brigade Group and three battalions of American construction specialists (Seabees, whose task it was to build the airstrip) were deployed through the convoy in such a manner that the dismissal of any one ship through enemy action could not seriously hamper the scheduled operations.[21]

The planners broke the invasion into two phases: an assault phase, and then a consolidation phase with the beaching and unloading of the remaining LCIs, and the LSTs and LCTs.

The operational plan envisaged the three assaulting battalions seizing the two plantation areas and then establishing a defense perimeter. Patrols were then to be sent out to locate the Japanese. The 30th Battalion was given the task of taking Pokonian Plantation and the southern part of Barahun Island. This would enable it to secure the entrance to the lagoon. The 37th Battalion was to seize the left-hand side of Tangalan Plantation and the 35th Battalion the right-hand side. It was intended that they would have the support of a troop of tanks.

In the amphibious landing phase it was considered an "urgent necessity" that the APDs be released "at the earliest opportunity." It was directed that all the landing craft of the 8 APDs were to be used to land 800 men in the Pokonian-Barahun area. The landing craft were then to return to the APDs, load up the remaining 800 men, and deliver them to the Tangalan area.

H-Hour was set at 0630 hours on D–Day. This was when it was anticipated that the first wave would hit the beach at Pokonian Plantation.

The successful landing and emplacement of antiaircraft guns were considered vital for the success of the invasion. These were to be "placed in position ashore with all possible dispatch under the direction of Commander Royal Artillery (CRA) NZ Division. LAA 40mm Bofors Guns will be 'stepped ashore' by troops and at least half the guns will remain in action on top deck of LSTs until the other half are in action ashore." Two troops of each light antiaircraft battery were deployed on the upper decks of the LSTs on which they were traveling for the protection of the convoy. Another troop was to have the first priority on the LSTs elevator so that it could be landed quickly.[22] The New Zealanders had bitter experience of operating under Japanese air attack on Vella Lavella and the Treasury Islands, and 29th Light Anti-Aircraft Regiment was given priority in the first echelon. Two full batteries of 40mm Bofors guns were allocated, and given the shortage of shipping space, this is indicative of just how seriously the Japanese aerial threat was taken.[23]

The emplacement of radar was to be given priority, and COMAIR SQUAREPEG had the power to require any other unit or organization to move in favor of the radar unit.

Field artillery was also another important asset, so 17 New Zealand Field Regiment was designated to deploy in the area of the Pokonian Plantation. One troop of 144 Battery was to be landed at Tangalan and then ferried across to Pokonian Plantation. Antitank artillery was to be deployed to cover the channel south of Barahun Island.

The New Zealand Engineers were given the task of landing on assigned beaches to support the landing operations. Priority was to be

Another view of the deck of an LST. Nissan Green Island 1944 [Archives Reference ADQZ 18905, WA117, 3/17 E 2 2], Archives New Zealand, The Department of Internal Affairs, Te Tari Taiwhenua.

given to dealing with the beached LSTs and prepare shore approaches and dump areas. They were also to assist with preparing antiaircraft positions and radar installations, to build dugouts for medical and signal units, and finally to construct roads and tracks.

The 22nd Naval Construction Regiment was specifically tasked with unloading the 3 LSTs and 2 LCIs and assist the New Zealand engineers on the landing beaches. New Zealand troops from all formations were directed to supply unloading parties for the LSTs—248 for LST-472; 259 for LST-354; 238 for LST 446; and 210 for LST-447.[24] Not even HQ 3NZ Division was exempt. They had to supply ten men. Predictably, the infantry supplied the bulk of the unloading parties; 37 Battalion, for example, provided one hundred and twenty-three men.

Intelligence summaries were prepared and distributed, including a Special Intelligence Summary covering information gleaned from the Commando Raid.[25] Lieutenant Colonel A. Murray of the Divisional Engineers had his staff construct scale models of Nissan. For 37 Battalion, Lieutenant McKenzie, who had been involved with the Commando Raid, helped construct a sand-table model of the terrain. Aerial photos were also used in its construction. It was expected that every man in the Battalion would have the opportunity of studying it.[26] On 3 February, Lieutenant Dean, an intelligence officer, lectured company commanders on terrain, and Lieutenant Col. Sugden outlined the brigade plan, whereby 30 Battalion would secure the entrance, followed by 35 and 37 Battalions landing in the vicinity of Tangalan. Lieutenant Zivaneth, the U.S. Naval gunfire officer, and a naval gunfire observation party consisting of Lieutenant Kelly, USMC, and seven Marines were attached to 37 Battalion. Lectures were given by Captain Brooker of the 3NZ Division Tank Squadron on infantry tank cooperation, and Lieutenant Bartos was sent to 14 Brigade as liaison officer and air support control officer.[27]

Heavy casualties were anticipated from an opposed landing and arrangements were made with the LST flotilla to receive these. Plans were also made to establish a medical dressing station as rapidly as possible on Nissan.

Food for the invaders was essential. A new type of ration was issued. The J ration consisted of a foot-square wax-sealed carton containing dried fruits, porridge, nuts, dried milk and biscuits. This was considered sufficient for four days for one man or two days for two. The food was palatable but required a little culinary imagination in preparation. Of more importance was the need for clean, drinkable water. Two-gallon tins of water were provided but had to be conserved.[28]

The logistical aspects of Squarepeg presented a problem of nightmarish proportions. The infantry and their supporting units were located on Vella Lavella, some 220 miles from the target. Various stores and equipment had to be loaded from Guadalcanal, the Russell Islands and Ondonga. Making matters even more complex was that heavy equipment and supplies for the rapid construction of airfields and roads had to be added to the items to be shipped.

Then to make matters still more complex, it was decided that the Valentine tanks of 3NZ Tank Squadron were to be deployed. Even then there was insufficient sealift for the NZ tanks, and so only 8 tanks under the command of Major R.J. (Jim) Rutherford were to be in the initial landings, with the remainder of the squadron to arrive five days later.[29] The huge amphibious vessels, the LSTs, were in short supply, and there was vagueness as to how the tanks would be transported. For Major Arthur Flint, a British Army officer sent to observe the New Zealand tanks, it was almost the last straw when it was proposed by the American planners that the tanks would be loaded onto one ship and the crews onto another, with two miles' distance between their landing zones. Flint was informed that "any fool could drive a tank!" He was also told that if he continued his objections there would be no tank involvement at all. Fortunately, matters were later resolved at a higher level, and the tank crews were able to drive their tanks off their LSTs. However, one consequence of the argument was that as a compromise the tanks were obliged to tow U.S. 90mm AA guns ashore.

To add to the chagrin of the tankers, when they arrived at the embarkation area of Kukum Beach, Guadalcanal, they discovered that no provision had been made for the trailers carrying their reserves of ammunition. Consequently, they were informed that there was no room for the trailers on the LSTs. Major Rutherford resolved the problem by suggesting that the trailers be placed on the engine decks of the tanks, and this was done.[30]

In the planning of Squarepeg, Barrowclough took the step of freeing up the specialist Seabees from routine tasks such as unloading landing craft, roadmaking and maintenance in order to allow them to concentrate on the all-important job of airfield construction.[31]

Barrowclough recognized that Squarepeg was fraught with risk. He considered that it involved "our stretching our necks to uncomfortably close proximity to strong Japanese forces on New Ireland and we have behind us very large Japanese forces in Choiseul, Bougainville and Buka Islands." He proposed that his forces be as strong as "humanly possible."[32] To that end, 8 Brigade on the Treasury Islands was designated as an "Area Reserve," but realistically, if the invasion miscarried, there was little chance of 8 Brigade's coming to their comrades' rescue.

The Demise of Battalion Combat Teams

Impressed by the flexible combined arms approach of the German Army, Barrowclough had developed the concept of battalion combat teams. These were small units of infantry backed up by supporting groups of artillery, communications, supply and medical personnel. The concept had been trialed by 14 Brigade in its operations on Vella Lavella. Although successful, the concept of battalion combat teams had the chief drawback that it spawned multiple command structures. It was not used by 8 Brigade in Operation Goodtime. It was abandoned for Squarepeg.[33] Squarepeg was a much larger operation than conducted on Vella Lavella, and the added complexity of amphibious operations made it undesirable to continue an unwieldy command structure.

Green Combat Paint

In the Commando Raid, the troops had applied green combat paint. However, for the invasion there was less enthusiasm to use it. As Harry Bioletti comments, "There is not the keenness to apply green combat faces this time, for experience had shown that it takes a week to remove it from the pores of the skin."[34]

The Invaders Prepare to Depart: The Barrage Balloons Are Floated

As the invasion convoy prepared to depart, specialist personnel from Barrage Balloon Unit, LST Flotilla Five, Navy 145, began inflating large, ungainly, special balloons tethered by steel cables to the ships.[35] Each LST floated one barrage balloon. The purpose of the balloons was to provide protection against attacking aircraft. The theory was that the balloons and their steel cable would provide an obstacle for aircraft, and if the ships got extremely lucky, might even bring down an aircraft unlucky enough to collide with their balloon or steel cable.

These barrage balloons had been a common sight in Britain during the early part of the war. They had had limited success in protecting British cities from the Luftwaffe, but no doubt boosted civilian morale.[36] However, the barrage balloons to be used by the ships of Squarepeg were different from their land-based cousins produced by Firestone. They had special fins so that they could be used with moving vessels. They were of a variety known as the "Type Z.K.S. Shipboard Barrage Balloon." Their inflation and operation were entrusted to specialists.

By the time of Squarepeg, the use of barrage balloons to protect shipping had become standard practice. They had been used in Operation Goodtime with some consternation caused to the invaders when the ghostly balloons appeared unexpectedly with the arrival of further echelons on the Treasury Islands.

As the Squarepeg ships gathered, the barrage balloons were inflated. Some, however, were not cooperative and were not fully inflated. The bal-

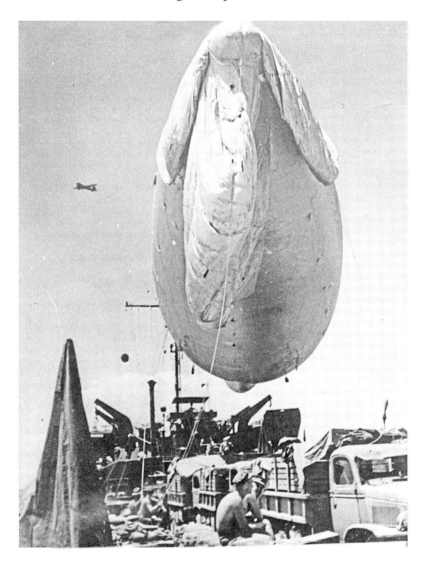

A barrage balloon is secured to an LST prior to its departure for the Green Islands, February 1944. Nissan Green Island 1944 [Archives Reference ADQZ 18905, WA117, 3/17 E 2 2], Archives New Zealand, The Department of Internal Affairs, Te Tari Taiwhenua.

loons were not without their hazards. When the second echelon returned to Guadalcanal on 22 February 1944, it was reported that "the balloon aboard LST-269 was struck by lightning and lost and the one aboard LST-39 was lost due to cable parting."[37]

The Fleet Ocean Tugs

Two seagoing tugs took part in Squarepeg. These were USS *Menominee* (AT-73) and USS *Sioux* (AT-75). Although slow and sluggish, the tugs were an important part of the invasion plan. They had the ability to assist landing craft that had difficulties in retracting or maneuvering. They also had fire pumps. There were no portable fire pumps except on the LSTs; the destroyers, with their firefighting equipment, had difficulty getting close in to shore. The tugs had proven their worth on Vella Lavella in October 1943, where they had helped in firefighting the burning LST-448. *Sioux* had taken part in Operation Goodtime with her sister tug USS *Apache* (AT-67) and had rendered yeoman service in salvage and towing operations.[38] The provision of these tugs is an indication of the care and forethought that characterized the planning of Squarepeg.

Five

Bloody St. Valentine's Day— The Ordeal of USS *St. Louis*

By early 1944 the *Helena* class light cruiser USS *St. Louis* had experienced an interesting war and had earned the nickname "Lucky Lou." Commissioned in May 1939, she had survived the Japanese attack on Pearl Harbor on 7 December 1941, bombarded the Aleutian Island of Kiska, fought alongside the New Zealand cruiser HMNZS *Leander* at the Battle of Kolombangara, and shelled Japanese positions on the Shortland Islands and Bougainville. Although *St. Louis* had been hit by a Japanese torpedo at the Battle of Kolombangara (13 July 1943), the damage had not been fatal, and by mid–November 1943 she was back in the thick of it.

On 14 February 1944, St. Valentine's Day, *St. Louis* was deployed as part of the escort group for the Squarepeg convoy. One of the escort task forces was commanded by Rear Admiral W.L. Ainsworth and the other by Rear Admiral A.S. Merrill, both extremely experienced and competent American naval commanders. Task Force 39, made up of 3 light cruisers and 5 destroyers, operated in the area to the east and north, whilst Task Force 38, consisting of 2 light cruisers and 5 destroyers, covered the area between the Green Islands and St. George Channel.[1]

The Japanese detected the approach of the invasion convoy at dusk on the evening of 14 February off the coast of Bougainville. A reconnaissance plane reported "a large convoy of thirty transports and eighteen cruisers and destroyers" headed in a northerly direction.[2] The Japanese commander's response had been to order an attack by 32 Japanese aircraft, although the darkness of night delayed the aerial attack.

At 1855 hours, sundown, on 14 February, six Vals were spotted. The Aichi D3A Val was a single-engine, fixed-undercarriage dive bomber, and despite its antiquated appearance was one of the deadliest shipkillers in the Japanese arsenal. These flew astern of the vessels and turned to the southeast, and then five of the aircraft split into two groups. One group

USS *St. Louis*, circa 1944. USS St. Louis Association.

attacked a destroyer. The other group of two planes attacked *St. Louis*. *St. Louis* zigzagged desperately, moving at 27 knots. The first plane dropped 3 bombs, which were near misses off the starboard bow. The second plane was more successful. Two bombs fell off the port quarter and were near misses. The third hit near the No. 6 gun mount, ten feet to port of centerline, penetrated into the living quarters and exploded, causing carnage. Twenty-three sailors were killed and 20 wounded, of which half were serious. Damage control teams fought the fire, but the ventilation system was wrecked, and the aft engine room had to be abandoned due to extreme heat and smoke. Control of the ship was transferred to the forward engine room. The ship maneuvered at 20 to 28 knots in the aftermath of the attack, but the gyro compasses had been affected and it took four hours for them to settle down. The ship slowed to 15 knots at 2125 hours with *Honolulu* protectively taking station ahead of *St. Louis*. An alarm was given at 0045 on 15 February that further Japanese aircraft were closing fast. Smoke screens were laid and evasive maneuvers were begun. Fortunately, the attack did not eventuate.[3]

Five. Bloody St. Valentine's Day

In war, the difference between life and death can depend on chance. Boatswain's Mate I/C Walter Brickhause told the *St. Louis Globe*,[4] "A coxswain named Parnett was trainer on a quad mount, and the bomb bent the outer edge of the trainer's seat he was sitting on and went on through the deck. Parnett wasn't even scratched but he went around for about a week with eyes as big as saucers!" This was the bomb that penetrated two decks and exploded.

John Hinds was a gunner's mate at the time the Vals attacked. He later commented that although he had received a lot of training, "When it's time to shoot for real it's over in seconds, especially when airplanes are involved." He added, "I was first loader on a quad 40mm at Green Island. I suppose I may have put 6 or 8 clips (4 rounds to a clip) into the gun, when a bomb from a *Val* dive bomber went through the deck on our gun platform causing the ammunition in the ready room under the gun to start exploding just like a string of firecrackers. Later the Captain came back to inspect the damage. He wanted to know who was sitting in the trainer's seat. One of the guys spoke up and said he was. The Captain then replied 'If I were you, I would go to Church Sunday, or better yet, I would go before Sunday.'"

Electricians Mate 3/C Bill Murphy, was one of the first on the scene of the bomb explosion:

> I was the second fire hose handler into the compartment. We could hardly see because of the smoke but we did see some movement not far from us. We found four men there, all mangled, but still alive. They died minutes later. Being an electrician, I helped kill live circuits and cut out circuits. I fought the fire and helped evacuate wounded and killed. There weren't many wounded, two or three I think. Most were dead. They said there was an officer in the next compartment with his head blown off, but I didn't see. There was plenty right there where I was.
>
> Those damn Japs knew we were hurt and they were trying to get us. The destroyers had put out a smoke screen and were maneuvering round inside it. There must have been about 30 planes in all, and you could always hear their roaring engines. One tin can on our starboard beam would run out of the smoke, turn outside, fire like hell and then duck back in. It was the worst night I ever spent, but I guess we have to expect such things once in a while. War sure is hell.[5]

For the crew, the damage was indeed like a scene from Hell. William F. Harral recalled, "My battle station was 'stretcher bearer mid-ship.' It was just forward of the 6 inch handling room by the forward turret. When we got hit, they called for stretcher bearers mid-ship to report back aft, so I went up there. Man, here's all these guys laying around there. Higgenbottom was the Chief there, Pharmacists Mate. Me and this other guy were trying to roll this body over, onto the stretcher, real easy, and he says,

'Put him in there! You are not going to hurt him. He's dead.' Yeah, OK. We did. That's where I grew up real quick."[6]

The crew faced an additional ordeal. William C. Chew remembered, "The hospital corpsmen and what not took all the bodies out, but we were constantly finding bits of flesh, in among the springs in some of the bunks that were left, or just pasted onto a stanchion or something like that. It took a long time to clean that place up. It really did."[7]

Ralph Koontz recalled that the bomb had taken off the arms and legs of a ship's electrician. "Took them off just like they'd done it with a saw. They couldn't find his arm and it started stinking down there where we eat. It smelled. They went down, the R Division took it [the air duct] off and found his arm." The unfortunate sailor survived his horrific injuries. "They put him in a basket and shipped him back off to his folks and he kept hollering, 'Kill me, don't let me go back,' he says. 'Shoot me. Do anything but don't let them send me back.'"

The dead sailors were moved to the main deck aft out of the sight of the survivors, and were then identified by identity tags, tattoos, names on clothing and dental charts. The bodies were then placed in canvas bags with two 5-inch shells to weigh them down, and a funeral at sea took place.

Having completed its escort mission, *St. Louis*, accompanied by the destroyer *Woodworth*, retired to Purvis Bay on Florida Island, British Solomon Islands, for repairs. In addition to her personnel casualties, *St. Louis* had suffered significant battle damage. Her War Diary recorded:

> [L]iving compartment B-205-LM completely demolished with all ventilation and electrical fixtures. All drainage and piping on the port side ruptured. Hole 6ft square in the deck of B-205 LM at frame 99, 15ft to port of centerline. Minor flooding in B-316–1 from ruptured sprinkling system. Numerous electrical fires with dense smoke. After engine room vent and supply ducts and damage to motors, remainder of after ventilation running on casualty power. B-205-LM-80% of fixtures demolished. 5[qm]/38 hoists 6 and 8 from lower to upper handling room of Mt. #4 knocked out of line and inoperative. Doors 2–93–1, 2–93–2, 2–103–1 and 2–103–2 blown off hinges. Bulkheads 93 1/2 and 103 second deck level pierced by numerous fragments and bulged. Near miss caused slow water leak with some indication of oil leakage into two voids under hanger, C-608-V, this leakage controlled by use of main drain. Both planes out of commission, port gasoline tank leaking, hull bent in at frame 123.[8]

American cruisers were robust, and heavily armored in parts. However, they had weak, vulnerable spots, and the Japanese bombs, both direct hits and close near misses, had inflicted significant damage. It is testament to the efficiency of the ship's damage control teams and crew that *St. Louis* was able to continue functioning. The loss of trained personnel affected the ship's combat efficiency. On returning to the relative safety of Florida Island, replacements were taken on board.

Although it was recommended that *St. Louis* be sent to a Navy dockyard for repairs, these were undertaken at Purvis Bay and *St. Louis* returned to duty. *St. Louis* would take part in the invasion of Guam, the Battle of Leyte Gulf, and Okinawa. She survived the war and was decommissioned on 20 June 1946.[9]

The casualties of the Japanese air attack were inflicted on *St. Louis* and LST-466, which received slight bomb damage. The Japanese, however, claimed one transport sunk and two cruisers, one destroyer and three transports damaged. They acknowledged that twelve of their aircraft had been lost, including the reconnaissance aircraft which had shadowed the invasion convoy during the night.[10]

Six

Invasion

En Route to the Green Islands

Units from the 14 Brigade and various American supporting units sailed from Guadalcanal and Vella Lavella. Of the total force of 5,782, some 4,218 were Kiwis.

Headquarters recorded: "The invasion convoy consisted of 8 APDs, 13 LCIs, 7 LSTs and 6 LCTs. These vessels travelled at varying speeds and accordingly set out for the Green Islands at staggered times. Progressively the faster LCIs and then the APDs closed their gap between the slower LSTs to form one impressive convoy under the protection of destroyers and scooting PT boats. Anti-aircraft gunners kept constant vigil and high in the sky above each LST sailed a silver barrage balloon tethered by a steel cable as a further deterrent to Tojo's dive bombers."[1]

Things did not go completely according to plan. One of the escort vessels was the *Adroit* class USN mine sweeper USS *Constant* (AM-86). *Constant* suffered from engine problems and was unable to fulfill her patrol function. The LST Flotilla Five War Diary acidly commented, "This inspired the vexatious muddle as to which was the escort and which was the escorted."[2]

The other aspect which was disturbing was the antiaircraft gunnery drills which the LST Flotilla practiced on 15 February at 1420 hours. The AA gun crews fired at a target sleeve towed by an Avenger torpedo bomber with disappointing results. This was attributed to a layoff of a month and half and many new gun crews being made up of inexperienced men untrained in AA gunnery. Eventually, the target sleeve was hit, no doubt to the relief of all concerned.[3]

As the convoy steamed towards the Green Islands, the destroyers set up a circular screen. The night was clear and the moon very bright. The invasion convoy was located by Japanese "snooper" aircraft at about 0143

Six. Invasion

Antiaircraft gunners on an LST bound for the Green Islands practice firing at a sleeve towed by an aircraft—with disheartening results, February 1944. Nissan Green Island 1944 [Archives Reference ADQZ 18905, WA117, 3/17 E 2 2], Archives New Zealand, The Department of Internal Affairs, Te Tari Taiwhenua.

on the morning of 15 February 1944. The Japanese aircraft dropped flares periodically and made a number of dummy or unexecuted attacks, and two actual attacks. The multiplicity of radar contacts and the shifting of ships in the convoy confused the American AA gunners and limited their response. To add to their woes, at 0315 *Waller* was about to open fire on a bogey when *Renshaw* reported that it was a friendly aircraft. Although fire was held, there was no actual confirmation the aircraft was an Allied one. Allied nightfighters were, however, active. The destroyers circled the invasion convoy protectively.[4]

The composition of the LCI Task Unit 31.4.2 gives a good indication of the measures taken by the U.S. Navy to protect the invaders. The unit consisted of LCIs 433, 444, 360, 445, 436 and 446. They beached at Kukum on Guadalcanal on 12 February and took on board fifteen men and four officers of 3NZ Division, Brigadier General Dumas (U.S. Army) as an observer, and two correspondents for *Yank* magazine. Escorted by the destroyers *Pringle, Sigourney* and *Philip* on the right flank and destroyers *Waller, Saufley* and *Renshaw* on the right flank with *Menominee* in the rear, the unit proceeded to Juno Beach on Vella Lavella. LCI's 443, 433, 444 (the tug) and 359 took on personnel of 3NZ Division together with equipment and supplies. The beaching had occurred at 1508 on 13 February 1944 and loading was completed by 1607. Then LCIs 360, 434, 445 and 435 beached at 1630 on Juno Beach and had their turn to take on board troops and equipment. Loading went smoothly and they retracted at 1715. It was then the turn of LCIs 436, 358, 446 and 357 to beach at 1730. By 1840 loading was completed and the LCIs anchored offshore.[5]

The loading operation was a carefully choreographed event, both in respect of the LCIs taking their turns on Juno Beach, and in terms of the soldiers loading men, supplies and equipment. The fact that things went so smoothly is testament to the detailed planning of both the U.S. Navy and the New Zealand Army.

By 2345 the Task Unit was underway with *Waller* in the lead and with six LCIs in column following *Waller* in line astern with another six in column line astern on the left flank. The Task Unit traveled at 10 knots.

Nothing ever goes quite according to plan, and this was no exception. At 1230 LCI-444 radioed that it had a man with appendicular colic, which required hospital treatment. At 1345 the LCI moved out of the column and the unfortunate man was transferred to the destroyer *Saufley*, which transported him to the Treasury Islands for medical treatment. This was done quickly, and by 1740 *Saufley* had rejoined the Task Unit and recommenced its screening role.

The morning of 15 February 1944 was to be a tense one for the sailors and their guests. At 0145 the crew went to general quarters, and as the night progressed, various white float flares were dropped by Japanese planes in the vicinity of the convoy and its course.

Following the intricate choreography of the naval planners, at 0420 the LCIs passed the LSTs and were in turn passed by an APD unit at 0533. No doubt to the relief of all in the Task Unit, at 0620 thirteen friendly planes were sighted and took station above the convoy.[6]

In the early morning light, a formation of B-25 Mitchell bombers, returning to base after having attacked Rabaul, flew over the convoy. It seemed like a good omen.[7]

Grim-faced NZ assault troops on the Green Islands landing. Note the steel helmets, Lee Enfield rifles and heavy kit bags. 15 February 1944. Nissan Green Island 1944 [Archives Reference ADQZ 18905, WA117, 3/17 E 2 2], Archives New Zealand, The Department of Internal Affairs, Te Tari Taiwhenua.

The Vals Attack—0645

As the APDs came to a halt in preparation for offloading the assaulting landing craft, fifteen Vals appeared and struck the LCIs and LSTs at the entrance channel at 0645. The attack came in with little or no warning because the radar operators were faced with the large number of friendly fighter and bomber airplanes and the movement of the ships, and it was hard for the radar operators to identify hostile aircraft.

Ron Tucker recalled that as his LST headed towards the Green Islands, Japanese dive bombers appeared overhead. The convoy was attacked several times. Fortunately, the dive bombers were not accurate. The Kiwis stood on the deck cheering as the dive bombers were driven off by fighters and AA fire. Some six Vals were thought to have been shot down. LST-486 suffered a near miss. The barrage balloons streamed by the LSTs may have hindered the Japanese pilots, but perhaps not in a way

Convoy of LCIs entering the lagoon of Nissan, the Green Islands, 15 February 1944. Nissan Green Island 1944 [Archives Reference ADQZ 18905, WA117, 3/17 E 2 2], Archives New Zealand, The Department of Internal Affairs, Te Tari Taiwhenua.

the defenders intended. At 0705 a plane was spotted by the crew of LST-207 approaching from astern at an altitude of twelve thousand feet. It rapidly approached, dropping to an altitude of three thousand feet, and despite the LST's AA guns it dropped two small bombs some two hundred yards forward of the LST. It was believed that "the plane was running above and along the line of balloons, using them to sight on, but due to the brisk breeze from port the balloons were some distance out to the starboard instead of directly over the vessels. This was believed to have caused the bombs to miss the vessel."[8]

The LSTs may have been derisively described as "large slow targets" by their crews, but nonetheless, they escaped lightly. In his War Diary for LST Flotilla Five, Captain G.B. Carter, USN recorded: "From 0645 to 0700 on the morning of the landing, 15 February 1944, the unit was subjected to sporadic attacks by Japanese, single engined, Aichi 99's ('Vals'), two of these attacks directed at LSTs. One plane was downed by near misses.

The falls of the starboard davit of LST-446 [were] severed by bomb fragments dropping boat with same sinking; later salvaged by beach party. Other small damage with one casualty in the unit; Myers, Wayne B., MOMM3C, USNR (LST-446) wounded in the right forefinger by bomb fragment."[9] Wilkinson later reported that of the fifteen attackers, only six were seen to drop their bombs. "The Vals had no fighter protection and our covering fighters pressed home their attacks to inside the gun range of the ships. Some ships withheld fire because of the proximity of friendly fighters attacking enemy dive bombers. By 0700 the attack was completed."[10]

On their return, the Japanese pilots erroneously reported a transport ship, two cruisers and a destroyer sunk and three transports damaged.[11] They recorded their losses as being twelve aircraft, including the snooper reconnaissance plane that had shadowed the convoy.

The Mine Sweepers and Fire Support Gunboats

It had been planned that three mine sweepers would precede the invasion force and would sweep the entrance to the lagoon. However, two of the mine sweepers experienced mechanical problems and were delayed by a critical forty minutes. They arrived just as the landing craft were approaching the entrance, and to avoid a traffic snarl-up, the landing craft preceded the mine sweepers. Fortunately, the entrance was clear of mines, and even more fortunately, the Japanese had not targeted their artillery on the entrance of the channel.

The mine sweepers belatedly began their task.[12] They had as an escort two Landing Craft, Infantry (Gun) or LCI (G). These were Landing Craft, Infantry that had been turned into gunships for the purpose of supporting the vulnerable landing craft as they made their approach to the landing beaches. They packed a 3-inch gun, one 40mm Bofors gun aft, four 20mm cannons and six .50 caliber machine guns.[13] They had first been used in Operation Goodtime and had proven very useful in suppressing Japanese defenses. On this occasion their role was to be a much more limited one.

The PT Boats Return to Green

It was fitting that the first vessels to enter the Green Islands were PT boats. "On the morning of February 15, Lieutenant Commander Taylor

Valentine Tanks of 3NZ Division Tank Squadron are landed on Nissan 15 February 1944. Nissan Green Island 1944 [Archives Reference ADQZ 18905, WA117, 3/17 E 2 2], Archives New Zealand, The Department of Internal Affairs, Te Tari Taiwhenua.

and Lieutenant Hardy, in PT 247 (Ensign R.B. Warnock, USNR) and PT 249 (Lt. (jg) M.S. Trimble, USNR) made a last minute investigation of the channel at 0200 to make sure there were no obstructions. They reported to the approaching task force commander that the coast was clear."[14] PT boats 176, 178 (Ron 11), 247 and 249 (Ron 20) went after machine gun nests on the shore.[15]

Landings

The invasion began at first light on 15 February 1944. The soldiers were offloaded from the APDs first and then from LCIs a short time later. They would be followed by the LSTs an hour after that, and then later on in the afternoon, the LCTs appeared. 30th Battalion landed on the lagoon side of Pokonian Plantation (Beach Blue), and the second wave of troops of 35th and 37th Battalions landed on the lagoon side of Tangalan Plan-

Six. Invasion

tation (Beach Red—north; Beach Green—south). Much to the relief of the landing troops, artillery had not been zeroed in on their landings areas, nor had they been mined. In fact, the invasion was initially unopposed.

This was just as well, because although the soldiers had received training, they were highly vulnerable as they disembarked from their ships, climbing down cargo nets into fragile landing craft and then undertaking the ship-to-shore movement. Amphibious operations, no matter how carefully planned, are messy affairs. The USMC historian, Joseph Alexander, has acutely observed:

> Chaos characterized even the best-planned beachheads in the Pacific War. Even in peacetime maneuvers, amphibious commanders found it extremely difficult to move large numbers of heavily laden troops from their transport ships, down the scramble nets into the landing craft bobbing alongside, and direct them through several miles of sea swells and plunging surf to the right beach, at the right time, and in the right order.
>
> The ship-to-shore movement is inherently hazardous. Men drown in the surf,

After the hard, thirsty work of unloading LCT-446, troops drink coconut milk, 15 February 1944. Nissan Green Island 1944 [Archives Reference ADQZ 18905, WA117, 3/17 E 2 2], Archives New Zealand, The Department of Internal Affairs, Te Tari Taiwhenua.

are squashed by shifting cargo, or get run over by combat vehicles. Enemy fire complicates an already difficult process. Landing craft are blown up or capsize in the surf. Instead of an orderly tactical displacement, the beachhead often resembles a shipwreck.[16]

A New Zealand signaler recorded his impressions of the landing:

At the first light of dawn everyone crowded the decks to catch a first glimpse of Green Islands standing as a dusky oblong mass on the horizon. The day was D-day, 15 February 1944. Under an umbrella of allied aircraft the ships commenced to move in a circle, over a wide expanse of sea, each craft riding in the wake of the one ahead. As the sun came up the foam glistened silver and the ships silhouetted into an unending line of grim defiance as they awaited their turn to land their troops and equipment on the coral atoll known as Nissan Island. What enemy land opposition awaited the force no one knew. Fewer than 20 minutes flying time away was Rabaul, New Britain fortress of 100,000 Japs, from which air opposition could be expected, despite the bomb loads which allied aircraft were depositing daily on their quickly repaired airstrips. The Third Division was now closer to Rabaul than the forces located at the southern end of New Britain.[17]

Barrowclough and his staff traveled to the Green Islands on an American destroyer. He recorded his impressions in his War Diary:

The destroyers cruised around opposite the entrance to the lagoon and the APD's came in close and the first flight of boats, 32 in number, were soon in the water and made their way towards the entrance preceded by a PT Boat and an LCI gunboat. The plan was to effect a landing without preliminary bombardment if that could be done. If strong opposition was encountered, however, the minutest plans had been made for a thorough bombardment of the Japs by destroyer's gunfire and by bombs dropped from SBD's and TBF's. As the boats approached the channel the destroyers were in a position to open fire immediately when called for and a squadron of bombers was cruising over the position also ready to attack on call. The boats moved through the channel without a single shot being fired. On reaching the lagoon they turned around and effected a landing on the beach at the Pokonian plantation just south of the lagoon entrance. In a very few minutes they retracted from the beach after unloading their troops and we could see them from the destroyer coming out through the passage to pick up their next load of troops. At the same time I received word by wireless that the landing had been effected. The second flight of boats was loaded and proceeded through the entrance across the lagoon some four miles to the Tangalan Plantation where again a landing was effected without opposition. The LCVP's which carried the troops ashore from the APD's then returned to their mother ships and these withdrew. The next flights ashore comprised the LCI's which were run on the beach and discharged their troops down ramps on the side of the bow. While this operation was in progress an enemy post some fifteen hundred yards south of the entrance on the Pokonian side opened fire on our troops as they were debarking. No casualties were caused and the post was soon driven back by patrols of the 30th Battalion.

The next ships to enter the lagoon were the LST's of which we had seven, all of which beached without incident, and the big task of unloading began. By this time communications had been established ashore and I therefore left the destroyer

Six. Invasion

Tangalan Plantation 15 February 1944. Note copra shed in background. Nissan Green Island 1944 [Archives Reference ADQZ 18905, WA117, 3/17 E 2 2], Archives New Zealand, The Department of Internal Affairs, Te Tari Taiwhenua.

and landed at Pokonian beach and set up my Headquarters there. I visited the various positions where the anti-aircraft defences and radar installations were being erected, and saw the progress of the unloading of the LST's that were beached on that side. Later I crossed the lagoon and saw the situation on the Tangalan side.[18]

The unit historian for 30th Battalion noted:

A little before 0630 hrs troops boarded the landing barges, and it was quite pleasing to see our air cover already overhead. After a trip during which every face registered tenseness, we hit the beach, glad that it was an unopposed landing. Equipment was hastily unloaded by the occupants of each barge. A little later, during the unloading of LSTs we were treated with an impressive gun show. A gun-boat had located a Jap barge camouflaged in a northerly direction and opened fire. Another LST coming in to the beach opened up with Bofer [sic] fire, guns manned by the NZ boys who "went to town" in fine style. "D" Company meanwhile withdrew to a safer area. (They were in the line of fire). The Jap barge was soon sunk by our superior fire.[19]

New Zealand artillerymen were part of the assaulting infantry groups and "went in as infantillery, those on Blue Beach [Pokonian] comprising a quarter of the storming party.... Observation parties landed from the batteries to assist the assaults, their guns following once the beaches were clear."[20]

As his landing craft headed into the lagoon through a gap in the coral, Ron Tucker felt that they were sitting ducks to any Japanese defenders and was much relieved when there was no fire. The ramp of his landing craft hit the beach and his comrades worked quickly to offload their guns and gear. To his consternation, Tucker found that his guns did not have clear lines of fire, and coconut trees had to be chopped down to satisfy the F.O. officers.[21]

The soldiers of No. 1 Platoon and Company Headquarters of 14th Brigade Machine Gun Company were on LCI-443, which led the LCI convoy. The landing was not smooth. "Although there was a lovely coral beach on which to land the captain of our craft had other ideas and instead we dove in towards a six-foot coral bank which necessitated our entering into the water waist deep before scrambling up the coral."[22]

A New Zealand soldier meets a Green Islander, 15 February 1944. Nissan Green Island 1944 [Archives Reference ADQZ 18905, WA117, 3/17 E 2 2], Archives New Zealand, The Department of Internal Affairs, Te Tari Taiwhenua.

Doug Ross, the platoon commander of B Company, 37th Battalion, recalled his introduction to Nissan. His platoon "was a forward unit in the assault which was unopposed. From assault boats into chest high water on to a beach into dense jungle and rather dense undergrowth."[23]

For other members of 37th Battalion, the arrival at Nissan was almost an anticlimax. *Pacific Saga* records the impression of one of the invaders:

> Then the plunge ashore into the unknown, expecting every moment to hear the rat-tat-tat of machine guns or the crumph of bursting mortar bombs. But our landing was unopposed and we quickly put into operation the plans we learned and discussed on Vella Lavella. Natives soon came trickling into the perimeter and were anxious to make friends. They told us all they could and we learned that the Japs were in strength at the south end of Nissan. This information could not be confirmed so we went through all the battle procedure we knew so well, small company perimeters expanded to a battalion perimeter and then a wheel across the island to form a stop line. And all the while intense patrolling and reconnaissance—probing, searching. This methodical search continued and by night we had cleared a considerable area and were dug in at the north end of the Tangalan plantation, a considerable distance from the Red 1 and Red 2 beaches that had been our starting point that morning.[24]

The first wave of assault troops landed without opposition. Gillespie wrote:

> In two hours perimeters had been established with the perfection of a well timed and executed manoeuvre. Potter and his staff went ashore in the second wave of assault troops and established advanced brigade headquarters in the Tangalan Plantation. As soon as the battalion patrols established their block lines beyond the bridgeheads, the LCIs beached, then the LCTs, and finally, in the afternoon the LSTs. Men and material poured ashore as each wave of craft was cleared and retracted from the beaches to make way for the next carrying parties, one hundred from each battalion removed materials as they came ashore to prevent congestion on the beaches. By half past ten that morning Divisional Headquarters was established in the Pokonian Plantation, a dank site under the palms made worse when seeping tide water turned it into a bog.[25]

Wilkinson later reported: "The LST's arrived at 0835, two going to Blue Beach, one to Red Beach and three to Green Beach. All the beaches with the exception of Blue One required a bulldozer to do grading work before their load could be unloaded. Fortunately, the bulldozers were able to do this speedily and the pontoon bridges carried by the LST's were not needed."[26]

The New Zealanders were not the only ones to land on Nissan. In the first wave landing at Pokonian Plantation was Lieutenant Harland D. Warren, USNR, the code and publications officer of Amphibious Radio Communications Unit 39. Warren was a passenger in LCI-436 alongside the New Zealand assault troops. He later recalled, "At about the same time

Bren gunners ready to defend supplies, 15 February 1944. Nissan Green Island 1944 [Archives Reference ADQZ 18905, WA117, 3/17 E 2 2], Archives New Zealand, The Department of Internal Affairs, Te Tari Taiwhenua.

an LST unloaded our radio equipment including an NZ Radio Jeep in the lagoon side. In about one hour we were in radio contact with the Task Force Commander."[27]

As Sergeant William Laurence and his men struggled in the surf to get their Bofors antiaircraft guns off their landing craft, he noticed three men in jungle green uniforms without insignia watching them. Laurence proceeded with some irritation to remind the trio that there was a war on and suggested that they get off their chuffs and help pull the guns ashore. The three men pitched in and helped. Later, after the guns were safely emplaced, Laurence was approached by a stout man waving a swagger stick. The man introduced himself as Brigadier Duff, Royal Artillery. He told Laurence that Barrowclough sent his compliments and was pleased with Laurence's efforts. Laurence was puzzled until the realization struck him that Duff had been one of the three helpers. Duff then confirmed that Barrowclough had been one of the three who had got their pants wet in the surf dragging the guns ashore.[28]

The Tanks Are Landed

The state of the art in amphibious operations may have advanced hugely in World War II, but there were still oddities about Squarepeg. The USN provided the transport of the New Zealand Tank Squadron, but they insisted that the tank crews be berthed separately from their tanks. That meant that the tanks had to be crewed immediately prior to the landing and were delayed in coming into action. Compounding matters, the tanks were loaded alongside 90mm AA guns, and these had to be offloaded first. The Tank Squadron was landed mid-morning on 15 February without incident.

One troop landed at Green Beach on the southern part of Tangalan Plantation and 3 Troop landed on Red Beach at the northern end. A D-8 bulldozer was the first vehicle landed, and it set about creating a small jetty. Arthur Flint noted, "About one thousand hours orders were issued to advance further and enlarge the beachhead. Tanks were to stand by to support any infantry making contact. I went forward up a track for about one hundred and fifty yards and then everyone dived for cover. The obvious inference being that the Japs were coming towards us down the track. I felt apprehensive I can assure you! After a minute the 'sighting' came down the track and turned out to be a Seabee with a theodolite over his shoulder and busy surveying!! We were not sorry!"[29]

In an almost anticlimactic way, the invasion proceeded smoothly without opposition from Japanese land or naval forces, and within two hours the landing areas had been secured. Defense perimeters were established and patrols sent out. The question was, what had happened to the Japanese?

New Zealanders prided themselves on their ability to overcome complex problems in a practical way. Sometimes, however, they were awed by American problem-solving ability. Frank Cox, a tank troop commander, saw "one LST heavily loaded stuck fast on the beach trying to back off. Bulldozers were tried with no success. A U.S. Navy destroyer was called up which sailed past at full speed creating a huge wash which ran up the beach and back again taking the LST with it!"[30]

The unloading process went so smoothly that by 1730 hours the last of the LSTs had left for Guadalcanal. The vessels had landed "fifty eight Jeeps, sixty seven trucks of various kinds, forty four guns (both field and anti-aircraft), seven tractors, eight bulldozers, two compressors, ten radar installations of various types, twelve water-distilling plants ready for operation, ten trailers, two wireless vans, eight Valentine tanks, four hundred

Unloading from LCI-443, 15 February 1944. Nissan Green Island 1944 [Archives Reference ADQZ 18905, WA117, 3/17 E 2 2], Archives New Zealand, The Department of Internal Affairs, Te Tari Taiwhenua.

and twenty six tons of petrol in drums, two thousand gallons of fresh water in tins and two hundred and sixty seven tons of rations, in addition to vast quantities of personal and unit equipment."[31]

What had undoubtedly helped in the success of the invasion was that the unloading process had been unhindered by the much-feared Japanese air attack.

> Bulldozers went into immediate action, shearing off trees and palms and improving the landing beaches. Earth which had not known the sun for unnumbered years reeked as it dried in the heat. By the afternoon the landscape of Nissan was vastly changed, as though a tornado had torn bits of it away. Trees and palms had toppled everywhere. Guns of the 17th Field Regiment; the 144th Independent Battery commanded by Major G.R. Powles[32]; and the 29th Light Anti-aircraft Regiment were ready for action and areas cleared of all vegetation to give arcs of fire. Signals personnel were linking up headquarters and units as they strung their lines from tree to tree and laid six miles of underwater cable across the lagoon. In twenty four hours Captain K.H. Barron had a wireless station working with Guadalcanal, nearly 500 miles away. Engineers turned their machinery into the jungle and began to push it violently aside. Seven miles of rough roads had been

completed by nightfall in the two plantation areas. Each arm of the service fulfilled its appointed task in that closely co-ordinated scheme. Field Ambulances sited and established their hospitals; Major Brunette was performing operations on wounded natives the following day. ASC companies organized dumps for food and supplies, for which they were responsible for everyone on the island. American units hauled their valuable radars and air control trucks ashore and into position.[33]

The seven miles of rough road that had been created were capable of taking jeeps and trucks.[34]

McIlroy's Mission

As the invasion unfolded, an unescorted USN four-engine long-range photo-reconnaissance Liberator, piloted by Commander John H. McIlroy of Squadron VD-1, circled overhead. Regular reports of the progress of the landing were sent to Wilkinson, who was in a destroyer outside the

Unloading on the Green Islands, 15 February 1944. Nissan Green Island 1944 [Archives Reference ADQZ 18905, WA117, 3/17 E 2 2], Archives New Zealand, The Department of Internal Affairs, Te Tari Taiwhenua.

Another view of troops boarding an LCI and unloading, 15 February 1944. Nissan Green Island 1944 [Archives Reference ADQZ 18905, WA117, 3/17 E 2 2], Archives New Zealand, The Department of Internal Affairs, Te Tari Taiwhenua.

lagoon.[35] On board there were two passengers—Lt. Colonel Floyd Skow[36] of the United States Army Engineers and the ubiquitous Associated Press reporter, Vern Haughland.[37]

Haughland watched the operation from the air and recorded, "From the time the Higgins landing craft started unloading until the last ship in the big convoy had disgorged its cargo, it was a beautiful show of precision and efficiency. The best the Japanese could do was to send three planes in at dawn to attack—all three were promptly shot down by naval antiaircraft fire—and two hours later to fire feebly from shore long after hundreds of troops had landed. Landing craft and naval units replied furiously and quickly put an end to that."[38]

Although the photo reconnaissance plane may not have had a direct combat mission, the flight was not without its dangers. Firstly, there was the danger of "friendly fire" from antiaircraft batteries. Then several fighter planes appeared but were identified as friendly. Starboard waistgunner Walter Theobold, Recondo Beach, California, let go with a burst at one plane before it was found to be one of ours. "It was a Corsair," he said. "I think I put a couple of holes into him but it didn't seem to do any harm."[39] The plane completed its mission. "The weather was clear which made the Navy photographers happy. The glassy smooth water also aided the operations."[40]

Gillespie made reference to McIlroy's plane: "Circling above the assaulting troops 'was a special liaison aircraft, used for the first time that day to acquaint the task force commander in *Halford* of the progress of the landing and, if necessary, direct gunfire against opposition."[41]

Air Operations in Support of Squarepeg

Ross Templeton of 4 Motor Transport Company, NZASC, recalled that immediately prior to the invasion he and his comrades were given a tot of rum and assured that air cover would be provided.[42] The assurance was correct.

Prior to 15 February, determined efforts had been made to eviscerate Japanese air power by attacking nearby Japanese airfields. General Kenney, USAAF, recorded:

> The final Kavieng attack to support Halsey's landing came on the 15th as he was making an unopposed occupation of Green Island. Forty B-24's ruined the remaining Jap airdromes, silenced three heavy anti-aircraft positions, and set fires that were still blazing two hours later. Sixty B-25's set fire to the town area, destroyed the airplane and engine-repair facilities, burned or sank ten float planes in the harbor, sank dozens of barges and harbor craft, and blew up a huge ammunition dump which released debris bringing down five of our strafers. Three of the crews were picked up in one of the most striking rescues of the war, when one of the Navy Catalina flying boats assigned to the Fifth Air Force for air-sea rescue service picked up all fifteen men in Kavieng Harbor itself, while under fire from the Jap shore batteries.[43]

The air effort in support of Squarepeg was multinational and multiservice. The RNZAF provided fighter cover from 0800 hours to late afternoon. No. 14 and No. 18 Fighter Squadrons, equipped with *Corsairs*, flew twenty sorties and kept eight fighters on patrol. By the time the New Zealand fighters arrived, the *Vals* had departed, and the New Zealand airmen did not encounter any Japanese aircraft on 15 February.[44]

One of the fighter squadrons providing cover for the landings was a USMC squadron VMF-216 equipped with Corsair fighters. The squadron was based on the Piva fighter strip on Bougainville. Two divisions of four planes apiece provided medium cover for the landings. The fighters left

The hard work of unloading an LST, 15 February 1944. Nissan Green Island 1944 [Archives Reference ADQZ 18905, WA117, 3/17 E 2 2], Archives New Zealand, The Department of Internal Affairs, Te Tari Taiwhenua.

Piva at 0530 and returned at 0950. They initially took station at ten thousand feet but were ordered by the FDO [fighter direction officer] to climb to twenty thousand feet.

By its very nature, air defense is porous, as the Japanese pilots were able to show on 15 February 1944. A USN assessment of fighter direction commented, "For the Green Islands invasion not enough fighters were provided to provide the CAP [combat air patrol] to unprotected groups being attacked. The fighter director team on the USS *Sigourney* recommended that each transport unit be assigned its own cover."[45]

Another facet of the air effort was close air support. In February 1944, close air support was still in its infancy. Nonetheless, Avengers from VMTB-143 were deployed in this role. However, their usefulness was limited by the thick jungle of the Green Islands and the lack of identifiable, worthwhile targets. No doubt to the disappointment of the pilots, it was not necessary for the planes to be rearmed when they returned to their airfield. It is indicative of the degree of planning for Squarepeg that close air support was made available. However, it proved to be unnecessary.

Although the emphasis was on daylight operations, the need for night fighters was recognized. VMF(N)-531 provided night fighter support on the first night. The "Gray Ghosts" had the distinction of being the first U.S. Marine Corps night fighter squadron. The squadron was equipped with a specially adapted two-engine Ventura, the PV-1N equipped with SCR-40 radar.[46] In the early hours of the morning of 17 February, Colonel Frank Schwable claimed the destruction of a Japanese Aichi E13A "Jake" floatplane just off the Green Islands. On the same night, Flight Lieutenant Jack M. Plunkett also claimed a "Jake." However, only one plane was lost by Rabaul's 958th Air Group. On 19 February, Lt. Colonel John Harghberger downed another Japanese aircraft twenty-five miles to the southwest of the Green Islands. The night was no longer safe for Japanese intruders.[47]

Fighter cover was provided from Bougainville up until 7 March 1944. By that stage, a fighter airfield had been built on the Green Islands, and American squadrons took over local defense.[48]

Overall, the air effort epitomizes Squarepeg in a nutshell. RNZAF squadrons No. 14 and No. 18, USN and USMC squadrons VD-1, VMF-216 and VMTB-143 provided air support during the daylight hours and a special night fighter unit VMF(N)-531 provided cover during the hours of darkness. The different services, nationalities and specialized units all meshed together to make Squarepeg a success during its most vulnerable and critical phase.

The Engineers

One of the intricacies of planning operation Squarepeg was the need to provide a satisfactory beaching area for the huge LSTs. An unorthodox plan was conceived whereby the engineer section attached to the 37th Battalion would blow up an overhanging coral cliff opposite Tangalan Plantation and the debris would provide a good, easy gradient suitable landing area and allow for the offloading of bulldozers and other heavy vehicles. The need was to get the bulldozers onto the plantation area so they could get on with the job of clearing an airstrip.

The LCIs carrying the engineers and their cases of TNT explosive landed at 0703. Time was tight and the LSTs were due to land at 0730. However, to the frustration of the engineers, valuable time was lost because an officer in a nearby LCM misunderstood signals and blocked the way forward.

An RD-7 tractor is unloaded on Nissan, 15 February 1944. Nissan Green Island 1944 [Archives Reference ADQZ 18905, WA117, 3/17 E 2 2], Archives New Zealand, The Department of Internal Affairs, Te Tari Taiwhenua.

An observer, Sgt. J.W. Burnie, recorded:

> The LSTs were gliding all too rapidly across the lagoon from the entrance and the precious minutes were getting fewer and fewer. The official photographer was standing by to record the doings, the Sergeant in charge of demolition becoming more and more agitated. At 0730 hours the charge went off—a failure! The resultant damage to the cliff face was inadequate to give the bulldozer the desired ramp.
>
> Hurriedly alternative action had to be taken. Coconut palms on the plantation edge above were felled and pushed over the cliff face to make a very rough slope up which the bulldozer from the LST was trying to climb within ten minutes of the first charge's failure. We had some doubts whether the dozer would make the grade but after some tense moments of teetering on the top of the pile, the big blade tilted forward and sufficient grip was obtained on the edge of the coral shelf to pull the machine up to the plantation.[49]

That was not the end of the engineers' work, however. The engineers began the job of cutting down coconut palms to clear arcs of fire for the AA guns. AA gun pits were constructed out of coconut logs and earth was bulldozed around them so that they "provided a safe area from the night sniping of the allied troops."[50]

The Signalers

One group that was less appreciative of the efforts of the engineers was the signalers. The signalers had to haul ZC1 radios, heavy cables, telephone wiring and the plethora of signals equipment onto the invasion beaches. Most of their gear was in the cavernous holds of the LSTs, and they had to wait for these behemoths to beach.

Once divisional headquarters was established at Pokonian, the signalers began to set up a telephone exchange and cipher section, and then began the tedious task of laying telephone cable. By 1400 the signalers had created a radio network linking Green Island with Allied stations on the Treasury Islands, Vella Lavella and Guadalcanal. By nightfall all unit headquarters were linked up and six miles of underwater cable had been laid across the lagoon.[51]

Assault cable was used to link Divisional Headquarters, 14 Brigade Headquarters, and various artillery headquarters. However, their efforts were to be frustrated by "the fatal fascination bulldozers have for telephone

Landing Craft, Tank-577 in the lagoon at Nissan, February 1944. Nissan Green Island 1944 [Archives Reference ADQZ 18905, WA117, 3/17 E 2 2], Archives New Zealand, The Department of Internal Affairs, Te Tari Taiwhenua.

cables." The linesmen were kept fully occupied repairing the damage of these giant machines as they churned the beach head into temporary roads. Wherever there was a cable, it acted like a dozer magnet.[52] A constant battle took place to lay telephone cables and keep these links operational in the face of the depredations caused by heavy vehicles and equipment.

The New Zealand engineers were not the only source of the signalers' woes. For 37th Battalion's signals officer, the day of the landing was one of acute frustration: "American naval construction battalions landed soon after us and rapidly got to work with their bulldozers, clearing lanes in the jungle to allow a start to be made on the survey for the air-strip. As fast as the signals officer erected or repaired his telephone lines, bulldozers tore them down."[53]

In the early stages of the invasion it was vital that communications be linked up between New Zealand artillery batteries and the advancing troops. A New Zealand signals team was assigned the task of laying telephone cable across the lagoon using a barge. The signalers laid about three miles of cable and then their line got snagged, which led to the loss of the spool of telephone cable in one hundred and sixty-five to one hundred and eighty-five feet of water. The New Zealand officer was desperate, for he knew that the infantry advancing in the direction of the mission would likely soon make contact with the Japanese defenders, and also night was due to fall. At 1700 hours the officer contacted Lieutenant Warren and, indicating it was an emergency, asked for walkie-talkie radio packs, one for the artillery and the second for the infantry. The situation was resolved, however, by the ingenuity of an American sailor, Motor Machinist's Mate Clement F. Marley, who was on board the barge. Marley suggested that a pulley on a rope be rigged up using the block and tackle that was used for operating the landing ramp on the barge. Marley arranged for the leading end of the lost telephone cable to be threaded through the pulley, and by retracing their path, they were able to pull the wire spool from the depths. By 1800 hours the situation had been fixed and the radio packs were recalled. Communications were established between the guns, and the infantry and artillery fire began on Japanese positions.[54]

Digging In

As night drew near, the invaders began digging foxholes. This sometimes proved especially difficult because of the hard foundation of coral that lay beneath the thin layer of surface soil. The troops at Pokonian had the worst of it: "Owing to the low lying nature of the terrain and the narrow width of the island—barely two hundred yards—the holes began to fill with seeping saltwater. In some instances, too, large land crabs decided that they had a more rightful title to the occupancy of the fox-holes than the person who had dug them."[55] The men of 37th Battalion experienced similar problems because "after a day of grueling patrols or man-handling stores we were pretty tired and the structure of the island was not conducive to good digging. Wherever we went we found about six inches to a foot of rotten vegetation and then granite-like coral of which every inch had to be won by hard work with a pick. We counted ourselves fortunate if we each got a trench one to two feet deep and long enough to lie in."[56] However, even then the soldiers could not feel secure because the vegetation surrounding them was so thick that they could not be certain that there were no Japanese defenders close by.[57]

Field Cookers

The New Zealand Army appreciated the importance of providing hot food to the troops. Field cookers were landed on 15 February. Hot food was taken to the troops within a few days thereafter.[58]

Japanese Resistance?

Several accounts of the invasion of the Green Islands, including that of the journalist Vern Haughland, make reference to Japanese fire directed at the invaders some two hours after the initial landing. Indeed, there is contemporary film footage of an LCI gun crew firing their machine guns at the Japanese.[59] All accounts agree that Japanese resistance was rapidly suppressed. But was there really Japanese resistance at this point?

Gillespie, in the New Zealand official history *The Pacific*, states very plainly that there was none, saying of the landing, "Not a shot was fired." He describes how, two hours after the landing, "perimeters had been established with the perfection of a well timed and executed manoeuvre." Potter and his staff had come in with the second wave and set up an advanced brigade headquarters at Tangalan Plantation, patrols had been sent out, and carrying parties had begun the task of moving items from the beach to stop congestion. "The whole landing had been completed without

LCI-444 approaches Tangalan Plantation, 15 February 1944. Nissan Green Island 1944 [Archives Reference ADQZ 18905, WA117, 3/17 E 2 2], Archives New Zealand, The Department of Internal Affairs, Te Tari Taiwhenua.

hindrance or confusion." He then goes on to say, "It was disturbed by only one outbreak of firing when a too imaginative officer, examining the lagoon coast from the deck of an LCI, picked up the two barges destroyed during the 30 Battalion raid. All the armament from the LCI was turned on them, to the bewilderment of 30 Battalion patrols working their way slowly through the jungle nearby."[60] If Gillespie is correct, what had sparked the firing? There was a clear danger to New Zealand troops on shore from the 20mm shells, which would have had considerable penetrative power into the jungle, and there would have been the risk of an ugly "blue on blue" situation with New Zealand casualties.

The firing at the Japanese barges was quite deliberate and furthermore was authorized by CTF31. The officer who sought permission to open fire was none other than Commander J. MacDonald Smith. His motives for opening fire on the wrecked barges are obscure—he may have been taking precautions in case the barges had become Japanese sniper or machine gun nests, he may have been paying tribute to the fallen of

Six. Invasion

RD-7 tractor with bulldozer clears track, South Pokonian, 15 February 1944. Nissan Green Island 1944 [Archives Reference ADQZ 18905, WA117, 3/17 E 2 2], Archives New Zealand, The Department of Internal Affairs, Te Tari Taiwhenua.

the Commando Raid, or he may simply have been venting his frustrations. Either way, the Japanese barges were hosed with a lot of lead.

Smith, in his report to his superior, laconically noted:

> 0819 on beach. Unloaded troops supplies and observers. Com. LCI (L) Flot.5 [i.e., Commander Smith] observed 2 Jap barges under cover of trees along shore line about one thousand yards south of Blue 1-A Beach. Requested and received permission from CTF31 [Wilkinson] to join in the fire.
>
> 0835 Directed LCI 436 beached about eight hundred yards from the observed barges to advise troop commander to keep troops clear of the target area.
>
> 0849 LCI (L) 433 retracted from beach, took position eight hundred yards off shore to fire on targets.
>
> 0858 LCI's 433, 436 LCI Gunboat 67 opened fire on target. 2 LST's heading into the beach also joined fire.
>
> 0911 Barges destroyed, ceased fire and directed gunboat to investigate area carefully for other possible barge before returning.[61]

No disciplinary action was taken against Smith, which raises the presumption that his actions were considered valid.

In fairness to Smith, he would not have known for certain that the Japanese had not occupied the area, and the revetment-like structure of the coral around the barges would have been an obvious place for the Japanese to take up strong defensive positions. Smith's actions may in hindsight seem excessive, but at the time could easily have been justified.

There were, in fact, Japanese barges in the vicinity, and which were fleeing northward. Gillespie notes that "the only action, however, fell to 144th Independent Battery which shot up some Japanese barges on the shore of Sirot Island."[62]

The Mosquito Fleet Begins Operations

Another indication of the intensive planning behind Squarepeg was that the PT-boats, designated "MTB-Green," were able to begin official missions from the night of 15 February 1944, in addition to their security

Marston matting is laid down to form a road, February 1944. Nissan Green Island 1944 [Archives Reference ADQZ 18905, WA117, 3/17 E 2 2], Archives New Zealand, The Department of Internal Affairs, Te Tari Taiwhenua.

patrols for Squarepeg. Special support ships, such as a Bowser Boat, were available for the PT-boats, landing craft and seaplanes, which enabled them to operate locally, independent of repair and refuel stations.

The First Echelon Withdraws

By 0933 the LCIs had completed their unloading and Task Unit 31.4.2 reformed with the destroyer USS *Waller*, leading the formation back to Guadalcanal. However, the withdrawal was to be eventful. At 0320 on 16 February 1944, LCI-443 reported that she had lost her starboard screw and was limping along on her port screw. A towline was established by the destroyer *Phillip*, but this parted. The destroyer USS *Renshaw* screened *Phillip* and her charge. Happily, by 1127 the towline had been re-established, and *Phillip* and LCI-443 began to rejoin the formation. Early in the morning of 17 February, the Task Unit successfully reached the safety of Guadalcanal.[63]

Night Jitters

The night fell quickly and for most it was an uncomfortable period. The 30th Battalion historian noted, "Throughout the night one man in each foxhole was awake for an hour at a time. A perimeter had been formed around the ADS [Advanced Dressing Station]. A few fired shots into the darkness imagining that they saw or heard Japanese. (No casualties on either side from this shooting.) Japanese planes were over at regular intervals during the night, dropping bombs in scattered areas and doing no harm. The ack-ack batteries are not operating yet, so the aircraft had an easy time. Very little sleep by anybody and I've decided I'd never be comfortable in a foxhole."[64] He was not quite correct, however. Five islanders had been killed by Japanese bombs. Some twenty to twenty-five bombs had been dropped by high-level bombers during the night of 15–16 February. Air raid sirens had warned of approaching Japanese planes a little after midnight, and there had been a series of air raid alerts over the succeeding six hours. The Japanese bombers were aiming blind because of the darkness. Their main effect on the invading troops was to deprive them of much-needed sleep.[65]

Most of the troops on Nissan were apprehensive as night fell on 15 February. The island had thick, dense undergrowth, and there had been no sign of the Japanese garrison. The Japanese had a well-deserved

Valentine tank of NZ Division Tanks Squadron, February 1944. Nissan Green Island 1944 [Archives Reference ADQZ 18905, WA117, 3/17 E 2 2], Archives New Zealand, The Department of Internal Affairs, Te Tari Taiwhenua.

reputation as superb jungle fighters who excelled at nighttime infiltration. However, it was not only the Japanese who came out at night:

> With the dark came jungle noises to which we were accustomed, but this time a new note was added—thousands of somethings started clucking for all the world like hundreds and hundreds of domestic fowls. The noise was more prolonged and increased in tempo and pitch until an almost hysterical crescendo was reached. The offenders were small, horned brown frogs or toads which appeared very much like dried leaves in the light of an electric torch and which infest the jungle of the Solomons. In the pitch-black night, hundreds of lamps glowed in the form of rotten phosphorescent vegetation and what with one thing and another the atmosphere was decidedly eerie. One feels intensely lonely, although surrounded by comrades in shelter trenches. One hears a rustle in the undergrowth and some of the jungle noises abate, a dark form seems to be creeping stealthily towards one blotting out patches of phosphorescence—yes, here it comes—this way—staring into the blackness one imagines others—Japs!—then a grunt—whew, a wild pig! There were dozens of the brutes nosing around in the dark, needless to say our feelings towards them were not friendly and sometimes our thoughts were blistering.[66]

The blackness of night did indeed strain the nerves of all concerned. "As darkness fell everyone endeavoured to make themselves as comfortable as possible for the night under ground level, but in a hard coral fox-hole with seeping water this was not easy. Once again the war of nerves commenced as the island came to life with scuffling pigs, croaking frogs and the many weird noises peculiar only to the jungle."[67]

The peace was not to last, however: "No. 2 Platoon, MMG Company landed on the southern part of Tangalan Plantation without incident and proceeded to dig fox-holes and settle in for the night. About 10pm what sounded like a major battle started on one of our flanks but it soon died down and the rest of the night was surprisingly quiet. Enquiries next morning disclosed the source of the 'major battle' as a private battle some trigger-happy Yanks had had with some of the many pigs that roamed the island—perhaps excusable as a browsing pig at night bears a remarkable resemblance to a Jap."[68] Gillespie comments, "Among the ground troops

Fresh water is unloaded on the Green Islands, 15 February 1944. Nissan Green Island 1944 [Archives Reference ADQZ 18905, WA117, 3/17 E 2 2], Archives New Zealand, The Department of Internal Affairs, Te Tari Taiwhenua.

there was some indiscriminate shooting during the first few nights, provoked in the darkness by herds of marauding pigs, but there was no sign of the Japanese."[69]

Invasion Success

By nightfall the invaders were well established. Barrowclough reported to his prime minister:

"This complete immunity from enemy interference lasted all day and was surprising as it was gratifying."[70] He added, "By nightfall every gun and vehicle, every single round of ammunition, every item of equipment had been unloaded and the whole convoy had safely retired, leaving us in well established positions on the atoll. Field and anti-aircraft guns had been emplaced, radars were already installed and in operation and defensive positions were manned."[71]

The big question was, what had happened to the Japanese? The islanders reported that some seventy Japanese were in the south, and patrols from 30 Battalion found indications that the Japanese had retreated south. Where they were and what their intentions were remained to be discovered.

Seven

The Push Inland

Patrols were sent out on the morning of Wednesday, 16 February 1944. As the infantrymen of D Company, 30th Battalion pushed forward, to their surprise they discovered, in the area of the wrecked barges, three 20mm Japanese guns which had been abandoned. Had they been used on the day of the invasion, they could have exacted fearful casualties.

Antiaircraft batteries were established. A "lone raider received a warm welcome."[1] Patrols from 30th Battalion pushed to a mile south of Pokonian Plantation. They also cleared Barahun Island. Patrols sent out from the Tangalan Plantation penetrated into the jungle in a northerly and southerly direction for about two miles but did not encounter any defenders.

For the soldiers of 30th Battalion the push inland was "heavy going for everyone through the undergrowth and sometimes across mangrove swamps especially so for signals personnel who trailed out combat telephone wire, and also for the medical orderlies carrying a wicker hamper of medical supplies."[2]

The men of 37th Battalion had a similar experience as they marched inland, but they had an advantage: "The lack of natural water on Nissan made it necessary to carry enough water with us to last several days, and this together with a full pack and digging tools made our next move of two miles to Lihon quite an effort in the steaming heat and sticky mud. We were fortunate in having three medium [actually light] Valentine tanks with us from the tank squadron and were able to use the paths they had smashed through the jungle during their patrols, thus dispensing with the necessity of cutting tracks through the dense growth."[3]

Gathering intelligence from the local inhabitants proved problematic. "The natives, when you mentioned the word 'Japs,' sucked in their breath and waved in a general direction further down the island. Numbers mean nothing to Nissan Island natives and indeed they probably have no words in their language for words above ten."[4]

On 16 February the two tank troops met, and in concert with the soldiers of 35th Battalion, moved south. The tanks helped the infantry by crashing through the vegetation and creating a pathway. To the undoubted frustration of the tankers, the local geography proved more of an obstacle than the Japanese. On the third day after the invasion, infantry patrols probing towards the area of the mission came across a steep ravine to the east of Torahotup. This blocked the pathway of the tanks. Rutherford thought there were three options: use explosives to blast a pathway through the ravine; alternatively, that his tanks be amphibiously transported across the lagoon to Pokonian Plantation; or thirdly that a way round the ravine be found.

Following the latter option, Lieutenant Holden's troop and an infantry platoon were sent along the southern beach in the afternoon. Their efforts were recorded for posterity by an official United States film reporter who was full of blood and fire and had been heard to exclaim, "I wanna take some shots of you guys crushing those little yellow bastards under your tracks!"[5] Alas, it was not to be. Although the tanks rolled along the southern beach and fired exploratory rounds into suspected areas of Japanese occupation, there was no response. The progress of the tanks was blocked by a rocky peninsula, and so they returned to south point.

The next day orders were received to travel to Green Beach. One of the tanks had broken down and so had to be left behind. The squadron moved across to 30th Battalion Headquarters at the village of Tanaheran. It seemed that the tankers were to be denied their opportunity to fight the Japanese.

The 35th Battalion reached the southeastern part of Nissan on 17 February. Its sister 37th Battalion penetrated to a mile of the atoll's northern tip. 30th Battalion continued to strike south.

As the soldiers of 37th Battalion moved northwards, they anticipated contact with the Japanese. "During our trek through the jungle, we had heard the noise of battle to the south but had not flushed any Japs ourselves and three days after our landing were able to declare north Nissan safe for democracy, although there were several reports of odd parties of Japs in our sector."[6] In fact, no area of Nissan could be guaranteed to be cleared of Japanese and the New Zealanders of 37th Battalion made intensive but unproductive sweeps for Japanese soldiers. Signal lines, motor transport and landing craft in particular had to be well guarded.[7]

To the delight of the soldiers, operations were less severe than they had been in the struggle for Vella Lavella. Field cookers were landed on the first day and hot food was made available to the soldiers.

W.A. Gamble, the unit historian for 30th Battalion, noted for Sunday, 20 February 1944: "Except for a few shots fired and a grenade hurled in the darkness the nights are uneventful. Pigs are fairly plentiful around here and I think in many cases it is these which are responsible for the casual shooting. Near our area is an old pig-sty (we're not proud) and I've noticed some of the boys have used the thatching of the roof as a cover for their foxholes, so even the pig has no privacy."[8]

"A Very Unsavory Spot"

Barrowclough noted in his diary:

> Div. HQ was originally established at the southern end of the Pokonian plantation in a very unsavoury spot, low-lying and surrounded by dense jungle which did not permit even a breath of air to get through. The weather was very fine and we seem to have selected the most uninhabitable spot on the whole island. It was not practicable to move it at once as I wished to make only one move and the area in which I desired to establish Div. HQ had not yet been cleared of Japanese. Moreover, the route to it across the lagoon passed over a good deal of shallow water where numerous niggerheads [coral outcroppings] made navigation difficult for LCV's and LCP's. Finally, the situation was on top of a bank and the landing of vehicles and equipment there was impossible until we had got some bulldozers down overland to prepare the landing ramp.[9]

The Second Night

Japanese aerial activity slackened off somewhat. There were four Condition Reds on the second night, but only a few bombs were dropped with no damage to the invaders. This time, however, the defenders had retribution. A patrol of night fighters from Bougainville succeeded in shooting down two Japanese planes.[10] Unlike the first night, when the Japanese planes came over "every anti-aircraft gun on Pokonian plantation opened up on them. Pieces of falling shrapnel rang their way through the trees in the bivouac areas."[11]

For the men of 37th Battalion there was considerable satisfaction watching the antiaircraft guns at work. "It was cheering to lie on one's back in a slit trench and watch thousands of anti-aircraft shells floating up into the night like bubbles of fire. In spite of our previous fears as to what the surrounding Jap air bases would produce for us, this was the last occasion on which he paid us any serious attention. This was because the American and New Zealand Air Forces had literally plastered his airfields during the month prior to our attack and just sat over them until our own airfields were in operation."[12]

For the companies of 30th Battalion the night brought problems. "A, C and D Companies bivouacked for the night in particularly hard coral ground where it was impracticable to dig fox-holes, forcing the men to build coral breastworks around their individual positions. Water was short and thirsty troops cut water vines in the bush to gain a few drops of bitter-tasting water."[13]

Unusual Rations

On Thursday, 17 February, the troops received an unusual distribution of rations—J Rations. These contained three meals for four men. Contents are as follows: four packs of cigarettes (ten in each), four tins of coffee, one pkt raisins, one lb milk powder, one lb peanuts, 80 oz Buddies (cereal), 11 oz dried apricots, 11 oz dried peaches, 4 lb 3.5 oz beef and pork loaf, four chicklets (gum), 4¾ biscuits, 4.5 oz cocoa, 4.5 oz lemon powder, four pkts candy, four 30 sheets toilet paper.[14] These rations were more substantial than the usual rations and reflected American tastes.

Eight

Japanese Resistance

Skirmish at Sirot—17 February 1944

Sirot Island had come to notice on 15 February when it was reported that a Japanese barge was at its northern end. LCI gunboats had been sent to investigate and had drawn Japanese mortar fire. It was believed that Sirot was a Japanese barge hide-out.[1] Information supplied by the islanders indicated that a number of Japanese had fled to the densely wooded island of Sirot, at the entrance to the lagoon. B Company of 30 Battalion, under the command of Captain D. Dalton, were given the task of checking out the situation and eliminating the Japanese. Although a skirmish was anticipated, it was decided that no chances should be taken, and Dalton's men were reinforced by No. 1 Platoon Machine Gun Company, 14 Brigade Defence and Employment Platoon, and 4 Field Security Section.

This force landed on Sirot on the morning of 17 February after an intense seven-minute barrage from the 25-lb guns of 144th Independent Battery. It was intended that patrols would sweep the island. The soldiers of 14 Brigade Defence and Employment Platoon under the command of Lieutenant E.G. Taylor soon found that the Japanese were no pushovers. The Japanese defenders had taken full advantage of the thick jungle and had set up machine guns. Taylor's platoon took the brunt of fighting a near invisible enemy of indeterminate strength. Corporal P.A. Davidson was in command of a section of infantry which pressed forward and became cut off. Davidson killed two Japanese, but as his Bren gunner, Lance Corporal C. Reid, dashed forward to position his machine gun, he was hit by Japanese fire and killed.

The New Zealanders went to ground and fired from behind trees and cover at any signs of movement from the Japanese position, and the Japanese responded in kind. Taylor's men over the next two hours proceeded to slowly tighten the noose around the Japanese defenders. Taylor was shot in the boot but killed a Japanese soldier who had fired at and killed Private I.N. Tolich. A Bren gun jammed and a Japanese soldier took advantage of the situation by leaning behind a tree, shooting the gunner and throwing a grenade which wounded two more of Taylor's men. Davidson then killed the Japanese soldier and destroyed a Japanese machine gun. It was a costly day for the New Zealanders—five men were killed and three were wounded.

Taylor's hard-pressed and exhausted men were relieved in the afternoon by No. 8 Platoon. It had been a bitter and costly close-quarters fight.

The Pacific records, "During the action some consternation was caused by a wounded and dazed member of Taylor's platoon who had wandered away from the fight, happily in the right direction, telling the passing barge which picked him up on the beach that there were 150 Japanese on Sirot. Fortunately, by the time the information reached headquarters the engagement was over."[2]

No. 1. Platoon of the MMG Company landed on Sirot and was given the task of guarding the beachhead perimeter. *The Tanks* noted: "Settling down to wait, the silence was suddenly broken by a roar of rifle fire followed shortly after by the arrival of a wounded and badly shaken New Zealand lad who shattered our calm by informing us that 150 Japs had broken through. This, to say the least of it, made our position a trifle precarious but apart from Private Stewart's snap shot at a wandering pig nothing untoward occurred and the infantry returned to say they had bagged 20 Japs."[3] There were twenty-one Japanese defenders who had sold their lives dearly.

For his bravery, Corporal Davidson was awarded a very well-deserved Distinguished Conduct Medal. Barrowclough summed it up in his diary: "It was quite a desperate fight as the Japs were cornered and fought to the last man."[4]

Clearing Nissan

Islanders reported that there were about seventy Japanese located in the Torahatup area hiding in the caves which were used for island burials.[5]

The soldiers from 30th Battalion found trekking through the jungle exhausting. As they moved to forward positions the lack of drinking water took its toll. "[O]nce again the good old coconut milk saved out lives. Without coconuts we'd have found it very difficult as water is very scarce here, we're limited to one bottle a day. The boys are very weary and look far from fresh in their mud and sweat soaked jungle suits. Dug in through heart-breaking coral which is everywhere here."[6]

By 18 February, 37th Battalion had cleared the northern area of Nissan and 30th Battalion had reached the southwest point. 35th Battalion pushed west along the southern coast area and only a square mile separated it from 30th Battalion. Just prior to the link-up of 30th and 35th Battalions, the area around the Mission was shelled intensively by 17 Field Battery. The link-up between the 30th and 35th Battalions was achieved on 19 February when men from the two battalions met in the area around the Mission. The New Zealand soldiers discovered a Japanese bivouac and a cache of Japanese weaponry. This included six 20mm antitank rifles, 150 rifles, and 150,000 rounds of ammunition. They also discovered caches of rice and food.[7] In the late afternoon on the same day, a patrol from 30th Battalion discovered a group of desperate Japanese trying to escape in a canoe. A firefight broke out and seven Japanese were killed with one New Zealander wounded.

Japanese defenders on Nissan sent a final radio message to Rabaul on 19 February. They said "we are charging the enemy and beginning radio silence."[8]

The lack of resistance led to an underestimation of Japanese strength in the southwestern part of the atoll. The New Zealanders would receive a rude awakening.

Nine

Tank and Infantry Action at Tanaheran

The most intense fighting on Nissan would occur near the tiny island village of Tanaheran. Located on the southwest coast of Nissan, some 150 yards from the coral cliffs, the area had dense thickets and large trees which provided ample cover for the Japanese. The New Zealanders had previously sent patrols through the area and had not encountered any Japanese. They began to think that the area was secure and lowered their guard. They would pay in blood for this assumption.

The Carrier Platoon under the command of Captain J.F.B. Stronach arrived at Tanaheran Village on 20 February. Stronach's task was to find a suitable spot for 14 Brigade Headquarters. At noon he decided to give his men a rest and to go for a swim. A soldier walked across towards the edge of the cliff, and to his shock a rifle shot rang out, with the bullet missing him. Assumptions about the security of the area evaporated. Two sergeants hastily gathered 15 soldiers, and assuming that the rifle shot had been made by an isolated Japanese straggler, they began to comb the area. To their horror the New Zealand soldiers were hit by intense rifle and machine-gun fire and two soldiers fell wounded.

Hearing the firing, Stronach raced to the scene. He quickly realized that this was no small group of cut-off stragglers but rather a considerable number of Japanese. Stronach quickly gathered together 28 men from various units and began forming a defensive perimeter with the aim of boxing the Japanese against the coast and preventing them from escaping. Once reinforcements arrived, the Japanese could then be eliminated.

An attempt was made to rescue one of the wounded soldiers, Corporal Roy Stannard, who lay exposed to Japanese fire. Stronach and some of his men crawled to within 10 feet of Stannard but could not get to him because any further movement brought a flurry of Japanese rifle and mortar fire. Stannard would have to wait.

Stronach was not the only officer in the vicinity. Lieutenant E.H. Ryan of the machine gun company quickly arrived on the right flank and organized his men to fire into the Japanese positions from "knee height to the tops of the trees. Because of the noise, it was impossible to pick up snipers hidden in the branches. So severe was the Japanese mortar fire that Lieutenant Ryan's machine-gunners were pinned in along the coast and the signal was sent for reinforcements. Soon afterwards he was wounded."[1]

Pat Beban, another soldier from the Medium Machine Gun [MMG] Company, was wounded by a Japanese sniper. Two sergeants carried him back to an advanced dressing station, but he died shortly afterwards.[2]

The New Zealanders had bitten off more than they could chew. However, help was on its way. At about 1400 hours the tank squadron liaison officer, Captain L.F. Brooker, sent a message to the tank squadron saying that an infantry patrol had made contact with a small number of Japanese on the south coast near a native village. Brooker suggested that two tanks be used. The commander of the tank squadron, Major Jim Rutherford, ordered two Valentine tanks of Number One Troop to go to the village. Rutherford, Major Arthur Flint, Chaplain Robertson, and the squadron intelligence officer, Lieutenant C.A.L. de Vere, climbed on the back of the two tanks, which were under the command of Lieutenant T.K. Evans and Sergeant R.H. Beetham, and prepared to leave.

At this stage the United States film reporter showed up again and asked what was going on. To which Major Flint replied, "You've got your chance now, mate, the Japs are attacking our B-Echelon and we're going down to rescue them." He muttered, "Goddamit, I must get some more film," and promptly disappeared down the track, never to be seen again.[3]

The tanks reached the western end of the village and a discussion took place between the tankers and Stronach and Brooker. Stronach said that his men "had accidentally contacted the enemy—accidentally because the area had been reported cleared by 30 Bn. One man of the Carrier Platoon had been shot and was either dead or wounded, and he had been left where he fell. Attempts to rescue him had been foiled by intensive enemy strength fire. At that time estimate of enemy strength was possibly six or seven and not more than twelve."[4]

The officers quickly devised a plan. Four Vickers medium machine guns [MMG] were to be set up on the east side of the village to provide covering fire through the trees while the two tanks of No. 1 Troop came forward. Evans and Beetham were told to watch out for the New Zealand casualty and to rescue him if at all possible.

At about 1430 hours the Vickers machine guns opened fire and the

Japanese replied with their automatic weapons. Japanese snipers sited in the forward area, possibly in trees near the village, began firing.

Tanks are formidable fighting machines—they carry powerful armaments and their crews are protected by steel armor. However, tanks also have important limitations and weaknesses. The armor that protects the tank crew also limits their ability to see what is happening around them. A tank commander who exposes himself to enemy fire by standing in the open hatch of his tank runs considerable risk of being sniped and an enemy grenade thrown through the open hatch. In combat, most tank crews prefer to operate "buttoned up," with all hatches closed despite the intense discomfort, heat, engine fumes and difficulties of escape should the tank catch fire. Tank crews in a buttoned-up state are totally reliant for their vision on the periscopes provided for the tank commander and the limited vision slit in front of the driver. In the tropical heat and humidity of the Green Islands, the level of discomfort was worse than ever. The close jungle and uneven terrain further limited vision. Not only was visibility limited, so also was movement. The great spreading flanges of the pandanus trees hampered the movement of the tanks. Although tanks give the appearance of strength and solidity, they are in fact quite fragile. A thrown track caused by vegetation has the potential to bring the tank to a grinding halt, immobilized and virtually helpless.

A tank that advances into an enemy position without infantry support usually very quickly turns into a burnt-out tank with a dead crew. The Japanese defenders lacked gasoline bombs, pole charges, satchel charges, mines or the usual equipment for attacking tanks. They did have long-barreled obsolete 20mm Type 97 antitank rifles, but these were of little use against the armor plate of the Valentine. They were also heavy and cumbersome to operate, and had a huge recoil (there is no indication that the antitank rifles were used at Tanaheran). The Japanese on the Green Islands may have had very limited antitank capabilities, but they certainly had determination in spades. They were about to demonstrate this. "Japanese snipers picked off a tiny periscope on one tank and fired at an observation aperture no larger than a bullet. Their accuracy was disturbing, as was evidenced by bullet marks on the heavy metal."[5] The sniper fire was so accurate that "Tom Evans lost four or five periscopes and his driver as well."[6] Considering that the tank crew's visibility was already limited by the terrain, the knocking out of periscopes made things even more difficult for the crews.

Two tanks were in the area, but the question was how they could best be used. Tank-infantry coordination is a complex business. Whilst the sol-

Nine. Tank and Infantry Action at Tanaheran

diers of 8 Brigade had conducted training exercises with the tanks, their compatriots of 14 Brigade had not. They had to learn the basics of infantry-tank cooperation on the job and in a hurry.

Brooker set himself up in one of the MMG posts and had walkie-talkie communication with the two tanks. Rutherford, Flint, Robertson and de Vere were positioned at the eastern end of the village near an MMG post.

The New Zealand machine guns raked the Japanese positions for about fifteen to twenty minutes. The Japanese intermittently returned rifle and mortar fire. The tanks now entered the fray and began firing three-inch howitzer shells and Besa MG fire into the Japanese positions. The Japanese snipers struck back, hitting one of the machine gunners in the head. He was moved to the shelter of an island hut and then evacuated by truck but died shortly after.

Arthur Flint recorded his impressions:

> The Vickers machine gunners moved forward and mounted their gun. At the same time, Major Rutherford, Padre, deVere, Vickery and I went through the village and took up positions behind the trees on the far side of the coral wall bordering the village. I was on the north side of the track immediately opposite a Vickers that was mounted on the south side. Ever since we had arrived at the village there had been intermittent rifle shots across the village but the direction from which they came could not be determined. There was a bright sky, no rain, but the usual gloom in the jungle itself. The two tanks in line-ahead came through the village up the track, past us and veered off right into the jungle and out of sight. In a minute or so we heard the tanks open up with Besa fire and the Vickers also commenced to fire. There were also occasional shots of two-pounder and three-inch howitzer. Fire was returned by the Japanese, both rifle and automatic, and this continued for several minutes.
>
>   Then there was an increase in the rifle fire, with ricochets off the trees, but it was impossible to judge the sources due to the general din. I then noticed that one Vickers across the path, and which had been firing long bursts, had stopped firing, and I then looked over and saw the gunner lying on his back behind the gun. Steam was rising from the gun. At first I though some accident had occurred with the gun, which had knocked out the gunner. It did not occur to me he could have been hit. I went over to him and saw he had been seriously hurt, most likely from sniper fire. He was then carried dying. He was then put on a truck and taken back through the village with the Padre and Captain de Vere. I lost sight of Vickery, and Major Rutherford went off to find Captain Brooker.
>
>   I returned to my tree. The tanks continued to fire, mostly Besa. At this stage two bullets hit the tree behind which I was sheltering and struck the ground near me. I found I was on my own and decided it was not a particularly healthy place! I moved rapidly back through the village to where I found Vickery. Shots, apparently from the trees, were still cracking overhead through the trees in the village. I returned again with Vickery to the east end of the village and we took cover behind the low coral wall that marked the village edge. We then moved further

into the trees along the track and again took cover behind a tree. The Japs then commenced to fire mortar, which fortunately burst in the trees above us, bringing down showers of foliage. The sniper fire intensified and the tanks were still firing. New Zealand rifle fire could also be heard from the direction of the village. The infantrymen moved away and the Vickers gun teams withdrew back through the village with their guns, Vickery and I with them, they having had some instructions to clear everyone from the eastern end.

Rutherford thought that the two Valentines were moving too far to the left. He crept up to the back of one of the tanks, and using a telephone set located at the rear of the tank, he was able to guide the tank onto a fresh line. The wounded machine gunner was moved by truck to the rear area and Padre Robertson accompanied him.

At this point the machine gunners moved back to the rear. Rutherford returned and called for No. 3 Tank Troop to be brought up to the fight.

It was 1600 hours and D Company of 30th Battalion arrived. Their commander, Major Bullen, was briefed by Lt. de Vere. The infantryman decided that he would not commit his men to action until matters were clearer. The infantrymen holding the perimeter at this point were the Carrier Platoon, personnel from B Echelon of the Tank Squadron, and the machine gunners who had returned with infantry weapons.

The two tanks of No. 3 Troop, commanded by Lieutenant D. Holden and Corporal H. Johns, arrived shortly afterwards.

> Holden and Johns found themselves in a clearing with a lot of people milling around. Trooper F.G. Aldrich decided to try to find out what was going on and climbed out of Corporal Johns's tank. Just then some bullets struck a tree behind him giving him the impression that they were surrounded. He dived under the tank where he was joined by some others. Reaching up he got hold of the tank telephone and learned from Corporal Johns that they had been ordered forward and to get back inside. So he immediately scrambled over the engine deck and back into the turret, and along with Holden's tank they set off into the fray. The three other tanks arrived about this time but they were retained outside the village near the north-eastern corner. Then Sergeant Beetham's tank came out carrying the wounded man. Apparently in trying to protect him Evan's tank had run over a branch on which he lay and in the act had lifted him onto Beetham's tank. The tanks continued to spray the area with all weapons while those in support concentrated Besa, canister and HE on suspected sniper posts in the higher levels. One tank even engaged in the practice of tree felling to deal with one sniper by firing a HE shell with cap on into the base of the suspect tree.
>
> At 5.45 pm Major A.B. Bullen decided to direct three-inch mortar fire onto the enemy to enable his company to reorganize and launch an assault. Evans' and Holden's Troops were withdrawn to the B-Echelon position north of the village covered by the other three tanks, which joined them shortly afterwards. Here all tanks replenished and stood by. The mortar fire fell first on the village and then moved back towards the Japanese positions in the gardens by the cliffs. This

enabled the infantry to get closer to the Japanese but the fire seemed just as intense as before. In the fading light the infantry were ordered to fix bayonets and, under a barrage of grenades, they carried the position. Lieutenant Holden's tank was guided to a position where a pocket of Japanese were believed to be but they were all dead. A further eight Japanese were wiped out by a section of 16th Platoon on the beach below, after they had escaped over the cliff edge and tried to make their way northwards. A total of fifty-two dead Japanese were found in the area the next day.[7]

The eight Japanese referred to had run into a picket commanded by Corporal L.G. Ratcliffe. He had killed six Japanese with his Thompson submachine gun. The other two "were dispatched as they rounded some rocks."[8]

The infantry assault on the Japanese defenders was not straightforward—the tanks were withdrawn seventy-five yards back to allow the three-inch mortar crews to fire rounds into the Japanese position to soften up the defenders:

> At 6pm an organized assault was made by the two infantry platoons and the MMG platoon but enemy snipers made this movement difficult. The MMGs advanced to within four or five yards of the enemy using grenades to good effect, but were unable to get any further. Ron Richards, using his borrowed Rising gun [Reising sub-machine gun], killed three Japs before having his thumb shot off. This wound was accompanied by a stream of abuse dealing in no uncertain terms with Tojo's parents, or lack of them, followed by a bitter tirade on his future inability to write to his girlfriend, much to the amusement of his pals.
>
> While waiting for the infantry platoons to swing in from the left No. 3 received the full weight of the enemy attention in the form of grenades which although making much noise, inflicted no casualties. Shortly after this, while moving over to Ron Richards, Lieutenant Ryan was shot through the buttocks, a rather unromantic type of wound, but nevertheless, painful—both were later evacuated.

The Third Division unofficial history, *Tanks, MMGs and Ordnance*, conveys the flavor of the combat for the tankers—

> There was an hour of hectic "busyness"—feverish swinging of periscopes, fire orders not according to the book, the thrill of the first shell fired at the enemy, straining of eyes desperately searching for an enemy who kept pouring a stream of bullets at you from a few yards away, and who infuriatingly remained invisible and kept his bullets going from the very spot, seemingly, where a moment ago you had planted a shell. There were the racket of the Besa and the pungent fumes that came back from it, the bellowing of the engine, and the crackle of the earphones, the flickering of the leaves where the Jap bullets came through and the tack-hammering on the turret where they struck. There was the view of leaves and vines and trucks that in an instant burst into a silver-splintered nothingness, when a bullet hit the periscope prism. In the hot reeking security of the turret there were the recoiling gun, the gunner who turned to grin when his shell smacked an indicated target and the cheerful shirtless loader who worked

heroically at the heavy shells and the refractory Besa. There was the backing and filling as your tank manoeuvred amid closely spaced coconut palms, scraping ominously over the hard coral as it heaved around, and the anxiety lest you break a track in there where you could least afford to break it. And there was the sickening fascination of that close range view of a wounded Kiwi climbing painfully on to an adjacent tank a few short feet from the Jap position, the slow suspense as the tank backed away to safety, the relief when he made it. There was a period while the tanks were reloading and the ground troops had a go. Machine-gunners moved closer in, infantrymen sniped from the doubtful shelter of coconut palms and mortars barked viciously. Jap .25 bullets cracked sharply about, and positions previously thought safe became untenable as concealed tree-top snipers opened up.

You became confused and a little fearful as they seemed to be all round you. You stared as our dead and wounded came trickling back.

Eventually it was over, the tempo had slackened as the enemy strength dribbled away. The infantry had gone in with grenade and bayonet and the remaining Japs had been scuppered. We rode our Vals back to the leaguer area, examined our battle scars and talked excitedly far into the night. Next day there was the visit to the scene of operations where the contorted and mutilated bodies lay everywhere—big, evil-looking men who had fought till they were wounded, patched themselves up with field dressings and gone on fighting till they were killed or until there was no more ammunition, only one grenade, which pressed tightly against the chest, sent them violently into eternity. You did not stay long in that macabre spot.

That is how it seemed to us at Tanaheran."[9]

Corporal Roy Stannard had been hit in the shoulder at the start of the action and had lain pinned down by Japanese fire. At 1530 hours he had climbed onto one of the tanks and had escaped. His commanding officer later commented, "His courage and patience saved his own life!"[10]

After they had seen action at Tanaheran, the tank crews were surprised to be on the receiving end of abuse from some of the infantrymen. The infantrymen were unaware that the tanks had been in combat.[11] The attitude is understandable, if unfair. The battle had largely been an infantry one with the tanks providing support.

The ferocity of the tank fire can be gauged by the expenditure of ammunition—sixty-two rounds of three-inch howitzer shells; ten thousand eight hundred rounds of Besa machine gun bullets; thirty-seven rounds of two-pounder H.E. shells; seven hundred rounds of Bren gun fire; fifty rounds of two-pounder canister fire; and eight rounds of two-pounder armor-piercing.[12]

The Japanese had fought desperately in small groups amongst the rocks and trees, taking full advantage of the cover. "One wounded Japanese, as our men approached him, placed a hand grenade on his stomach and committed suicide."[13] The New Zealanders did not have it all their own way, however. Captain P.R. Adams was killed by a Japanese sniper. Four of his comrades were also killed and seven were wounded.

The tanks' fire undoubtedly suppressed the defenders. The four tank commanders later acknowledged that "no enemy had been actually sighted. All fire had been directed at movement of undergrowth, suspected positions and tree tops. Also general strafing of area. Their fire arc was limited by the approx positions of our own Infantry blocks on coast."[14]

However, it was also appreciated that the New Zealand tankers had learned the hard way what their Australian counterparts in Papua New Guinea had already discovered: "infantry must move forward to contact the enemy and definitely locate their centre of resistance before tanks can be effectively employed."[15]

Although the tanks' fighting abilities had not been properly challenged by the Japanese, nonetheless, it was felt that the tanks had been useful—they had traveled at roughly the same speed as the infantry searching for the Japanese and "heightened the morale of the infantry considerably; the wireless transmitter in the tank was useful for keeping battalion headquarters informed of activities at the point of contact with the enemy; the tanks also crushed out a track by which stretcher cases could be more easily carried back and over which jeeps could sometimes bring forward supplies."[16]

The fighting at Tanaheran had a sequel. Some Japanese were able to escape the New Zealand tanks and infantry. Barrowclough recorded in his War Diary: "The canoe with the escapees was sighted next morning a mile or two off shore and we sent a PT boat out with instructions to capture the occupants if possible. The PT boat approached the canoe at speed with the idea of overturning it with its wash and then fishing out the three occupants. Two of the Japanese, however, opened fire on the PT boat as it approached them and the gunners on the PT replied, killing these two Japs. The other who was lying in the bottom of the canoe was thrown into the sea when the canoe overturned. He was badly injured and suffering from bruises he had received when he fell over a cliff when making his escape."[17]

The battlefield had an irresistible attraction for souvenir hunters. Barrowclough noted: "The success of the operation on the afternoon of the 20th soon became generally known and numbers of American soldiers appeared from everywhere hunting for souvenirs. Most of the legitimate souvenirs had already been taken by our troops, guns, swords, rifles etc but this did not deter these American visitors who thoroughly turned over the dead bodies even extracting the teeth of the dead [for gold fillings]. We put a stop to this ghoulish business and sent them packing."[18]

Halsey's Visit

One of the first Allied planes to land on the lagoon at the Green Islands was one of the famous "Black Cats," the PBY-5A Catalina flying boat. The pilot had received a hurried order to land at Torokina. However, it was not a combat mission, but simply to transport passengers. They were not ordinary passengers, and the crew busied themselves scrubbing the plane and bringing in cushions and comforts for their guests. Admiral Halsey, his chief of staff Admiral Carney, Admiral Fitch, Brigadier General Riley and various other American officers boarded the big flying boat. Admiral Fitch at one point took over the controls of the seaplane. They arrived on the afternoon of 20 February and landed in Nissan's lagoon at 0100 hours and departed at 1430 hours. Barrowclough noted in his diary, "They seemed pleased with the progress we were making."[19]

Admiral William ("Bull") Halsey, USN, checks his watch. Major General H.E. Barrowclough is at right. Nissan Green Island 1944 [Archives Reference ADQZ 18905, WA117, 3/17 E3 3], Archives New Zealand, The Department of Internal Affairs, Te Tari Taiwhenua.

Pinipel and Sau

Nissan Island may have been cleared, but a reconnaissance patrol that visited Sau on 21 February found a Japanese bivouac. Soldiers from 37th Battalion and No. 3 platoon, MMG Company were sent to Pinipel on 23 February and laid down a mortar barrage on Sau and raked it with machine gun fire. An infantry company, B Company, 37th Battalion, then landed on Sau. One of its infantry patrols encountered a small group of Japanese defenders equipped with a light machine gun and grenades. The New Zealanders killed eight of the defenders and did not suffer any casualties. That luck was not to last. A further group of six Japanese were found and four New Zealanders were injured by Japanese grenades. All the Japanese were killed.

Doug Ross, an officer with 30 Battalion, recalled: "We had a couple of Nisei attached to 30th Battalion when the platoon got into action on Pinipel in the Green Islands. We were supposed to use the Nisei [Japanese-American soldiers] to invite the Japanese to surrender. I did not call them up because I got carried away in the heat of the moment."[20] However, a Nisei interpreter with the New Zealanders offered a group of Japanese good treatment if they surrendered, but the response was a thrown grenade. The Japanese holdouts were all killed. To the surprise of the New Zealanders, the Japanese were found to be almost naked. They had used their clothing to tie a makeshift raft together. Some 14 newly made paddles were found alongside their raft.[21]

> Patrols were subsequently sent to Sau in late March, but there were no indications of recent enemy occupation. One old bivouac was discovered and numerous documents were sent back to the battalion for deciphering. The remains of the dead Japs were still where they had fallen, and the island was no pleasant spot. (It might be mentioned here that under normal circumstances the dead Japs would have been buried by "B" Company. However, the bodies were so badly mutilated that handling them would have been a very bloody task. As there was no fresh water and no disinfectant available, the Japs had to be left where they were. A short burial service was held for them by Padre Harford).[22]

Another account of the clearance of Pinipel and Sau is provided by the history of 37th Battalion, *Pacific Saga*:

> Included in the 37th Battalion sector were the northern-most islands of the Solomons group. These were Pinipel and Sau, which lay to the north-east of Nissan, the whole forming the Green Islands. They were the last islands of the Solomons as yet not invaded and we felt quite pleased that we had been chosen to round off, as it were, the Solomons campaign. Natives had reported the presence of Japanese on these islands and we were instructed to round up the intruders. A

strong reconnaissance patrol under Captain Adams was sent to locate suitable landing beaches and gain any further information possible and the report made very detailed planning possible. Two companies with mortars, medium machine-guns and an artillery liaison group were dispatched under command of Major Trevarthen. The first landing was made on the north-east end of Pinipel and all of the usual precautions were taken. Here and at most other places we had to wade ashore waist-deep but as we were almost continually wet through by perspiration or rain we didn't mind that. Although only about waist deep for most of us, the depth was quite a trial to some of the shorter chaps. One little chap waded out with equipment on his head. The water came up to his eyes and every now and then he bobbed up for air. At the ramp of the ship he stumbled and it appeared that the weight of his gear would carry him under, so an officer leaned out and helped him up. The little chap came aboard yapping like a terrier: "I'd have been well all right!" quoth he.

The natives at our first meeting proved too friendly and were over-anxious to please. Their replies to our questions told us that there were many "Japanese mans" on Pinipel. Pressed further, they admitted that the Japs had left one, two, three moons (months) ago. We also found that there were from five to twenty-five Japs on Sau (the smaller island) and that these had not left. Armed with this useful information, B Company set sail across the lagoon to test its accuracy. The landing beach was well neutralized by Lieutenant "Stove-Pipe" Jack Forward and his 3-inch mortars, assisted by medium machine-guns from the 14th Brigade Machine Gun Company. The skipper of the LCT begged permission to use his 50-calibre and 20-millimetre machine-guns, so the detachment commander set him the task of firing on the tree-tops adjacent to the landing beach to get any snipers lodged therein. An unopposed landing was effected and shortly after the crackle of rifle and machine gun fire and the thud of bursting grenades told that Captain Ron Keith and his company had made contact with the enemy. All opposition was quickly overcome and although we did everything possible to get prisoners, as usual, the Jap wasn't having any, and fought to the last breath. Although they were heathens, Padre Harford performed our burial service over them and we withdrew to the landing beach to dig in for the night. Digging here was a pleasure as this island was almost wholly composed of coral sand. The only casualties in this brush were four wounded.[23]

Ten

Aftermath and Consolidation

The Second Echelon

On 19 February the second echelon (31.5), made up of 8 APDs, 10 LSTs and 2 LCIs set off for the Green Islands escorted by seven destroyers and a tug. They arrived on the morning of 20 February and by 1115 hours had unloaded their cargo. By 1700 hours all had set off for Guadalcanal without incident.[1] Fine weather helped with the unloading process.

It is indicative of how smoothly run the landings were that although LST-117 grounded at the entrance to Nissan, it managed to quickly clear itself, beached without assistance, and in fact unloaded ahead of schedule.[2]

The arrival of 35th Field Battery, and 208th and 214th AA batteries and a radar unit, added to the strength of the island's defenders. It did, however, precipitate a crisis. One of the LSTs accidentally severed the underwater lines of W110 cable which had been laid with such effort by the New Zealand signalmen. In an example of inter-Allied cooperation, the American Naval Headquarters made alternative circuits available.[3]

Japanese Holdouts

The fighting on Pinipel and Sau on 23 February was the last organized Japanese resistance. However, there were still isolated Japanese holdouts. Barrowclough noted in his diary, "22 Fd Amb surprised everybody by capturing a prisoner who was moving about in that portion of the jungle to which they had been allocated."[4] Not all of the Japanese holdouts were quite so docile.

A Seabee with Company C, 93rd NCB, Bob Conner, recorded in his diary for 3 March 1944: "Might not have felt so secure here where we are living now had we known that there were three Japs living about 300 yards behind us. One of them was killed this morning and the other 2 are still at large. They had very clever shelters built out of branches and leaves. Tonight we even notice the pigs routing around in the woods and wonder if it is really a pig. Maybe some of the pigs after all."[5] The following day Conner noted, "Scuttlebutt today was going the rounds that one of the 37th's men was found on his dozer this morning with his throat slit, presumably by a Jap. How true that may be no one knows."[6]

A New Zealand mechanic with the ordnance radar maintenance section had an unpleasant shock one morning as he was shaving. A Japanese sniper's bullet hit a tree about two feet away from his razor.[7]

Corporal James of 37th Battalion noted in his unit diary: "Further sightings of odd Japs continued to be made, but none were in our sector of the island. Three were seen in the 93CB area south of the strip. A patrol gave chase and shot one of the Japs, but the others escaped. Patrols were sent out after a Jap reported in the vicinity of South Point, but, in the words of the Intelligence summary, 'there was not trace of that elusive infidel.'"[8]

Even after the island was supposedly secured, encounters with Japanese soldiers continued to occur.

> One such encounter involving the New Zealand signallers which did much to brighten the routine and conversation of the camp at unit headquarters was the meeting face to face of a lone Jap by a member of the headquarters company in the camp area at 2 o'clock one morning. The Jap made full use of the nearby jungle and quickly disappeared but he was obviously one of the few still at large on the island who, under cover of darkness, endeavoured to raid ration stores for something edible. The episode proved too much for the cooks who were quickly out of their beds in an enthusiastic but unsuccessful manhunt. As a searchlight to penetrate the jungle they carried with them a six-volt car battery powering a detached headlight![9]

For the surviving members of the Japanese garrison, the prospects were indeed bleak. Isolated from their commanders and comrades, and frequently sick and wounded, they found the prospects for inflicting harm on the invaders was limited and the focus became one of surviving each day. The jungle, although lush, is essentially a desert of sorts, and unless a soldier had survival skills of a high order, the prospects dwindled to a choice between trying to raid the enemy's food stocks or starvation. The Allies controlled the air and sea around the Green Islands and there simply was no escape.

War is full of tragedy and mischance. Sometimes it seems that some men are fated to die even when they seem out of immediate danger. Such

Ten. Aftermath and Consolidation 123

Personnel of 4 Field Security with native guides and Japanese prisoner, 31 May 1944. Nissan Green Island 1944 [Archives Reference ADQZ 18905, WA117, 3/17 E3 3], Archives New Zealand, The Department of Internal Affairs, Te Tari Taiwhenua.

was the case with one unfortunate Japanese soldier captured on 8 March 1944 on Nissan.

> Unusual circumstances surround the story of how a Jap was captured by a "D" Company patrol and later shot by another out with a patrol from No. 16 platoon, which was camped with Coy. Headquarters on the lagoon side of the island. They had not travelled far when an unarmed Jap was encountered and taken prisoner. The Jap offered no resistance and appeared resigned to capture. He was wearing shirt and shorts, but had no boots or shoes. When taken back to the company lines, he bowed and scraped like the Pooh Bah of "Mikado" fame. The food given to him he ate ravenously. The prisoner knew no English, but he gestulated and pointed towards the coast, as if he wished to be taken there. As there were other Japs thought to be in the vicinity, it was decided a patrol should take the prisoner out so that all possibilities could be investigated. Lieut. E.C. Robinson led the party, and when nearing a small native village which seemed to be the objective, the prisoner was sent a few yards ahead, as a precaution against a trap. The next moment, there was a burst of fire, and as the Jap dropped, CPL. [Corporal] L.N. Dunlea and a small party from No. 14 platoon came on the scene. CPL. Dunlea reported that his patrol had set out from the coast, and coming to the village, had

found a Jap bivouac in which were clothes, boots and several cartons of American cigarettes. Anticipating that the occupant would return, the patrol lay in wait. When the Jap was seen making his way back alone, he was fired on and killed. CPL. Dunlea, of course, was unaware that he was already a prisoner. Buttons on the Jap's coat showed that he had been attached to a naval unit, and it was unfortunate that an opportunity to gain enemy information was lost in such a way.[10]

Defensive Zones and MacArthur's Communique

On 28 February an Operations Order was issued by 14 Brigade HQ defining the defensive zones to be held by each unit. There was always the possibility of a Japanese counterattack, or that Japanese units retreating from Buka would try to pass through the Green Islands.[11] Effectively, however, the invaders had now entered a garrison phase.

General Douglas MacArthur confirmed that the islands were now secure in his own personalized, inimitable style. He issued a communiqué declaring:

Personnel of 3NZ Division Tank Squadron do maintenance. Cleaning a Bren LMG, 28 February 1944. Nissan Green Island 1944 [Archives Reference ADQZ 18905, WA117, 3/17 E3 3], Archives New Zealand, The Department of Internal Affairs, Te Tari Taiwhenua.

Ten. Aftermath and Consolidation

> We have seized the north end of the Solomons Archipelago. New Zealand and American ground troops, covered by naval and air forces, have landed on and occupied Green Islands.
>   This is the culmination of the successful series of flank movements, commencing in the New Georgia Group, which have gradually enveloped all enemy forces in the Solomons. These forces, estimated at 22,000 are disposed through Choiseul, the Shortlands, Bougainville and Buka Islands and are now isolated from their source of supply at Rabaul. The starvation and disease which are certain to ensue from the military blockade will render the position hopeless. With their airfields destroyed and their barge traffic paralyzed, the relief of these scattered garrisons is no longer practicable, and their ultimate fate is sealed. For all strategic purposes, this completes the campaign for the Solomon Islands.[12]

For once, MacArthur was correct.

Casualties

The Allied casualties from the Commando Raid and Squarepeg amounted to 10 killed and 21 wounded. American casualties were 3 killed and the same number wounded.[13] Some 120 Japanese were estimated to have been killed. It is hard to be exact with Japanese casualties—many chose suicide by leaping over the cliffs and their bodies were washed out to sea or taken by sharks. Bob Conner came across Japanese bodies in the course of his journeys around the island.

Consolidation

THE THIRD ECHELON—25 FEBRUARY 1944

The third echelon, consisting of six escorting destroyers, 11 LSTs and 3 LCIs bringing 2,577 soldiers and a tug, arrived at beaches 8 and 9, Pokonian, on 25 February.[14] Barrowclough noted in his diary: "The LSTs flew barrage balloons much to the bemusement of the soldiers. Heavy rain set in and conditions were very muddy and trying. Again there were 11 LST's in the convoy and some of them were very heavily loaded. It was with difficulty that we got them all away by about 5.30pm."[15]

The new arrivals included the headquarters company of 22nd Field Ambulance together with attached ASC personnel. They were landed at the original beachhead on Pokonian Beach and transferred by LCTs to the mission at the southern end of the lagoon. Things were not quite as secure as the troops would have wished: "A reconnaissance party to the camp site, a few hours prior to the arrival of the main body on this first

View of surgical ward, 22NZ Field Ambulance, at Tanaheran, 1944. Nissan Green Island 1944 [Archives Reference ADQZ 18905, WA117, 3/17 E3 3], Archives New Zealand, The Department of Internal Affairs, Te Tari Taiwhenua.

day, had discovered a Jap soldier lying unconscious behind a fallen tree and suffering from head wounds inflicted in the fighting a few days before. He was the 22nd's first and only prisoner."[16]

However, the security problems of the medical personnel did not end there. "Early the following evening three Japs, armed to the teeth, marched through our camp along the cliff track and scared the wits out of unsuspecting camp constructing ambulance men. The Japs were just as nonplussed, and each party ran from the other—our men to get rifles and report the occurrence, the Japs to beat it to temporary safety."[17]

The Third Echelon returned to Guadalcanal on 27 February with casualties, a Japanese prisoner and fifty-three islanders.

The Fourth Echelon—1 March 1944

The fourth echelon, consisting of LSTs 39, 117, 118, 123, 124, 125, 219, 247, 269 and 353, loaded up at Guadalcanal on 24 February and arrived at dawn on 1 March 1944.

Ten. Aftermath and Consolidation

Barrowclough recorded in his diary:

> Fourth Echelon arrived in extremely bad weather. Low visibility prevented the entry of the LST's until long after daylight. Heavy rain played havoc with existing roads and in many places the roads had entirely collapsed. This greatly delayed unloading operations though the control we had evolved for speeding unloading proved very effective. Had it not been for this I doubt whether we would have unloaded the ships before dark. As it was, one ship had to over carry 30 tons of cargo, much of it consisting of piping which was urgently required for the tank farm. Another ship (which was the first to be unloaded) was unable to retract from the beach and eventually the fleet had to leave without it.[18]

Further echelons would follow. What is so noteworthy is the commitment of the scarce LSTs to the buildup of stores equipment and personnel on the Green Islands. It is also noteworthy how quickly the LSTs were unloaded and turned around to head back to Guadalcanal and repeat the cycle.

Camps

As soldiers poured onto Nissan, camps had to be set up. Often these had to be carved out of the jungle using picks and shovels, and where available, bulldozers. For the Kiwi ordnance men it was heartbreaking having built a camp to have to move again and repeat the construction process because room was needed for American personnel.

Argus Unit Seven and Radar

One of the priorities for the invaders was to establish radar installations. These encompassed Long Range Air Warning Radar (a New Zealand–designed and –developed set), an Early Warning Radar (an experimental set developed by New Zealand scientists), surface search sets, and a Radar Reporting Circuit. These tasks fell to Argus Unit Seven.

The Argus units derived their name from Greek mythology. Argus Panoptes was a giant with a hundred eyes and was all-seeing. The purpose of the Argus units was to provide comprehensive air and surface radar warning facilities during the initial phases of setting up a U.S. Navy base. It also had the task of coordinating fighter control. On the Green Islands the success of Operation Squarepeg rested on the shoulders of Argus Seven's men. Without adequate warning, the invasion force was vulnerable to Japanese air and naval attack.

Twenty-seven officers and one hundred and forty enlisted men arrived with the combat troops or followed on in LCTs and LSTs. The commander's report noted: "On D Day (15 February) the personnel and equipment were beached and proceeded to installation sites with a minimum of confusion—in some cases pushing ahead of the New Zealand perimeter (opposition being slight). All tactical equipment with the exception of the 527 [G.C.I. Radar] reached installation points using their own or the Unit's transportation power. All personnel had foxholes by dark."[19]

The problem with the 527 Radar Set was that although it had been unloaded without incident from the LST carrying it, the path to its installation site was through swampy ground. The equipment was dispersed under trees. There was a wait till the engineers could clear a roadway to the site on the western side near Pokonian Plantation. By 1630 hours the first pieces of equipment were delivered and installation began. An additional problem was that the site had no air raid siren, and when air raids were imminent, warnings had to be shouted down the beach. Phone lines were installed the following day. Calibration tests were undertaken and the radar came into operation.

The operation of the Long Range Air Warning Radar Set provides an example of inter-Allied cooperation. Two New Zealand officers were in charge of the New Zealand–developed set, but twenty-five men from Argus Seven were used in its operation.[20]

Not all the radars were successful, however. The 602 Radar, which had an average range of some 30 miles, suffered parts failures. In its first night of operation on 15 February, three of its five transformers burnt up; on the following day, the indicators went bad and tubes also burned out. Because of these factors the 602 radar was only used as a standby and within ten days was dismantled.

A Light Warning Radar Set operated by two New Zealand Ordnance Corps technicians was also landed on the Green Islands. This was a British model, A.A. No. 4 Mark III, mounted in a large cabin on a Ford 4 × 4 wheel drive with a fully loaded weight of five tons. It was a very flexible piece of equipment; because of its mobility, it was able to travel over the roughest and muddiest roads without difficulty, and was set up within 30 minutes of being landed. The radar unit gave "remarkably good results," being able to pick up large flights of bombers out to a distance of 80 miles and single planes at 50 to 60 miles.[21]

A New Zealand radar maintenance unit arrived at Lunga Point, Guadalcanal, en route to Nissan. Two launches came alongside their ship. "The radar men were considerably impressed with the Royal New Zealand Air Force guard and the heavily armed picket in the launches, and took them to be an efficient escort for important equipment that was on board. The radar section was still more impressed, however, to learn that the guard was concerned solely with the preservation of 4,000 cases of beer the ship was bringing for the Kiwis in the Pacific."²²

The Disposal of Japanese Dead

One of the important priorities was the rapid disposal of Japanese corpses. There was an important sanitary reason for this, in that tropical diseases were endemic to the Solomons and dead bodies threatened the health of the invaders. Normally, this was done by using a bulldozer to bury the bodies. However, another method was to dispose of them in deep water. The *Pacific* records: "After the action on Nissan Island Irwin [Major R.M. Irwin, commander of 6th Field Hygiene Section], a strong swimmer, disposed of seventy dead Japanese by towing them behind him with ropes, two at a time, into deep water when the barge stuck on a coral reef."²³

Captured Japanese Equipment

One of the more unusual tasks the ordnance personnel had to do was to pack up captured Japanese weapons and equipment for shipment back to the rear area so that it could be examined. "In one day—the fifth day after landing—the following were some of the items captured:–100,000 rounds of ammunition, five 20-millimetre anti-tank guns, six machine guns, several mortars, three radio sets, an outboard motor, gas masks, many Japanese packs, split-toed shoes and a quantity of food." The Kiwis were impressed by the sophisticated nature of the Japanese equipment, especially the quality of the Japanese periscopic sights and lenses. Some sake was also amongst the booty, but this was considered "not so good, and tasted harsh, like a cheap unmatured brandy."²⁴

The Type 97 antitank rifles were a source of curiosity to the New Zealanders. The Japanese could have used the heavy weaponry to decimate the Allied landing craft as they came through the narrow channel on 15 February, the day of the invasion. It is a mystery why they did not seize this opportunity, and it may point to lack of command and control on the part of the Japanese garrison.

For many soldiers, hunting for souvenirs was their chief preoccupation in the early days of garrisoning the Green Islands.

Men hunted the jungle after the day's work and were rewarded by finding masses of Japanese equipment left by the deceased or hiding enemy. Rifles, helmets, anti-tank rifles, machine-guns, flags, letters, mess cans half full of rice, clothing, and web equipment were eagerly acquired by the souvenir hunter. Mess tins, with the owner's name scratched on the aluminium in Japanese characters were highly prized. Rifles of 0.256

Captured Japanese 20mm automatic antitank rifles are shown off by NZ soldiers, 29 February 1944. Nissan Green Island 1944 [Archives Reference ADQZ 18905, WA117, 3/17 E3 3], Archives New Zealand, The Department of Internal Affairs, Te Tari Taiwhenua.

bore were, of course, most sought after and these, with about three or four inches of barrel sawn off, made good carbines. The anti-tank rifles, being cumbersome, were not in great demand, but one enterprising youth in the unit sold one to a Seabee for one hundred dollars.[25]

Ammunition Storage

Of more practical concern for the invaders was the storage of ammunition. Unless carefully stored correctly and insulated from the tropical environment, ammunition had a tendency to "sweat" and become unstable and therefore unusable. What the New Zealanders had not taken into account were the Nissan termites. These attacked the reserve ammunition boxes so badly that many had to be dumped.[26]

Airfield Construction

The construction of an airfield was a top priority and construction work began at a frenetic pace. Floodlights were among the first items

Ten. Aftermath and Consolidation

landed, and from D–Day onwards these were used, producing a blaze of light visible for miles during the hours of darkness. (This is what had also occurred on the Treasury Islands.[27]) The normal use of blackout precautions was thrown to the winds as the Seabees labored round the clock. Reliance was placed on the radar units to give timely warning of any incoming Japanese air or naval units. The Seabees rapidly cleared areas for an airfield. By the end of February, a fighter airfield was almost complete, and surveys for a bomber airfield were well underway. On 4 March an emergency landing occurred. Priority was given to the construction of a bomber airfield, and by early March 1944 there was an airfield of five thousand feet. It was expanded to seven thousand feet by the end of the month, and a later extension to seven thousand three hundred feet.

The payoff came on 7 March 1944, when an air strike on Kavieng staged through the Green Islands. Twelve fighters from No. 14 Squadron and eight from No. 18 Squadron, RNZAF, equipped with bomb racks in place of their belly tanks, took off from Torokina in the early morning, landed at the Green Islands to refuel, took off again at 1000 hours, bombed Rabaul township at 1100 hours, and safely returned.[28]

On 6 March, Corporal James noted in his unit diary, "After being delayed for 24 hours by the heavy rain, the airstrip came into operation this morning, when 36 planes including N.Z. Warhawks landed and then provided day cover for the unloading of the Fifth Echelon. Later in the day more planes arrived making a total of 51. To have the strip serviceable just 20 days after our occupation was a remarkable undertaking by the C.B.s, particularly as considerable blasting was necessary in the hard coral."[29]

The aviation historian William Wolf wrote: "On 1 April the first SBDs and TBFs shared the field with VMF-114 and VMF-212 F4Us. By 15 April 13 BG B-24s landed on Green en route to Truk. The field became so crowded with aircraft and construction equipment that the SBDs and TBFs would taxi with their wings folded. The Green Island airfields flew COMAIRSOLS missions to isolate the next objective, the Admiralties in the Bismarcks."[30]

The Seabees saw their second airstrip christened in blood: even as they were completing it, a heavily damaged Liberator attempted a landing, but crashed and disintegrated.

The construction of the airfields provided Allied air commanders with new options for reducing Rabaul to rubble. As aviation historian Bruce Gamble notes, "Two naval construction battalions completed a five thousand foot runway on Nissan Island just three weeks after it was invaded. The first fighter units soon commenced operations, initially using the new strip for staging, but as soon as billeting and support facilities were prepared, squadrons moved in to stay. Shifting the emphasis to the dive-bombing role, the fighters took over the role of 'cleaning out the fringes' of Rabaul."[31]

As the number of aircraft increased, so also did their need for supplies. Barrowclough reported, "[W]ithin four weeks of our landing we were operating so many aircraft from The Green Island airbase that the weekly consumption of aviation gasoline alone exceeded a quarter of a million gallons and at that stage all of it was manhandled ashore in 40 gallon drums."[32]

Headquarters observed:

> The take offs of the bombers woke light sleepers as they assembled overhead in the early hours of the morning en route to bomb the powerful enemy base at Truk. At night tall sticks of light from searchlights pierced the blackness over the island as a guide to the overdue planes, but many a searchlight operator must have known that his beam was but a silent memorial to men who had paid the supreme sacrifice that day.[33]

THE FIFTH ECHELON—6 MARCH 1944

The Fifth Echelon arrived on 6 March 1944. For the New Zealand soldiers its arrival was like Christmas morning. The 37th Battalion historian wrote:

> The Fifth Echelon brought forward ship loads of parcels and papers which had accumulated at Base over a period of four months. There were parcels for everyone and the more fortunate collected armfuls of them—but much of the foodstuff was past the stage of being edible. One man reckoned that his [news]papers came to over two hundred, and while this may have been a record, there were many not far short of this mark.
>
> Tents were chock-a-block with parcels piled in all corners, and stacks of papers lying scattered about everywhere. It would be several days before there would be a restoration of tidiness.[34]

PT Boat Base

A PT boat base was built on the Green Islands and Squadron 10 took up residence. Boats began operations against New Ireland and New Britain in February 1944. On 1 March 1944, twenty-nine PT boats together with destroyers sortied into Rabaul Harbor and the coastal areas around Cape Gazelle, Cape George and Namatanal in New Ireland. Sadly, the two daring sorties produced only meager results. The PT boats only found a solitary barge in the heavy, driving rain. The destroyers, however, did succeed in shelling their targets. Thereafter, nightly patrols hit the Japanese supply line, sinking barges and effectively removing any Japanese threat of counterinvasion or infiltration.

PT-boat 174 engaged in "some heavy barge busting activity" and had field modifications to allow it to take a 40mm gun on the bow. "Substantial strengthening of the deck frames" was required.[35]

Seaplane Base

A small seaplane base was built in June 1944. The Green Islands were used as a base by VP-44 and VP-91 for "Black Cat" operations until August 1944. These involved black-painted Catalina seaplanes which carried out nocturnal anti-shipping strikes, particularly against Japanese shipping in Rabaul and New Ireland.[36]

Black Cats and PT boats

The Catalinas and PT boats formed a dynamic team for nocturnal attacks on Japanese shipping. The seaplanes would use their radar and searchlights to locate Japanese shipping and would then spotlight the shipping or drop flares. The PT boats would then attack using their armament to sink the boats.

Naval Advance Base

Support facilities in the form of Naval Advance Base, Green Island (FPD SF 3202) were built in July 1944.

Jarman's Team

Captain Jarman's hydrographic team landed on the Green Islands and were given further work. Jarman recalled:

> My group spent one day making a hydrographic survey of Pinapel [sic] Island Lagoon. This island was not very important to the High Command in the Green Island Caper. We did discover one side of the lagoon was shallow and offered an excellent spot to beach a damaged or sinking vessel.
>
> My small group remained at Green Islands from "D" day, February 15, 1944 to near the middle of March 1944. During this period, a complete hydrographic

survey was made of Nissan Atoll, all shoals and channels were buoyed, two permanent tide stations were established, and party members acted as pilots in getting supply vessels through South Channel. The commander of NABU-11 seemed to rely rather heavily on my group for assistance in establishing the Naval Base. The base demolition squad was turned over to me and I was told to use it as I saw fit. I had this squad reduce all dangerous coral heads, and pointed out high spots in the entrance channels that needed reducing. Two members of NABU-11 were given instruction and training in piloting supply vessels into Nissan Atoll through South Entrance Channel. Another of the base units was instructed in how to obtain data from the tide staffs and interpret it.[37]

The American Response to Squarepeg

The New Zealanders had proven their usefulness as allies in the South Pacific on Vella Lavella and the Treasury Islands. The success of Squarepeg set the seal on that. Vice Admiral Wilkinson, the Commander of Task Force 31, extolled the virtues of the New Zealanders: "The performance of the ground forces, both military and engineering, was characterized by the record for efficiency hitherto established by the 3rd New Zealand Division. All landing and combat operations were conducted in an aggressive and skilful manner."[38]

Admiral Halsey, in his inimitable and hyperbolic style, was fulsome in his praise of the participants of Squarepeg. He reported that Squarepeg was "thoroughly planned and was executed with the utmost precision and team play. Rear Admiral Wilkinson (CTF31) conducted the amphibious operation without a hitch and on a perfectly executed timetable. General Barrowclough of the 3rd New Zealand Division (Commanding General of the Landing Force) exercised command of all operations ashore, under the principle of unity of command, and his forceful and intelligent leadership and coordination resulted in early activation of the Green [air] Fields. From conception to completion I consider that the Green project was a remarkably fine combined operation in every sense of the word."[39]

Barrowclough, for his part, found himself as Commanding General on the Green Islands in command of not only New Zealand but also American troops. As John Crawford notes, "He dealt with the American forces under his command in a considerate and effective manner, which ensured that a harmonious spirit pervaded the operation."[40]

Culture Shock and Nationalism

American generosity solved a myriad of problems. Ron Tucker, a New Zealand artilleryman, recalled that on Nissan his unit found themselves short of tea, a vital commodity to their fighting effectiveness. He went to the neighboring American camp and asked the cook if they had any loose tea they could spare. The cook loaded up an 18-inch pot and handed it to Tucker, explaining, "We don't drink tea—drop the pot back."[41]

The two different nationalities may have had a common language, but they nonetheless came from different cultures. Ross Templeton was amazed that American soldiers fought over the shards of shrapnel from Japanese bombers that had pierced his tent.[42]

The main area where the two nationalities had differences was over food. The New Zealanders grew to loathe the American supplied Spam, Chili Con Carne, dried eggs and beans, and sauerkraut. John Rose, a New Zealand Quartermaster, commented, "I am fairly easily pleased. However, a lot of farm boys took a while to get used to Chilli Con Carne and Spam—known as 'South Pacific Army Meat' by the troops. Fruit juice was a great innovation—there were always cans of juice, fruit salad and that sort of thing."[43] The authorities found to their dismay that the food problem was not one of insufficient food, but rather food wastage. Fresh food was supplied every now and then and devoured. Studies showed the troops had a protein diet too high for the tropics, but overall the health of the troops was not damaged.[44]

The other area of difference was the provision of equipment. New Zealand had been hard hit by the Great Depression. Equipment was in short supply and had to be used till it disintegrated. In contrast, the Americans seemed to have been luxuriously supplied, even down to ice cream making equipment. The New Zealand signalers had to make do with heavy World War I–era heavy cable for communication purposes. "It was an eye opener being with U.S. forces because of their light field telephones and disposable wire."[45]

In the same way that the Americans simply saw the Kiwis as "Limeys" or Britishers, the Kiwis were unable to distinguish the regional differences of the United States and simply referred to all Americans as "Yanks."

One area of commonality was in regard to clothing. American-supplied jungle suits and cotton clothing suitable for the tropics were supplied to the New Zealanders. The New Zealand soldiers began to look very similar to their American counterparts. This caused at least one humorous incident on Guadalcanal when New Zealand troops were unloading supplies. A New Zealand ASC commander was incensed to see a soldier casually watching the unloading process and proceeded to verbally chastise the offender. The New Zealander was undoubtedly mortified when the soldier replied in an American accent that he had been there a while and had just come to watch the unloading.[46]

Handicrafts were a way for the Kiwis to relieve the boredom of garrison duty, and there was a trade in these. Robert W. Conner, a Seabee with 93rd NCB, wrote in his diary, "Bought some shell beads for Lib that one of the New Zealanders made."[47]

To simplify command arrangements, New Zealand and American units were kept segregated. This limited contact between the nationalities. For John Rose there was little contact with the Yanks. The only ones he came in contact with were on a transport barge run by the U.S. Navy. "There were two or three young US sailors—a skipper, basic engineer and one other. They looked eighteen years old. By our standards they were young and immature. They had comics sticking out of the their back pockets. They seemed very excitable to us. They did not have the taciturn balance that Kiwis had."[48]

Beer and Moonshine

One thing that the young men of both American and New Zealand cultures shared was a fixation with alcohol. The consumption of large quantities of alcohol and the ability to hold your liquor were considered to be the mark of manliness. The problem was that in the advanced forward areas like the Green Islands, the authorities tended to give priority to ammunition, equipment and food supplies rather than alcohol.

Even when alcohol was available it tended to be strictly rationed. The beer ration for the Kiwis was one can of beer per week. Even then the quality was sometimes dubious. Barrowclough observed that one brand, "Cascade," was so bad that the soldiers had been heard to say that they would rather go without than drink that particular brand.

Because of the alcohol shortage on the Green Islands, the inevitable happened, and illicit stills were set up. Both the United States and New Zealand had rich histories of the creation of illegal alcohol distilleries. Both nationalities rose to the challenge, and moonshine was conjured out of diverse materials such as pineapple juice, raisins, potatoes and virtually anything else that would ferment.

Ross Templeton, a New Zealand driver, recalled that a cache of rum disappeared. The question became "Who stole the rum?"[49]

Ten. Aftermath and Consolidation

"Wharfies for the Yanks"

One of the common complaints of veterans of 3NZ Division was that they had to undertake hard physical labor both loading and unloading an interminable flow of supplies. This was inevitable given the need to develop the Green Islands as an advanced base. In his report to Wellington, Barrowclough stated:

> New Zealanders and Americans toiled through the steaming days and stifling nights unloading and transporting thousands of tons of supplies of every description. It is impossible to over estimate the magnitude of the work involved in unloading this cargo. Some of it came in LSTs which could enter the lagoon and drop their ramps on the various beaches. No sooner had the huge bow doors opened than men swarmed into the cavernous holds and in sweating teams dragged out vehicles and loose cargo through oceans of mud to the dumps ashore. Most of the cargo, however, arrived in larger ships which could not enter the lagoon. These had to be unloaded into smaller landing craft, which pitched and tossed alongside the larger ships in the heavy ocean swell that was running.
> The agility and skill of the soldiers in performing this dangerous task would have done credit to experienced sailors. All services of both nations worked with commendable zeal.[50]

Stevedoring was hard, dangerous, physically demanding work. It was also unglamorous and unrewarded. Some Kiwi veterans later complained that they were simply "wharfies for the Yanks." Nonetheless, it did have its benefits. The 37th Battalion historian recorded: "March 12–14. Unloading parties, which worked in relays from dawn until late at night, kept many of us occupied during the next few days. It was hard work, particularly for those handling petrol drums, but there was some compensation when working at ration dumps. No objection was made to the men eating and drinking as much as they liked, provided they did not take the rations away with them—of course no one did that...."[51]

A good example of the complexities of unloading ships is provided by the Seventh Echelon, consisting of five LSTs and two AKs which were scheduled to arrive at daybreak on Thursday 16 March 1944. This required considerable manpower to unload and store materiel.

Air Raids

Air raids occurred on a regular basis, mainly at night. "Piss Call Charlie" often disrupted sleep with his desynchronized engine and randomly dropped bombs. The Japanese pilots' damage reports must have made spectacular reading, for Bob Conner noted in his diary, "Tokyo Ann has announced for the second time we have been here that the Green Islands have been bombed into oblivion."[52]

Water

One of the problems that confronted planners was the acute shortage of clean, drinkable water on the islands. The Commando Raid had revealed that there was no drinkable water on Nissan. As soon as the New Zealand Engineers became aware of this, "rough attempts were made by some engineer officers to make condenser sets for sea water."[53] Provision was made for each man to carry a full water bottle and bulk water supplies of two gallons per man were intended to be landed.

For the first five days, the troops had a very limited ration of drinking water. *Pacific Saga* notes that even this water was tainted: "Much of the water we had brought with us tasted strongly of kerosene or oil from the containers. Bathing and washing of clothes was done in the sea or at best in very brackish water from shallow wells."[54] It was intended that the problem would be resolved by setting up distillation plants converting seawater into drinkable water. These distillation plants were landed and were in operation by the end of the first day. Through the use of Cleaver-Brooks distillation units, some two hundred and fifty gallons of fresh water an hour was obtained. "This water was quite clear and not salty to the taste, nor did it need any chlorination."[55] However, the demands of fighting in the tropics meant that the troops had to be continually rehydrated. They fell back on the remedy of drinking coconut milk.

The coconuts were high up in the palm trees. The men of 37th Battalion resorted to enlisting local help: "To get them we would way-lay a diminutive native boy, give him something in the way of food from our jungle ration and point upward. He would then tie some vine loosely about his ankles and shin up a fifty foot coconut palm in a matter of seconds. Then for a while it rained coconuts. We were very partial to the milk and became quite adept at preparing the nut for drinking—three or four chops and it would be ready."[56]

Doug Ross recalled: "There was an abundance of coconuts on the Green Islands and the big ones had a lot of milk in the centre which was important because of the shortage of water. It was very pleasant."[57] He added, "My lasting memory is that we survived, thanks to an abundance of coconuts whose milk virtually kept us alive!"[58]

Ten. Aftermath and Consolidation

Sgt. L.R. Varnham, Graves Registration Unit, tries water divining, 1944. Nissan Green Island 1944 [Archives Reference ADQZ 18905, WA117, 3/17 E3 3], Archives New Zealand, The Department of Internal Affairs, Te Tari Taiwhenua.

Diviners made efforts to locate water and suggested a place to dig. After excavating to a depth of thirty feet, the engineers were still dry, so the attempt was abandoned and the hole later used as a rubbish dump.[59] "A diviner's life was not always a happy one, since majors and sergeant majors were known to threaten one at least with ceremonial burial in his own well."[60] Wells were bored, but unfortunately the water was brackish and suitable only for clothes washing. Attempts were made to catch and store rainwater. Tins were placed around the edges of tents to catch rainwater, but drinkable water was to remain a constant problem. The shortage of drinking water was exacerbated by the sudden dramatic increase in the number of inhabitants after the invasion had occurred and air and naval bases were constructed.

A total of five thousand gallons of drinking water a day were produced by the airfield and mission headquarters plants.[61] Drinking water was the priority, but water was needed for other purposes, and it was this shortage that caused problems with the troop's hygiene: "It was difficult to get a good wash. This no doubt, accounted for the heavy RAP parades, the record attendance of seventy five in one day being reached despite an official assurance that troops in the Pacific 'were fit and well and longing for another fight.'"[62]

As *Pacific Kiwis* records, "Every downpour of rain was the signal for the men to hop out in the nude and standing under a pandanus or coconut tree, give themselves a good lather. Tins of every size and shape were used to catch water off tent flies to use for ablutions and in washing clothes."[63]

David Williams recalled, "On this coral atoll there were no streams and there were a number of condensers, petrol driven, converting sea water to fresh. The many vehicles had first claim for their radiators and each man had a ration of a water bottle (I think). It rained heavily every morning and we would use it for a shower. It usually stopped just as you had soaped up! Bamboo guttering for our tents and empty petrol drums helped."[64]

The experience of 37th Battalion was typical: "Water was still on the scarce list and we were still washing ourselves and our clothes in the sea or bracking water. We must have developed quite a distinctive aroma, but as we all smelt the same none of us noticed anything wrong. The engineers gave us very valuable help in constructing several wells and with the usual ingenuity of the average New Zealand soldier we rigged up showers—very brackish, but very welcome, none-the-less."[65]

Tea

Because the Green Islands are close to the Equator, the heat was severe to those unaccustomed to it. For the World War II generation of New Zealanders, tea was of prime importance. John Rose recalled billy cans of hot tea being supplied to the troops. No milk was supplied. The hot, sugared tea was a great reviver.[66]

"Ogpu"

One of the more unusual units on Nissan was "Y" section, a group of New Zealanders consisting of an officer, Lieutenant Coates, and five men. Their duty was to maintain a 24-hour watch and intercept Japanese Morse code messages from Japanese garrisons round the Pacific. The unit

Ten. Aftermath and Consolidation

acquired the nickname "Ogpu," a joking reference to the name of the Russian Secret Police. It was hard, tedious work to log the Japanese messages. They had to record accurately and at high speed the Japanese Katakana language, a language made up of 78 characters. In one month over 400 were intercepted. The messages were sent on to Japanese language experts at headquarters for analysis.

Command Arrangements

David Williams commented, "Potter had a difficult job on the Green Islands. Big brother was just down the road."[67] Having Barrowclough and his headquarters staff in close geographic proximity to Potter's own brigade headquarters was bound to create tensions. There was also a degree of tension between Barrowclough and Potter. Barrowclough was in peacetime a lawyer, whereas Potter was a professional soldier in the Permanent Force of the New Zealand Army. Consequently, there was resentment at Barrowclough's being in command.

The Provosts

The 3NZ Division's military police, the Provosts, were among the first to land on Nissan on 15 February 1944. Their task was to act "as provost for the NZ command, with the addition of providing traffic and general patrols at the airfields."

The Green Islands for 5NZ Provost Company was not easy billet. The military police had long and arduous hours of travel over newly formed roads because the units they were policing were very spread out. The police found that they had "unwillingly acquired a new companion— this was a horned toad who made the night hideous with his unending croak." The only times when he remained silent would be after heavy rain—"then his silence was all the worse, we would not sleep for listening for his unholy row!"[68]

The General, the President and "Murder Incorporated"

Major General Barrowclough was fond of playing chess. One of his opponents was one Richard Milhous Nixon, a lowly lieutenant with

Richard Nixon (right) on the Green Islands, 1944 (courtesy Richard Nixon Presidential Library and Museum [National Archives and Records Administration]).

SCAT.[69] South Pacific Combat Air Transport Command had gained the unenviable nickname "Murder Incorporated" because of the number of planes and crews that disappeared without trace.[70] Nixon would one day become the president of the United States. After the war, Barrowclough and Nixon would meet again at an official dinner when President Nixon visited New Zealand.

Lieutenant Nixon, USN, had been involved with SCAT on Efate, New Hebrides, Espiritu Santo, Vella Lavella and Bougainville before ending up on the Green Islands on 1 March 1944. Nixon, as commanding officer, was in charge of another lieutenant as executive officer and seven enlisted men. Their plane attempted to land on the newly created fighter strip on the Green Islands but was waved off because of a "soft spot" on the runway. The next day Nixon tried again but found his plane had to wait while an aircraft damaged in a raid on Rabaul had to make an emergency landing. His was the second plane to land on the Green Islands.

The SCAT unit rapidly began operations with reasonably comfortable

Ten. Aftermath and Consolidation

accommodation, including a Quonset hut and tents. Crewman Joseph Tolman recalled, "Although we were not under aerial attack, the Japanese marines left on the island would snipe at the Seabees from time to time."

The Seabees rapidly repaired the soft spot in the fighter strip and they then began construction of a bomber strip. This was completed in the nick of time as aircraft located on Torokina had to relocate to the Green Islands airfield in order to escape a Japanese attack. Japanese soldiers attacked the Allied perimeter at Torokina and the airstrips came under Japanese artillery fire.

The Green Islands were a red-alert area requiring the rapid unloading of aircraft. Nixon directed unloading and reloading operations with an average ground time for aircraft of eight minutes.

Nixon became legendary for his skill at poker, and a participant, Lester Noble, recalled, "Nixon was a careful player. He never lost big."[71] Although poker and gambling seemed at odds with his Quaker religion, Nixon enjoyed these activities.

Nixon ended his sojourn on Green Island in mid–1944 when he received orders to report to Espiritu Santo, probably to set up a new air transport unit bound for the Marianas. Fitness reports record Nixon's performance as officer in charge of the SCAT unit on the Green Islands as "exceptional."[72]

SCAT provided a regular transport link between Nissan and Guadalcanal for personnel and cargo. The New Zealanders used SCAT for medical evacuations to 2NZ CCS and 4NZ General Hospital. About half a million pounds of cargo was handled in April 1944.[73]

"Lucky Lindbergh"

One of the most distinguished visitors to the Green Islands was Charles A. Lindbergh, the first man to have flown in 1927 from America to Europe solo. A genuine American hero, Lindbergh had besmirched his record by becoming associated with isolationists in the prewar period and for visits to Nazi Germany. Determined to contribute to the war effort, Lindbergh sought combat assignments which were predictably denied. This did not deter Lindbergh, who capitalized on his expertise at long-distance flying and fuel management. Lindbergh wangled an assignment as a civilian technical expert with the United Aircraft Company, studying the performance of the F4U Corsair fighter. He taught Corsair pilots how to reduce their fuel consumption and increase the range of their aircraft.

Lindburgh soon began accompanying the pilots in order to better understand the operational aspects of combat flying. On 2 May 1944, Lindbergh flew his first unofficial and unapproved combat mission from the Green Islands with three other Corsair pilots bound for Rabaul. Later Lindbergh flew bombing and strafing missions over Kavieng before moving on to New Guinea, where he worked on developing fuel management techniques for the twin-engined P-38 Lightning to extend its range. Surprisingly, for a civilian, the forty-two-year-old Lindbergh flew fifty combat missions while in the Pacific and shot down one Japanese aircraft.[74]

One of Nixon's regrets was that he did not accept Barrowclough's invitation to have dinner with Lindbergh—he had a poker game engagement.

Dorothy Sawyer, Nurse

One of the more welcome and unexpected visitors to the Green Islands was the SCAT nurse, Dorothy Sawyer. There were no females on the Green Islands garrison, so the young, pretty Dorothy Sawyer made quite an impact when she and her flight crew were obliged because of bad weather to overnight. Nixon, as senior SCAT officer, laid on dinner in the mess tent and took the guests to a makeshift club, a lean-to attached to the back of one of the Quonset huts. The copilot, Nielson, recalled, "Dorothy was put up for the night in Dick's Quonset hut office, and two guards were assigned. The hut was about 20 feet long and 10 feet high and had a lock on the door."[75]

Nixon later recalled Sawyer's arrival: "[E]verybody was excited beyond belief because the first nurse was arriving and there were literally thousands, not hundreds—the Third New Zealand Division was gathered around—and the rest ogling this nurse that was come off. Now this nurse as you can see, is very attractive. But I am telling you, if that nurse who came off that day had been a female chimpanzee, they would have still

Top: The most popular person on the Green Islands—SCAT nurse Dorothy Sawyer (identified as Lt. Ann Ganzeuhl in NZ Archives). Left to right: Major General H.E. Barrowclough, Brig Gen F. Harris, USMC, Lt. Ann Ganzeuhl, Lt. Col. P.L. Bennett, and an unidentified Allied soldier, 6 March 1944. Nissan Green Island 1944 [Archives Reference ADQZ 18905, WA117, 3/17 E3 3], Archives New Zealand, The Department of Internal Affairs, Te Tari Taiwhenua. *Bottom:* Dorothy Sawyer surrounded by admirers (courtesy Richard Nixon Presidential Library and Museum [National Archives and Records Administration]).

Ten. Aftermath and Consolidation 145

whistled and oohed and aahed because they hadn't seen any girls for a long time."[76]

Nixon's Hamburger Stand

Nixon found that he could get hamburger meat on occasion for his flight crews. He also "found that you could liberate some from time to time. The Seabees sometimes did that and I ate in their mess. And so I knew how to make hamburger from my old days. And the flight crews would come in, and I–I set it up so—and I fried the hamburgers there and gave them hamburgers when they came in. And on occasion we'd give them a bottle of Australian beer. Now, understand, this is at the end of the flight, not before. And that was excellent beer. That wasn't very often, however. So consequently, I was the most popular officer in the South Pacific because of that hamburger stand."[77]

Nixon and the Seabees

Nixon later professed a fondness for the "hard hats," the construction workers, stemming from his wartime experiences. He recalled his admiration for the men of the 22nd Seabee Battalion who kept on working in the middle of the night under floodlights in order to get the airfield finished, sometimes ignoring air raid warnings. Nixon recalled:

> I got to know them very well and ate with them because I was the head of a small detachment—Army, Navy, Air Force were all members of it. I being a naval officer, was the officer in charge, being a lieutenant and the ranking officer. And so I was able to select the mess we could use. Well, I turned down the Marine mess because the Marines can fight but they couldn't cook. They were terrible cooks. I turned down the Army mess because they were almost as bad cooks as the N–as the Marines. The only other mess was the Seabee mess, and it was the best. It wasn't because their cook was good, but the Seabees, you know, they had access to a lot of things. They could put in a—they could put some flooring in your tent. They—they could make various utensils and so forth. And so they could trade for meat and other vittles for their mess. And what they didn't trade they stole. And they were very good.[78]

Bob Hope's USO Troupe Visits the Green Islands

Bob Hope, the famous American comedian, formed a troupe that toured bases in the South Pacific giving shows to Allied soldiers. The troupe traveled more than thirty thousand miles and gave more than one hundred and fifty performances.[79]

On 1 August 1944, the Hope troupe arrived on Nissan. The troupe consisted of Bob Hope delivering his trademark rapid-fire one-line jokes and banter with the audience; the mustachioed comedian "Professor" Jerry Colonna; the accordion/guitar player Tommy Romano; Bob Hope's friend and gag writer Barney Dean; and two very pretty women. These two were the most popular part of the show. The singer Frances Langford had a trademark song, "I'm in the Mood for Love," which invariably brought forth the response from some wiseacre in the audience, "You've come to the right place, lady." Frances Langford would become famous for singing the theme song of Disney Studios, "When You Wish Upon a Star." The second female was a young blonde dancer, Patty Thomas. Hope would stand next to the scantily clad Patty Thomas and would joke, "I just want you boys to remember what you are fighting for."

The troupe did a show on Nissan and then went by PT boat to the PT boat base. They then went on to visit the Acorn-10 Hospital to cheer up the staff and patients. Hope later recalled that when he visited hospitals he and his comedian sidekick Jerry Colonna would ham it up and be as loud as possible. Normally hospitals were quiet places and they wanted to amuse the patients.

Bob Hope knew how to work a crowd. Norman A. Schneidwind of VP44 later recalled, "I remember Hope made all the officers move to the rear of the audience before he would begin the show."[80] Undoubtedly Bob Hope's troupe did wonders for morale, reminding the soldiers that they were not forgotten. However, the presence of the unattainable, glamorous Frances Langford and the gyrations of Patty Thomas would have heightened the men's sexual tensions.

The Jack Benny Troupe

Also in 1944, the American comedian Jack Benny took his troupe to the Green Islands, where they did a show. The troupe consisted of Jack Benny, Larry Adler, Jean Brummer, Martha Tilton and the Hollywood actress Carole Landis.

PT Boat Disaster—29 April 1944

One of the saddest aspects of the Pacific War was the frequency of "blue on blue" attacks, so-called friendly fire incidents, where personnel were accidentally killed by their own side. Fighter pilots would sometimes fail to properly identify their targets and would let loose with the awesome firepower of their planes. Such a tragedy occurred on 29 April 1944. Aircraft from the Green Islands attacked three PT boats, PT-346, 347 and 350.

The unfortunate incident began when PT-347 ran aground on a reef near Rabaul. PT-350 arrived and began attempting to pull off her sister ship. At about 0700 hours two fighter aircraft began strafing the PT boats. PT-350 hit back, shooting down one of the planes. Unfortunately, the attacking aircraft were not Japanese. They were American Corsairs.

A third PT boat, PT-346, arrived to help. A crewman on this boat, Ollie J. Talley, recalled, "When we arrived (about 12.30pm) we saw 350 and they was all shot up.... You could see the [Japanese soldiers] on the beach from there. We were ordered to blow up 347 if we couldn't free the boat."

PT-346's crew came alongside and tried to secure a heavy rope around the stranded boat. At about 2 p.m., planes were sighted. Talley recalled, "We recognized them. We knew they were Corsairs, Hellcats and Dauntlesses. We thought it was our air cover so we went back to trying to get the boat of the reef."

The planes were USN—four Corsairs, six Avengers, four Hellcat fighters and eight Dauntless dive bombers. They then attacked, thinking that they were striking at Japanese gunboats. Talley remembered, "The first bomb went right under my engine room and blew my engines and batteries all out of whack.... When I climbed out of there, I saw the skipper had been mowed down."

Lt. James R. Burk "was fatally wounded while holding up an eight foot American flag in an attempt to save his crew by alerting the pilots that they were attacking an American vessel. As he lay dying on the deck, his last order was for Navy Corpsman John Frkovich to take his life jacket. The medic reluctantly pulled on the Mae West and lived to help other wounded sailors that day."

The attack left Talley's boat sinking with its radio knocked out. Talley remembered, "We had no guns left.... I'm still on the boat, trying to get this cork life raft off when he comes in. He dropped his flaps and put a one thousand pound bomb right in the middle of our boat. When it blew, it knocked me right out of my shoes." It got worse—for the next hour and a half the planes completed strafing runs. "It seems like every plane that came was lining with me. I'm sure the other guys had the same feeling."

Talley continued, "I'd see the smoke go out of the guns up there, then the bullets would start hitting the water ahead of me." Talley dived under water to escape the strafing runs. Eight crew of PT-346 sank beneath the waves, including an Army officer who had come along as an observer.

At 5:30 p.m., survivors were discovered by a USN seaplane which was looking for a Hellcat pilot who had been shot down. Talley was among those rescued and taken to the hospital on Green Island. He had a shrapnel wound behind his left ear and his left knee was injured. The other survivors had to wait in the water till 10 p.m., when two PT boats arrived.

The lightly built craft were particularly vulnerable to air attack and had to rely on their speed and evasive maneuvers. This attack was devastating, with PT-346 suffering nine killed and nine wounded, leaving only two crew members unharmed. PT-350 suffered three killed, five wounded, and seven crew members unharmed. PT-347 was the most fortunate, suffering only two killed, three wounded, and with ten of her crew unharmed.[81]

Milton Bush comments, "Squadrons VMF215 and VMSB236 were involved, as well as several PBYs from Green. The Fleet Commander declined to file any charges over the innumerable mistakes."[82]

Islanders

The islanders had been deprived of medical treatment because of the Japanese occupation. On the second day of the invasion, about twenty-five islanders appeared in Allied lines and sought medical treatment. An Argus report noted, "The majority of those were cases of yaws, which had been totally neglected and untreated. There were also shrapnel wounds from bombings, filariasis, leprosy and other troubles. The New Zealand Medical Command handled the natives in an outstanding manner."[83] A New Zealand driver, Ross Templeton, was horrified to see one of the local island women had only one breast—the other had rotted off.[84]

Some one thousand, one hundred and forty-seven islanders were removed by convoy to Guadalcanal when the empty vessels of the second echelon returned on 20 February 1944. This was done for their own safety because of Japanese air raids, and also because of the water shortage and the need to clear space on what was becoming an increasingly congested island. At least two of the islanders were stretcher cases. A child was born during the voyage. The War Diary of LST Flotilla Five noted, "Natives reported very cooperative but many in ill health due to malnutrition, disease and lack of medical treatment since occupation by the Japanese. LST doctors busy entire trip treating the sick among them."[85]

The Pacific records, "The natives were given medical treatment, which they sorely needed. When most of them were evacuated to Guadalcanal, a few hundred able-bodied men and boys were retained as a labour corps under Archer. Two hundred other natives on Pinipel, their tropical diseases aggravated by years of neglect, received regular treatment from Major W.W. Hallwright, Deputy Assistant Director of Medical Services, and officers of the field ambulances. A diet of army rations, including some of the more despised dehydrated items, soon restored a gloss to their ebony skins."[86]

Not all of the islanders were removed, however. Some two hundred islanders were kept as a labor corps.[87] There were also those on the outlying islands. The 37th Battalion carried out a patrol on Pinipel Island that brought them into contact with the islanders. The 37th Battalion clerk recorded:

> April 3: After sixteen days on Pinipel Island, Lieut. C.D. Standage's party of fifty men returned to the battalion. The platoon and attachments were divided into three sections, two of which were out on patrol each day. The island was searched thoroughly and there was no sign of Japs having been there since the expedition in February. The natives did all they could to assist the party and even formed themselves into an unofficial military organisation. They carried out coastwatching with remarkable thoroughness and the leader was mighty proud when he marched into the officer's tent to pour [sic] over the map. "Me walk here, here and here—see nothing," he would say, with finger moving along the map in impossible places. One native attached himself to Lieut. Standage as a personal bodyguard and he rarely let the officer out of his sight.[88]

The New Zealand medical historian, T. Duncan M. Stout, noted, "New Zealand medical officers gave treatment to the native population on Nissan and Pinipel Islands. Several weekly visits were made to Pinipel on landing craft and the 200 natives were given injections for yaws and other medical treatment. A great improvement in their health, both physically and mentally was noted."[89]

New Zealand medical personnel (from HQ 3NZ Division Medical, 24 NZ Field Ambulance and 4 Field Security Section), faced a range of medical problems and did what they could to help. It is noteworthy that on the visits to Pinipel, the New Zealanders were accompanied by Solomon Islanders, who assisted with translation and medical examinations. It was found that there was a high incidence of malaria among the islanders of Pinipel Island.

The islanders were no doubt appreciative of the medical assistance.

Ten. Aftermath and Consolidation

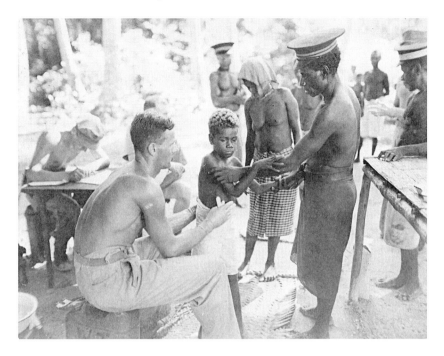

Major Hallwright, DADMS, examines a native child, May (?) 1944. Nissan Green Island 1944 [Archives Reference ADQZ 18905, WA117, 3/17 E3 3], Archives New Zealand, The Department of Internal Affairs, Te Tari Taiwhenua.

There were limits, however. On 4 April 1944, Major W.W. Hallwright, DADMS, examined a crippled island girl for a suspected tubucular knee joint and wanted the child evacuated to Guadalcanal. However, the family would not agree to this.[90]

Relations between the islanders and their guests sometimes had their odd moments. Larry Katz was a radioman on the PBY Catalina seaplanes of VPB-29 which were moored on the Green Islands and serviced by tenders. The seaplanes operated as "Black Cats" or alternatively "Dumbos" (strike aircraft or rescue aircraft). Although the islanders' village areas were supposed to be off limits, Katz recalled an occasion when he and his crewmates had gone "on a beer bust" and then tried to do some trading with the islanders.

> While there we went to one of the native huts for a trading session. We would trade with the natives things that we had for their trinkets like shell bracelets, necklaces, or stalks of bananas or anything native. We would trade razor blades, sheets, pillow cases (they called them LOP LOP). I had an I.D. bracelet that my

mother gave me with Naval Wings on one side with my name and on the other side engraved was "Mother." While in the hut one of the natives that we were trading with spotted my bracelet and started pulling on it gently. He wanted it and in return he took both hands of his and put the two forefingers and thumbs together forming a shape like a triangle. He then called out to someone in the back of the hut and a young native girl came out.

You know what he wanted me to do; he wanted me to trade the bracelet for the young girl for my pleasure. I looked at both of them and kept shaking my head from side to side in the no position. At that time all my buddies behind me kept yelling out "Larry, I'll give you $10.00 for that bracelet, $20.00, $30.00," and up…. Make a long story short. I did not trade that bracelet for anything.[91]

Garbage and Sanitation

One of the by-products of the invasion was the creation of garbage. That posed sanitation and health problems on such a small land area. As roads were developed, garbage dumps were set up along the cliffs, and chutes were created so that garbage could be disposed of into the deep water.

However, this only partially addressed the problem—the disposal of coconuts and food waste was inadequate, and this in turn led to an explosion in the size of the fly population, which threatened the health and comfort of the garrison. Gradually, as campsites became established, the fly population lessened.[92] By 1944 the New Zealand Army had learnt through bitter experience in the tropics the importance of hygiene. Brigadier Duff, prior to the invasion, had placed emphasis on "the disposal of 'K' ration wrappers, unused food etc continuously from the time of first embarkation. Only thus and by immediate construction of latrines can the fly menace be countered at the outset."[93]

Sanitation was of critical importance. The island was small, and great care had to be taken with field hygiene to prevent the outbreak of disease. Barrowclough was acutely aware of the problem, and he was also aware that although an area had been designated as a garbage dump, garbage was still building up in other areas and creating a hazard. Barrowclough called a meeting of officers, including Americans. He outlined the problem and then pointed to an American officer and asked what orders the officer would give to his men. To Barrowclough's astonishment, the American replied, "I guess, General, I will tell them to get it out of sight." Barrowclough coolly replied that if one of his officers had said that he would cease to be an officer.[94]

Native pigs proved to be a problem because they dug up garbage that had been buried.

Construction Projects

The New Zealand engineers helped the Seabees with the construction of the bomber strip on Nissan. This was completed within six weeks. The completion of the airstrip gave the engineers "that righteous glow of co-operativeness whenever we heard the dawn patrol go out."[95]

Roads were constructed on Nissan. Beginning with pieces of Marston Matting at Pokonian Plantation on the day of the invasion, the 26th Heavy Equipment Company created miles of road. "The initial reconnaissance for the nine mile stretch from Pokonian to the Roman Catholic Mission was not without excitement. Blissfully unaware of any Jap concentrations, the recce party was blazing a way through the jungle for the bulldozer 100 yards behind. In doing so they caught up on the scouting parties and as things suddenly opened up they found themselves flat on their stomachs on the fringe of the fight."[96]

For the first three or four days following the invasion the roads were reasonably solid, albeit full of jagged pieces of coral. As heavy vehicles were used during periods of continual rain, the use of the roads became increasingly difficult. The roads became extremely muddy so that vehicles without chains became useless.[97]

Nor did the engineers only build and maintain roads. "The engineers were of considerable help to the infantry for, in addition to their construction of supply roads from the landing beaches and carrying out many other tasks, they erected boobytraps around the perimeters of the forward troops every night, thus giving the men greater security for sleep."[98]

Dangerous Coconut Trees

One of the unintended consequences of the fighting on Nissan was that some of the coconut trees became so riddled with bullets and shells that they became unstable and dangerous. The author of *Pacific Pioneers* noted that in "the Torahatup area the twenty-five-pounders [i.e., artillery guns] had shelled the Jap headquarters and the results, at least as far as the betel-nut palms were concerned, proved disastrous when a wind blew. We were hardly surprised when an American QM tent (acquired) failed to stand the combined weight of three betel-nut palms across it."[99]

Wharves and Jetties

In order to be a useful forward base, arms, ordnance and supplies had to be offloaded. The problem was that the Green Islands lacked the

20 Field Company, 3NZ Division Engineers, at work on LCT pier at Halis. Cranes lift coconut logs into place, 1944. Nissan Green Island 1944 [Archives Reference ADQZ 18905, WA117, 3/17 E3 3], Archives New Zealand, The Department of Internal Affairs, Te Tari Taiwhenua.

facilities to handle cargo. There was a landing stage at the mission, and this was used for LCIs and LCVPs. The engineers constructed a wooden jetty at Pokonian for the use of the field ambulance.

Nissan has a shallow lagoon about eight miles long by three miles wide. Entry is difficult because of the coral reefs surrounding it. The LSTs had to heave-to off the Green Islands. Liberty ships could not get into the lagoon because of their draft. It was necessary to offload supplies from the Liberty ships to LCTs, which would then deliver the cargo to shore. This was a slow, tedious process and needed to be speeded up. To solve the problem it was decided to create two docks with cranes for side unloading, one at Halis and the other at Salipal. Timber was obtained locally and milled by 37th Field Park. Bulkhead piers were created capable of handling two LCTs. During the construction of the Halis pier, American officers were amazed that the logs for the cribbing were positioned not by cranes but by "submersible sappers."[100]

Theaters

In order to provide the troops with entertainment, 20th Field Company carved out a jungle theater at Torahatup on Nissan. The 20th had plenty of experience at constructing jungle theaters—they had previously built them on Guadalcanal and Vella Lavella. Torahapup was to be their piece de resistance, with tiered seating capable of holding half a brigade. Shows were put on as well as films. Newsreels even featured the invasion of the Green Islands. A veteran commented on the newsreels, "Here we saw ourselves as others saw us; landing on a waterless island and littering the jungle trails with dead Japs, LSTs giving birth to endless streams of lorries [trucks] and dozers, the first few coconuts falling to the airstrip builders."[101]

The Seabees Tragedy—10 June 1944

Heavy construction projects always entail risk. On 10 June 1944, five Seabees from 93rd NCB—Frank Sanchez, Marcel W. Simmons, Joseph H. Sowa, David J. Walters, John D. Walters and Andrew Zorn—were killed when several cases of dynamite exploded accidentally. Bob Conner observed that "several were equipment operators and not on the dynamite crew. The identification of the fellows has been very hard since it is having to be done by bits of clothing and personal items."[102]

The Green Islands Become a Backwater

The war was moving northward and the Green Islands became a backwater. A sign of this was the arrival of Liberty ships on 10 April 1944. Corporal G.A. James noted in his diary that this was the first time American merchant ships had traveled so far north since the outbreak of war. "Included in the cargo was a large parcel and paper mail for the New Zealanders and many cases of American beer. We hoped to share in the disposal of the latter."[103]

Barrowclough reported:

> With the completion of the airfield and their ancillary services we were able to devote a little more time to the improvement of living conditions for the troops on the island and the development of roads. The United States Service of Supply brought forward and installed refrigerating machinery and it is now possible to

obtain occasional supplies of fresh meat and vegetables. The change in diet was most welcome. So were the arrival of a cargo of beer and the provision of picture shows. Life began to assume a more normal routine. The landing of American troops in Emirau Island resulted in our ceasing to be in the van of the South Pacific area and we were justified in relaxing to some extent the state of preparedness against enemy attack.[104]

Barrowclough took the opportunity of removing some of his older commanders because they were unfit for the stresses of combat in the tropics, but also to give younger men the chance of promotion. One of the officers removed on 22 March 1944 was Lt. Col. Cornwall. His personnel file notes that he was "placed on the NZ Roll on account of age. The GOC records his appreciation of the services of this officer."[105]

Shipping

As the size of the Allied garrison grew and military facilities were developed, there was a constant stream of troopships and supply ships. These included USS *Cassiopeia*, *Talbot* and *Unicol*. These ships were highly vulnerable. For example, the cargo of the attack transport *Cassiopeia* in February 1943, had one thousand, nine hundred and forty-two tons of bombs and aircraft ammunition; one thousand, two hundred and seventy-six tons of rations; two thousand, seven hundred and thirty-eight drums of aviation fuel; eighty-five drums of aviation lubrication; pontoon sections for the PT base; one hundred and sixty-six tons of net D boom material; twelve tons of gas tanks; one thirty-three foot rearming boat; and twenty-five × three thousand, two-hundred-lb. cement blocks as well as mixed cargo for the Army, Navy and 17th Weather Squadron.[106]

The Problems of Static Garrison Duty— No "Club Med"

Health Issues and Diseases

During the period February to April 1944, the sickness rate for the New Zealanders on the Green Islands went up to 35 percent due to the constantly high temperature, manual work in the jungle, and lack of washing facilities, in particular the absence of fresh water![107]

For the troops on Nissan, tropical sores and dermatitis were common afflictions. One particular misery was inflicted by a furry caterpillar that produced a secretion which led to severe itching in its victims. The Argus Seven Report commented on the desirability of bringing medical supplies for treatment of infection at an early stage: "Almost without fail, every small abrasion or laceration becomes secondarily infected unless these are treated adequately and early. These lesions must be kept covered by sterile dressings until completely healed." The report writer attributed three main reasons for the prevalence of infections: "1. The lack of body cleanliness, due to the extreme shortage of water for bathing, washing and laundry purposes. 2. The general condition of the average individual in a forward area is somewhat run down, due to the excessive amount of work and the irregularity of sleep. Heat rash has been common and bothersome to many and often these lesions become secondarily infected. 3. The presence of large numbers of flies in the area. If the lesions are not covered they probably introduce infective material."[108]

The New Zealand signalers found that although there were no serious instances of illness in their unit, very few men escaped skin complaints or dermatitis. The consequence of this was that "men were to be seen with their bodies highly decorated with coloured daubs of the remedial lotions used. Long trousers were obviously the cause of much skin trouble and the order authorizing wearing of underpants in their stead was a great improvement." The New Zealand Army, in its Kafkaesque wisdom, had previously outlawed shorts to be taken into the forward areas.[109]

Ants proved to be a particular problem on Nissan. "A large brown species with a vicious bite appeared in huge colonies near the ordnance workshops camp. When disturbance of the ground revealed millions of these pests, tents had often to be moved."[110]

Ross Templeton, a New Zealand driver, had a particularly uncomfortable time. He developed a case of "Dhobi's Itch," an inflammation around the area of his crotch. There was no fresh water for washing, so his condition became aggravated. There was no toilet paper available in the early days and he used leaves to wipe his bottom. This in turn aggravated his condition. He recalled that he had dysentery when he landed on Nissan and would squat down and to his horror would leave a pool of blood. This lasted for 10 days and then began to ease off. He recalled that it was "most unpleasant."[111]

Pacific Kiwis records: "the constant sweating had brought on an outbreak among the troops of boils, septic sores, ringworm, prickly heat and rashes. Particularly prevalent were cysts under the armpits and those men so afflicted were dubbed 'Corsairs' by their mates, because of the manner in which they held their arms—something akin to the upswept wings of the well-known Corsair fighter plane."[112]

Hookworm was prevalent. George Laing recalled the somewhat blunt approach of the medical authorities to the problem: "All ranks tested for hookworm. 'You have an infection of 10%,' said the Doc. Any [men with a] higher rate are being sent to hospital at Guadalcanal. Asking what is a hookworm we are told that it can enter your body through the pores of the skin, then grows to a quarter of an inch and hooks on to the liver. Off to a field hospital where the treatment is a pill to anaesthetize the hookworm and a massive dose of salts to solve the problem. No further test will be necessary."[113]

John Rose, a quartermaster officer with 14 Brigade, recalled, "On Green Island there was a problem with Hookworm. It penetrated the skin of the feet. At one point the soldiers were compulsorily drenched with tablets. They were big tablets which came in boxes marked that they were only for use on dogs."[114]

T. Duncan Stout notes, "The natives of the Island were heavily infected with hookworm (ankylostomiasis) and the infection probably occurred in the first few days after landing when troops were sleeping in fox holes or on ground that had been infected by natives."[115]

Malaria was a constant threat in the Solomons. The troops were supplied with Atabrine, a malaria suppressant, in tablet form. One whole tablet was taken daily. The tablets were bitter tasting and sometimes caused headaches and nausea. Word had spread among Allied units that the tablets turned their users' skin yellow (true) and led to impotence (false). There was therefore considerable consumer resistance to taking the tablets.[116]

David Williams, a New Zealand officer, recalled: "Our battalion accepted the need and the officers had no problem with it. Atabrine was administered on parade and you watched each man swallow it. We started with a dose of 4 tablets a week (½ daily & none on Sunday) rising to six (one a day, none on Sunday). When in action we had to rely on buttoning up clothing and putting repellent on exposed skin. When tents and mosquito nets arrived we used them."

John Rose recalled, "There was not much in the way of malaria based casualties. There were strict instructions—get 'em to stick out their tongue and watch them swallow it. If one of your men got malaria then you copped it."[117]

The Allies took precautions as best they could. The wearing of shorts was prohibited between 1800 hours until 0700 hours the following day,

Private E.J. Blacklock, No. I NZ Malaria Control Unit at Yotchibol spraying stagnant water, 10 May 1944. Nissan Green Island 1944 [Archives Reference ADQZ 18905, WA117, 3/17 E3 3], Archives New Zealand, The Department of Internal Affairs, Te Tari Taiwhenua.

swimming at 1745 hours was prohibited, repellent lotion was to be used, and troops were required to sleep under mosquito nets.[118] The need for vigilance was well founded in respect of the Green Islands. Thirteen *Anopheles* mosquito breeding sites were found. Breeding grounds were found in the area south of Pokonian, where there was a salt swamp. The

U.S. Malaria Control Unit dealt with malaria suppression on the right-hand side of the atoll and 1 New Zealand Malaria Control Unit (1NZMCU) worked on the left.[119]

Unpleasant Climate

Being so near to the Equator, the Green Islands have a tropical climate. Rain fell almost daily and often all day.[120] Torrential rain and electrical storms were a frequent occurrence, which made life miserable for the troops. Roads were washed out and campsites became boggy morasses. Being able to keep dry was an effort in itself.

Boredom

Once the excitement of the landing and combat with the Japanese had faded, the troops settled into the humdrum existence of garrison duty. *Pacific Saga* sums this up: "As we had previously experienced at Vella Lavella, the Green Islands operation proved a comparatively short period of intense activity and stress, followed by months of accentuated quiet and our life now settled down to routine patrols, working parties, and the construction of defensive works. Those of us not engaged on these tasks set to work clearing jungle around the camp sites, forming paths and roads to get us out of the perpetual mud and slush, and generally improving living conditions."[121]

Inevitably, the switch from being in a frontline combat situation to the boredom of static garrison duty affected morale. One New Zealand veteran, Harry Bioletti, recorded that things settled into "another one of those dreary waiting periods which the men of the 3rd [New Zealand] Division had come to know so well. You looked at the well handled photo of the wife on the ration-box dressing table and thought, 'It won't be long soon!' When not on working parties over at the other side of the lagoon the boys squelched around the muddy area in underpants and boots, the almost uniform dress of officers and men alike, dropping into tents to hear the latest rumors, or hiking off down to the YMCA tent for a cup of stewed tea. Cards—cribbage and bridge—occupied leisure hours and the reading of well thumbed magazines and out of date newspapers!"[122]

John Rose commented, "Boredom is always a problem once an area has been cleared. What do you do? There is a limit to the number of times you can practice jungle drills unless you have an opportunity to try it in real life."[123]

Ten. Aftermath and Consolidation 161

Doug Ross recalled his time on the Green Islands: "Green Island will always remain in my memory as an occasion that tested one's ability to overcome boredom." There were "no areas for sport except swimming, coral reefs were murder on the flesh. Table tennis [was] a big winner.... [There was] no variety of diet and even meals were boring!"[124]

Even swimming had its drawbacks. Soldiers were warned, "Sharks and barracuda are an extreme danger around the whole coast of Squarepeg and neighbouring islands." Whilst swimming was not prohibited, soldiers were ordered to swim in groups of three at a minimum.[125] Recreational hunting of the local pigs and goats was forbidden due to the prevalence of animal tuberculosis. The meat was considered unfit for human consumption.[126]

Appreciating the importance to morale of alleviating boredom, the New Zealand Army did what it could. Amphitheaters were built for the screening of films. Quiz games, card sessions, chess debates and even mock trials were held. Concerts were much looked forward to. One particularly welcome concert was put on by the swing band of the 33rd NCBs, who traveled across some rough roads to play on a specially constructed stage. The Seabees' piano had to be brought across the lagoon by barge.[127]

The lengths the New Zealanders went to in creating their own entertainment is illustrated by "The Ancient Order of the Fraternity of Jungle Bums," an informal organization created by a wireless section. Initially, this simply involved off-duty personnel meeting nightly in a tent, but as the organization grew in size, an outdoor rotunda capable of seating forty men was carved out of the jungle. The nightly program consisted of participating in a community sing, listening to the section's jungle band, and enjoying supper of tea, coffee or cocoa made over an open fire—in fact, membership of this select band could only be gained by regularly contributing "acquired [stolen] rations to the larder."[128]

Some of the more adventurous Kiwis sought a more dramatic cure for the monotony. The New Zealanders saw American planes taking off from the airstrips on the Green Islands and made friends with American aircrew. Johnny Bull, a trooper with 3NZ Division Tank Squadron, struck up a friendship with the crew of a four-engine USAAF Liberator and asked a crew chief if there was any chance of going up on a test flight. The American replied that the bomber was due to leave at 7 the next morning and that there was room on board for two extra passengers. Bull accepted the challenge, together with his friend "Chuckles" Eccles. They made their way to the airstrip the next morning, where the crew chief signed them on as extra gunners on the B-24 *Dixie*. The bomber took off and completed its patrol. However, the pilot was "browned off" at the absence of Japanese and decided to take a look at the island of Lamotrek, slightly to the northwest of the Japanese base of Truk. The island was supposed to be uninhabited, but the aircrew discovered a building partially hidden by the jungle and a row of seaplanes lined up along the beach.

The pilot turned the bomber and

> came in from the north with a steep power dive. Over the line of beached planes *Dixie* streaked at an altitude of fifty feet, and every one of her ten .5 guns blazed away. When the bombs went every man could feel the plane shudder, pitch about and then right herself, as the skipper fought with the controls. The Japs had been caught napping for not one round of ack was fired. The buildings were well and truly strafed and the radio tower was not forgotten. Here a Nip, finding his cabin aloft a little too warm, decided to evacuate down the ladder. He had barely left the top rung before he collected a burst of .5s right in the middle and a laughable figure he cut as he somersaulted to the ground thirty feet below.

The B-24 Liberator was a heavy four-engine strategic bomber designed to deliver a payload of bombs from medium or high altitude. Although equipped with a formidable armament designed to ward off enemy fighters, the Liberator was in no way designed as a ground attack aircraft.

It is an accepted, unwritten rule of aerial ground attack that only one pass should be made over enemy positions—to do more is to invite intense enemy fire and risk destruction of a fragile and complex piece of machinery. All it takes is one "golden bullet" to bring down an aircraft. However, the American pilot was blind to these realities.

> That was the first of the four runs the skipper made on the target, but in subsequent runs the Nips were not so backward with their flak. They threw up everything, but it did not save them for *Dixie* with her machine guns blazing and bombs dropping, was on the mark every time. The place was a blazing inferno. Seven of the planes on the beach ceased to exist, whilst the other two were very much the worse for wear. Apparently a petrol dump had been blown up, and the buildings were rapidly being consumed by the fire. *Dixie* at the end of the third run had a lot in common with a pepper pot. The port outboard engine was out, and was spewing forth dense smoke in an alarming manner. The navigator's instrument panel was badly damaged, the port inboard engine was beginning to show signs of wear, and little holes were everywhere in the fuselage. Despite the fact that only three motors were running the skipper decided to go in and drop the two remaining bombs. He went in at the usual 50 feet and again through a gauntlet of lead. The trees whirled past underneath, almost close enough to touch, and as the bombs exploded the plane seemed to lift and then, bumping and jarring, headed down straight for the sea. All thought this was the end, and it almost came as a surprise when only a few feet from the water the skipper regained control and lifted her gradually away.

Ten. Aftermath and Consolidation

Incredibly, none of the crew was hurt, but the damaged aircraft would have been easy prey to Japanese fighters. The pilot decided to head for the safety of Allied-held Emirau Island rather than return to its base at Nissan. The problem was that Emirau had only a short fighter airstrip and the Marine Air Group located there were amazed at the arrival of the huge, bullet-riddled bomber. They were even more amazed when the two New Zealand tank crew got off the plane in their distinctive black berets. It soon became clear that the Kiwis were "stowaways." After undergoing debriefing, the aircrew met the legendary Major Joe Foss, one of the highest-scoring American air aces of the Pacific War. Foss presented each one with a bottle of brandy. An evening of "laughter and raucous singing" followed. However, the Kiwis faced a problem. Their absence on Nissan had been noticed and it eventually became known that their Liberator *Dixie* had failed to return. Divisional headquarters was duly notified. In the meantime a plane was sent from Nissan to pick up the aircrew on Emirau. On arrival back at Nissan, the Kiwis were charged with being absent without leave. They appeared before their commanding officer and were fined $30, the equivalent of twenty-two days' pay. Later on they received a visit from their commanding officer who, full of curiosity, wanted to know the details of their adventure. Annoyed at being fined, the two replied, "Well, if you want to know what happened, it will cost you thirty bucks."[129]

Alarms

The New Zealanders remained close to Japanese forces and vigilance had to be maintained. On 15 March 1944 at 0044 hours the phone rang in the orderly room of the MMG company. The orderly's "peace of mind was further shattered when a voice informed him that a Jap counter-invasion from New Ireland was imminent and could this company please do something about it. Ensued much bursting into tents, more profanity and a general feeling of unbelief. Gunpits had to be completed, [machine gun] belts filled and trucks refueled, but even so the privates lingered on their cots until the prospects of a fight had been properly reviewed while the despairing Sergeants pleaded and threatened that these things should be done. After about an hour the reception committee was ready so we all retired to bed until such time as friend Tojo should appear—no one was unduly surprised when the projected invasion failed to materialise."[130]

The Neutralization of Rabaul

The main reason for seizing the Green Islands had been to secure an advance base from which to isolate the main Japanese base at Rabaul. Airfields and naval bases were created and the bombardment and interdiction of Rabaul began in earnest. There were, however, to be further links in the chain encircling Rabaul. General Douglas MacArthur's forces landed on Los Negros and Manus Islands in the Admiralty Islands on 29 March 1944 and after a month of tough fighting eliminated the five thousand Japanese defenders. The next step was the capture of Emirau by 3rd USMC Division on 20 March against surprisingly weak Japanese opposition. This effectively completed the encirclement of Rabaul and left some fifty thousand Japanese troops in New Britain and New Ireland with a further thirty thousand in Choiseul and Bougainville. The isolated Japanese troops were in no mood to surrender.

A continuous Allied air offensive against Rabaul began in early January 1944 with a focus on destroying the Japanese airfields on the Gazelle Peninsula, New Britain. The Japanese fought back with fighter aircraft against the Allied heavy, medium and light bombers. Allied fighter aircraft included Corsairs, Hellcats, Lightnings, Aircobras and Kittyhawks. By 19 February the aerial attrition had taken its toll, and Japanese fighters ceased to contest the skies over Rabaul. A systematic bombardment began of Rabaul, and by 17 March 1944 it was calculated that Rabaul had been 67 percent destroyed. By May 1944 this estimate had risen to 90 percent and the harbor had effectively been closed to Japanese shipping.

The RNZAF played its role. No. 20 (Fighter) Squadron equipped with Corsairs arrived on the Green Islands on 26 October 1944. It had been preceded by Nos. 3 and 14 Servicing Units, which arrived on 3 October to find that most of the area they were to take over consisted of "a dismal wilderness of heavy tropical undergrowth."[131] The men set to work creating facilities until prefabricated huts arrived from New Zealand. The Kiwi fighters carried out defensive patrols, "Dumbo" escorts, and offensive fighter sweeps over New Ireland, where they shot up targets of opportunity. They replaced two American Corsair squadrons which were redeployed to the Philippines. No. 20's tour ended on 19 November and it was replaced by No. 18 (Fighter) Squadron, which was based on the Green Islands to give its pilots operational experience. It was in turn replaced in December 1944 by Nos. 14 and No. 16 Fighter Squadrons.

On 29 October 1944, No. 1 (Bomber Reconnaissance) Squadron, RNZAF deployed to the Green Islands. Initially the Venturas undertook

Ten. Aftermath and Consolidation

RNZAF personnel at the Green Islands pose for the camera in front of RNZAF Corsairs, December 1944. Green Island Emirau Los Negros 1945 [Archives Reference ADQA 17263 AIR118 58/64 22], Archives New Zealand, The Department of Internal Affairs, Te Tari Taiwhenua.

weather flights and reconnaissance missions over Rabaul, but in early December they began "night heckles" over Rabaul, raids which were designed to keep the Japanese defenses on edge and make life as miserable for the defenders as possible. The Venturas were not equipped with bomb sights, so their accuracy was dubious.[132] Coordinated strikes with American aircraft based on Emirau were launched against Rabaul. The squadron left on 5 January 1945.

A Black Day for the RNZAF—15 January 1945

RNZAF Corsair fighters were based on the Green Islands and regularly took part in fighter sweeps and escorting bombers attacking Rabaul. On 15 January, thirty-six Corsairs took off from their Green Islands airfield with the mission of attacking the Taboi wharf and nearby floatplane anchorage at Taboi on Rabaul. By this stage of the war, the Japanese fighter defenses had been eviscerated and the most basic threats were from Japanese antiaircraft defenses and the weather. On this day a chain of events would unfold which would lead to the severest loss for the RNZAF in the Pacific War.

The strike unfolded as planned, but Flight Lieutenant Francis G. Keefe's Corsair was hit by flak, setting his plane on fire and wounding him in the arm. Keefe had no choice but to bail out.

Air-sea rescue facilities had developed hugely over the course of the war, and as Keefe swung from his parachute he had every hope of being rescued even in Rabaul's harbor. Landing in the water, Keefe discarded his parachute and dinghy, believing that the dinghy would attract Japanese gunfire. He began swimming towards the mouth of the bay. His comrades strafed Japanese gun positions.

A USN Catalina seaplane in its "Dumbo" role attempted to land and rescue Keefe but was driven off by heavy gunfire. Keefe floated in the harbor. In the afternoon another attempt was made to rescue him. A dozen

RNZAF Ventura takes off from the Green Islands, December 1944. Green Island Emirau Los Negros 1945 [Archives Reference ADQA 17263 AIR118 58/64 22], Archives New Zealand, The Department of Internal Affairs, Te Tari Taiwhenua.

RNZAF Corsairs escorted an RNZAF Ventura, which dropped bamboo rafts close to Keefe. The pilots saw that Keefe seemed to be motionless, lying face-down in the debris. They sadly concluded he was dead and began the trip back to the Green Islands.

The fighters encountered a storm front. Twelve fighters entered the maelstrom but only six emerged. The others had either collided, become disoriented, or because they were at low altitude, had crashed into the sea. No trace of the missing six was ever found. To compound the tragedy, a seventh Corsair disappeared on the flight back.[133]

Ironically, Keefe had survived and was picked up by the Japanese. He died, supposedly of blood poisoning, some two weeks after his capture, but more likely from ill treatment by his captors.

Assault Drones

The Second World War was very much a war of scientists, a "Wizard War," and huge advances took place in technology. One such advance was the use of unmanned drones to attack enemy targets. Although primitive by today's standards, the drones were still capable of packing a significant punch. The twin-engine drones, manufactured by Interstate TDR, were made of steel tubing and plastic and were "nothing more than an oversized radio controlled model airplane with a wingspan of forty five feet and length of thirty."[134] The drones were equipped with a television camera in the nose, a gyro stabilizer and radar altimeter, and were guided by radio control to their target by an operator in an Avenger.

Special Task Air Group (STAG) 1 was formed after proving the viability of the concept. The aviation historian Bruce Gamble states that four strikes were flown against Rabaul in October 1944. "Flying from Nissan in the Green Islands, each strike consisted of four drones for a total of sixteen sorties against Rabaul. A great majority either missed due to radio interference or malfunction, or crashed en route…. The last strike, on October 27, resulted in one direct hit on a secondary target, and a couple of hits on buildings near their intended target. The following day the programme was officially terminated."[135] The USN concluded that "obviously in its present state of development the assault drone is far less accurate and effective than the more ordinary bombing methods."[136] It would not be until the late 20th century and early 21st century that the drone would evolve in a deadly weapon of modern war.

Future Operations for 3NZ Division: Withdrawal and Disbandment

Squarepeg had been uniformly successful and 3NZ Division had demonstrated to its American ally that it was very proficient in amphibious operations. Both 8 and 14 Brigades had successfully carried out one amphibious operation, and much had been learned from the experience. Barrowclough commented to his superior officer in Wellington, Lt. General Edward Puttick, "I have now got a very efficient planning and movement control staff which breaks the back of most of our loading problems."[137] The men of the Division had experienced combat and demonstrated their skills in fighting the Japanese. The Division had also demonstrated that it could work alongside American personnel of different services. Having reached this point of proficiency, the Division was clearly a useful asset for future operations in the Pacific.

The question was where the Division could be best employed. With the taking of the Green Islands, another link had been forged in the steel belt around the Japanese base at Rabaul, and its potency had been severely degraded by air and sea blockade. However, there was still work to do. Emirau seemed a possibility, but it was some distance from the Green Islands, and the ability to provide fighter cover for the invaders was problematic. Shipping shortages were also a major problem, and the planned invasion was postponed. Another possible target was the Japanese base at Kavieng in New Ireland. It had a sheltered anchorage and the potential for development of airfields. 3NZ Division was designated as the area reserve for the Kavieng operation and a target date set of 1 April 1944. The operation was to involve a USMC Division and was given the code name Forearm. Major General Barnett, U.S. Chief of Staff, commented, "Original plans for the Forearm and Merchantile operation and the consolidation of those positions envisaged the necessity of retaining the 3rd NZ Division in the combat area of that period."[138]

However, by this stage New Zealand's manpower problems were evident, and a reduction in the size of the Division seemed imminent. Because of the uncertainty of the future of 3NZ Division, its role was canceled. Understandably, the American planners had to have certainty because of the huge planning and logistical effort that was required.

In 1944 one of the problems that New Zealand faced was that it could not sustain two infantry divisions, and the hard choice had to be made whether 2NZ Division in Italy or 3NZ Division in the South Pacific would be disbanded or allowed to be run down. There were also pressures to

Ten. Aftermath and Consolidation 169

provide men for food production. Although the process took time, 3NZ Division was withdrawn from the Solomon Islands and disbanded. The men had anticipated further combat, possibly in New Ireland, and in early April 1944 were surprised to discover that since men were required in farming, butter and cheese production, freezing works, coal mining, sawmilling and food production, they would be returned to New Zealand. Quotas were set up and forms filled out giving details of marital status, work experience and an indication of willingness to work in particular sectors. For most it was a case of marking time and a rundown of infrastructure. Those soldiers who were not interested in the manpower scheme were categorized "Z," which rapidly became known as "Zombie," or the living dead.[139]

For most soldiers, however, the choice was obvious. As Corporal James observed, "We had little time to make up our minds—but very few needed long. The thought of returning to New Zealand after long months of monotonous existence was the turning point for many who were in doubt."[140]

The names of two hundred and eighty-seven men of the first draft of 37 Battalion to return to New Zealand were announced on 14 April, and the following day a staging camp was set up. There was, however, some uncertainty as to when precisely the soldiers would leave. On 20 April, tents were dismantled and sent on ahead, leaving the men with only their ground sheet shelter halves for protection. Predictably, the rain fell almost continuously. Bed cots were packed up on 27 April, leaving the soldiers with "only the wet ground for a couch." They did, however, have the consolation that they would soon be leaving. On 28 April the 287 men tramped to the beach in teeming rain, and as they left, Lieut. Col. Sugden commented that the mud and sludge would give them a taste of what was in store for many of them in the cow yard.[141]

The Green Islands had one final gift for the departing Kiwi troops of the MMG Company:

> [A] first class thunderstorm. A high wind came up of almost hurricane force and as a result trees came crashing down and many tents gave up the ghost and collapsed. Apart from some discomfort, no one suffered any injuries which was surprising. Another storm blew up on our last night on Nissan when all our tents had been packed away. The hardy ones who had slept in the open were soaked to the skin and driven to seek the dubious shelter of the mess hut, which had been left standing, only to become the prey of the numerous cookhouse rats which infested that area. Consequently, it was a bedraggled bunch who, on 29 May, clambered up the side of the USS *Naos* from the landing barges and thankfully looked their last at Nissan Island.[142]

The New Zealand signalers were among the last to leave. To their dismay they found that the prevalence of hookworm meant that they had to have blood tests before they could leave. By the end of May they began preparing to hand over all of the land and submarine circuits that had been installed with such effort to their successors. One feature which had been useless now acquired a value: the twenty-three-foot-deep hole that had been dug in a vain attempt to find water became a useful firepit to burn debris.[143]

A rear party was given a bare three hours to dismantle their station in darkness and pack it into a van for shipment on 6 July 1944.

There would have been few soldiers sad to leave the Green Islands.

The Australians

The New Zealanders handed the Green Islands over firstly to American control in the form of the African American troops of the U.S. 93rd Division, and then eventually 23 Australian Brigade took over garrison duty to the end of the war. By the latter part of 1944 the war had moved northwards and the Green Islands were a backwater. Much to the disgust of the Australian commanders, MacArthur directed on 2 August 1944 that Australians garrison Emirau, the Green Islands and New Georgia Islands with a minimum of an infantry brigade.[144] The Australians did not find the boredom of garrison duty any more satisfying than the New Zealanders. However, the adventurous could still find some excitement. In an escape from the monotony of guarding airfields, the men from the 27th Battalion on Green Island participated in seaborne raids from PT boats against the neighboring Japanese-occupied islands.[145] Their Australian commander, Brigadier Arnold Potts, a veteran of the Kokoda Campaign, Papua New Guinea, found being relegated to the backwater of what the Australian commanders referred to as "the Outer Islands" to be very hard to take. He pestered his superiors for an offensive role for his men, including an attack from Green Island against an estimated thirteen hundred Japanese in northern Bougainville. Fortunately, Pott's high-risk ideas were squelched, but the duty remained.[146]

As the Australian official history remarks, General Savige "restrained the enthusiasm of Brigadier Potts."[147] General Savige persuaded his superior General Sturdee that a smaller garrison was sufficient, but it was not until 20 March 1945 that MacArthur approved the reduction in garrison size. One company of the 8th Battalion remained on the Green Islands.

Ten. Aftermath and Consolidation

They did not, however, have long to suffer—in June, approval was given to their redeployment to Torokina, Bougainville.

With the redeployment of American units to take part in the Philippine campaign, the Australians took over on Bougainville. The war had moved northwards, and by June 1945, RNZAF operations on the Green Islands ceased. Fighter bomber operations ended in mid–May 1944 and support units were redeployed. Air operations against Rabaul and in support of the Australians on Bougainville continued up until the Japanese surrender.

Eleven

Significance and Legacy

Squarepeg required considerable effort and resources. The question has to be asked, "Was it worth it?" The answer must be "yes." Dividends were rapidly evident of a strategic nature.

The immediate effect of the allied seizure of the Green Islands was that the Japanese supply lines running from Rabaul and Kavieng to their garrisons in the northern Solomons were slashed. At one stroke, some 20,000 Japanese on Choiseul, Bougainville and the Buka Islands were cut off from supplies.[1]

For the Japanese on Bougainville, the loss of the Green Islands was catastrophic. The Japanese High Command had envisaged a strategy of holding a perimeter in the Pacific and then, when it was opportune in late 1944, launching a devastating counterattack. Troop strength had been built up on Bougainville and orders were issued for a renewed attack on the Allied enclave at Torokina. Ironically, the seizure of the Green Islands triggered a premature Japanese attack. The attack was prompted by the knowledge that rations for the soldiers were only expected to last until the end of March 1944. The decision was made to launch the attack so that the Japanese could fight to the best of their capabilities before starvation set in. The loss of the Green Islands meant that the supply situation on Bougainville could only worsen![2] The attack, launched on 8 March 1944, cost the Japanese some five thousand, four hundred dead and seven thousand, one hundred wounded.[3] Thereafter, the Japanese on Bougainville faced starvation, exhaustion and disease. Likewise, the Japanese garrison on Rabaul and the islands that the Allies had bypassed.

The seizure of the Green Islands, along with operations against Los Negros, signaled the end of the Solomons campaign, for all practical purposes. Allied air forces, particularly the Royal New Zealand Air Force, would relentlessly pound Rabaul. As *The Pacific* notes, "The great arsenal of Rabaul, which had been pounded for months with increasing violence as each move brought it within easier range of aircraft, was now encircled and impotent. Any remaining Japanese forces scattered through the jungles of the Solomons and New Guinea were completely isolated and left to 'wither on the vine.'"[4] The Japanese troops there were, in Stephen Taafe's evocative description, "to spend the rest of the war scratching at the top of an American-designed and built coffin."[5]

Of all of the operations undertaken by 3NZ Division, Squarepeg was the largest. The force consisted of 14 Brigade together with divisional troops and Barrowclough's headquarters. Despite its magnitude, the operation remains virtually unknown to the general public. There are a number of reasons for this—wartime conditions meant that operational security needed to be maintained and the Japanese kept guessing as to the Allied order of battle; journalists and photographers had limited access to the combat zone and restrictions were placed on their work; the light casualties meant that it was not likely to have much of an impact on the New Zealand nation; and the invasion was overtaken by the more dramatic events such as the Central Pacific drive and the end game in Europe.

Despite its lack of recognition, the invasion was successful, and the Green Islands were developed as air and naval bases. Squarepeg, with the exception of the Australian campaign on Bougainville 1944–5, marked the end of the Solomon Islands campaign. The isolation and neutralization of Rabaul enabled MacArthur's soldiers to move up the coast of New Guinea and provided a solid foundation for the American invasion of the Philippines.

Arguably, Squarepeg can be seen as a high point in joint operations between the various services. It is also noteworthy as being an exemplar of cooperation between the Allied nations. Both Barrowclough and Wilkinson were deserving of more recognition for their achievements. Instead, Squarepeg has faded into obscurity. Within the New Zealand Army there is little remembrance of Squarepeg. The more glamorous exploits of 2NZ Division in the Desert War and the Italian campaign have tended to completely overshadow its sister division, 3NZ Division in the Pacific.

The New Zealanders provided the soldiers for Squarepeg, but the Americans provided the ships and logistic support. It was necessary for the New Zealanders to work alongside the Americans and they were successful in doing so. This was a significant step in the American–New Zealand relationship. It is arguable that the operations of 3NZ Division paved the way for a beneficial U.S.–NZ relationship in a postwar world in an American-dominated Pacific.

For New Zealanders, one outcome of their involvement in the Solomon Islands Campaign was a greater awareness of the Solomon Islands and their strategic significance to New Zealand. In 2003 the Solomon Islands descended into the condition of a "failed state," and New Zealand peacekeepers, both soldiers and civilians, were deployed through the multinational organization Regional Assistance Mission Solomon Islands (RAMSI). By 2013 the situation had been stabilized to the point where soldiers were withdrawn. Most of the soldiers would have been unaware that they were treading in the footsteps of their forebears, the soldiers of 3NZ Division.

For the Americans who garrisoned the Green Islands, their tenure was one of boredom interspersed with tension from Japanese air raids. Their contribution to the war in the Pacific has been overshadowed by the ghastly battles of Iwo Jima, Okinawa and the Philippines. Likewise for the Australian garrison which succeeded them.

For the Japanese who fought on the Green Islands, they fought valiantly, but their sacrifices were in vain and simply a small part of a lost war, the Great Pacific War.

For the families of those killed, the trauma and grieving would have repercussions that spanned generations. For those wounded or who had their health broken, the consequences were similar.

The islanders had suffered severe disruption from the Pacific War. They had found their peaceful home devastated by war and the intrusion of Allied personnel, however welcome that may have been. Most had been removed from the Green Islands and were only able to return once the Pacific War had receded. The skeletons of infrastructure and debris of war still remain. The Green Islands have once more receded into obscurity.

Chronology

Prewar
Marist missionaries establish a mission, dispensary and school on the Green Islands. Three copra plantations are established, one at Barahun and two on Nissan.

1941
7–8 December—Japanese forces strike at the U.S. Pacific Fleet at Pearl Harbor and invade Malaya. The Great Pacific War begins.

1942
23 January—Japanese forces seize the Green Islands.

1943
13 July 1943—Naval Battle of Kolombangara.
18 September–9 October—14 Brigade, 3NZ Division clears Vella Lavella, New Georgia Group, Solomon Islands of Japanese troops.
27 October—8 Brigade 3NZ Division seizes the Treasury Islands, Solomon Islands. (Operation Goodtime)
20 December—Conference between Halsey and MacArthur at which MacArthur suggests Halsey invade the Green Islands.
31 December—The plan to invade the Green Islands is given the codename Operation Squarepeg.

1944
10/11 January—Four PT boats from Torokina carry out a survey and ascertain that the South Channel was able to take Landing Craft, Tank.
24 January—Admiral Halsey directs the seizure of the Green Islands and designates 3NZ Division to undertake the task.
30 January—Commando Raid force departs from Vella Lavella. Arrives at the Green Islands at midnight.

1 February—Returning Commando Raid personnel disembark at Juno Beach, Guadalcanal.
2 February—77 Japanese reinforcements arrive from Rabaul.
4 February—Operations order issued to 3NZ Division for Squarepeg.
5 February—Operations order issued for Task Force 31. The original Japanese defenders return and 102 move into a cave on Pokonian and then to the mission.
10 February—Briefing held for commanders, medical officers and firefighters of LSTs of the first echelon.
12 February—Briefing held for the commanders and medical officers of the LSTs in the second echelon.
13 February—Most of the amphibious craft involved in Squarepeg arrive at Vella Lavella and loading begins.
14 February—APDs arrive and commence loading troops. At 1855 Vals attack and damage USS St. Louis.
15 February—Operation Squarepeg—Transports arrive at the lagoon entrance at 0620. Troops of 14 Brigade land on Nissan at 0655. At 0645, 15 Vals attack the LCI and LSTs off the channel entrance. LSTs beach at 0835. LCTs arrive at 1335. Last of the shipping departs at 1730.
15 February–6 March—Arrival of 33rd NCB.
15, 19, 24 February—37th NCB arrives.
19 February—Construction begins on airstrips.
15–25 February—93rd NCB arrives in four echelons.
20 February—The second echelon arrives, bringing 4,715 soldiers and 6,315 tons of equipment. 30 Battalion encounters dug-in Japanese forces at Tanaheran Village. Valentine Tanks assist with the elimination of the Japanese.
23 February—Japanese defenders on Pinipel and Sau Islands are eliminated.
25 February—Third echelon arrives. 11 LSTs, 3 LCIs bring 2,577 troops.
26 February—22 field ambulance personnel capture a Japanese soldier.
29 February—General Douglas MacArthur's troops land on Los Negros and Manus, of the Admiralty Group, establishing another link in the Allied chain encircling Rabaul.
1 March—29 PT boats from the Green Islands, together with destroyers, mount sorties into Rabaul Harbor. Fourth echelon arrives.
4 March—Halsey orders that the Green Islands constitutes an independent island command under Major General Barrowclough. Command of the Green Islands passes to Barrowclough from Wilkinson.

Chronology

5 March—A damaged U.S. plane makes an emergency landing on Nissan from Bougainville, together with 20 U.S. planes.

6 March—Lt. Cmdr White, 22 Naval Construction Regiment directs all construction equipment be used to build a bomber airfield by 1 April 1944.

6 March—Thirty-six planes, including sixteen RNZAF planes, land on the airfield at Nissan in the morning, followed by a further 15 in the afternoon. Fifth echelon arrives. 9th Special NCB, Company C, Gang 24 Stevedores arrive with headquarters personnel.

7 March—The first airstrike on Kavieng to stage through the Green Islands comes in from Piva, Bougainville.

13 March—Squadron VMF-223 "Bulldogs" send 20 fighters to the Green Islands.

14 March—VMF-223 assigned to Marine Air Group 14, 1st Marine Air Wing.

15 March—VMF-223 ground crews arrive to service VMF-114.

16 March—Seventh echelon arrives at the Green Islands.

20 March—USMC seizes Emirau, completing the encirclement of Rabaul.

29 March—A damaged B-24 Liberator is the first plane to land on the new bomber strip, but crashes on landing and all the crew die.

17 March—17,000 troops on the Green Islands.

22 March—Arrival of PATSU with Richard M. Nixon.

3 April—Departure of 15th NCB echelon.

7 April—VMSB Dive Bombing Squadron 341 (SBDs) arrives.

11 April—USS Cassiopeia arrives with supplies.

24 April—USS Wharton evacuates the first group of New Zealand troops to New Caledonia.

29 April—U.S. aircraft (VMF-215) from the Green Islands strafe PT boats 346, 347 and 350 killing 25 and wounding 24.

7 May—"Bulldog" Squadron aircrew return to relieve VMF-114; VMF-114 departs.

28 May—USS Naos leaves for New Caledonia with NZ troops.

30 May—USS Mintaka leaves for New Caledonia with NZ troops.

Midnight 29–30 May—Command of forces on the Green Islands passes to American control.

May/June—Arrival of VMB-423 ground echelon.

June–Spring—VMB-423 (PBJ/B-25) Squadron.

June—VMB-413.

June—MAG 24/14 leaves and 423 ground echelon moves.

June—U.S. Army Coast Artillery station on Barahun.

June—[Seabee Maintenance Unit] CBMU-552 arrives from Ellice Islands.
10 June—Five Seabees of 93rd NCB die in an accidental dynamite explosion.
Early summer—U.S. Army takes over from 3NZ Division.
15 June—The Main Body of HQ, 3NZ Division's staff sail from the Green Islands for New Caledonia on USS Rotanin.
16 June—USS Coos Bay departs.
21 June—Arrival of VMB-423 air echelon.
24 June—VMF-433/VMB-223 ground crew depart.
1 July—VMSB-341 returns.
3 July—CBMU-553 arrives.
16 July—arrival of VMB-433.
By July 1944, all authorized construction on the Green Islands was complete, and CBMUs 552 and 553 reported to take charge of general maintenance and miscellaneous construction. Late in 1944, the maintenance units began dismantling structures for removal. By January 1945, the majority of the naval facilities had been rolled up and were awaiting shipment to forward areas.
July/August—Departure of 33rd NCB.
1–2 August—Bob Hope does 6 shows on the Green Islands at various camps.
14 August—VMB Air leaves for Espiritu Santo.
15 August—VMSB leaves for U.S.
15 August—Jack Benny show on the Green Islands.
20 August—1944 Departure of VMB-433.
44 August—PT RON 28 is on Green.
4 October—1944 Departure of 37th NCB.
20 October—The official order to disband the 3NZ Division was given by Major General Barrowclough.
25 October—Departure of 93rd NCB.
20 October—No. 1 Bomber Reconnaissance Squadron (Venturas) RNZAF arrives.
20 October—23 Brigade, Royal Australian Army under Brigadier Arnold Potts takes over garrison duties from U.S. 93rd Division on the "Outer Islands," including the Green Islands.
Between 26 October to May 1945 No. 14, 15, 16, 17, 18 and 20 Fighter Squadrons, RNZAF are rotated through the Green Islands.

1945
17 January—No. 2 Bomber Reconnaissance Squadron (Venturas) RNZAF arrives.

14 January—No. 1 Bomber Reconnaissance Squadron RNZAF leaves.
17 March—No. 2 Bomber Reconnaissance Squadron (Venturas) RNZAF leaves.
20 March—CBMU 552 arrives at Hollandia from Green.
15 April—VPB departs.
June 1945—All RNZAF operations on the Green Islands ends.
12 June—VMB 423 leaves for Emirau.
15 June—VPB 53 departs for Samar.
1 August—CBMU 553 departs for Leyte/Samar.
10 August—The Green Islanders return to the Green Islands.
15 August—Japan surrenders.

Glossary

AA—Antiaircraft, also "Ack Ack."
AA & QMG—Assistant Adjutant and Quartermaster General, i.e., senior administrative military officer (also "A & Q" NZ).
AAA—Antiaircraft artillery.
Acorn—United States Navy code name for a CB unit tasked with constructing, operating and maintaining advanced plane and sea-plane bases.
ADC—Aide de Camp. A military assistant to an officer of high rank.
Adjt—Adjutant.
Adm—Admiral.
ADMS—Assistant Director Medical Services (NZ).
ADS—Advanced Dressing Station (i.e., a medical facility located further back from Regimental Aid Posts).
AK—United States Navy acronym—cargo ship.
AKA—United States Navy acronym—auxiliary cargo transport, attack.
Aldis Lamp—An Allied signal lamp utilizing high-intensity light to flash messages in Morse code to a recipient.
Amb—Ambulance.
AMCU—Anti-malarial control unit.
Amphibious Operation—An attack launched from the sea by air, naval and landing forces with the aim of landing on a hostile shore.
ANGAU—Australian New Guinea Administrative Unit.
ANZAC—Acronym for "Australia and New Zealand Army Corps" from World War I, but also used in reference in World War II to refer to the Australia–New Zealand defense area. During World War II Australia and New Zealand, despite being part of the British Empire, did not have a unified command organization.
AP—Armor-piercing ammunition; also ammunition point, a place where ammunition is collected for operations; also U.S. Navy acronym for a transport ship.

Glossary

APA—United States Navy acronym—auxiliary ship cargo attack. Large U.S. transports used to transport troops, including troops of 3NZ Division.

APc—USN acronym—coastal transport ship.

APD—United States Navy acronym for Auxiliary Personnel Destroyer. A "four stacker" obsolete American destroyer modified by the removal of funnels to provide accommodation area for troops. Originally designed to provide fast transport for USMC raiding parties in line with the raiding philosophy developed by the USMC in the interwar years. APDs were used in World War II for the transport of elements of NZ 8 Brigade and NZ 14 Brigade to Japanese-held areas in the Solomons.

AR—All ranks, i.e., officers and enlisted personnel.

Arcadia—Allied code name for a conference held in Washington, D.C. 22 Dec. 1941–14 Jan. 1942. The meeting between Winston Churchill and Franklin D. Roosevelt confirmed the "Germany First" policy. At this stage of the war, the British tended to dominate their American counterparts.

Archives NZ—Archives New Zealand, Wellington, New Zealand.

Argus—U.S. codeword for radar units involved in fighter control, e.g., Argus Unit Seven deployed on Green Island in 1944. This involved New Zealand radar sets and operators as well as specialist U.S. personnel. The USN purpose for Argus units was "to provide during the development stage of a United States naval base a comprehensive air warning, surface warning and fighter direction organisation which will co-ordinate all radar operations under the area commander." Typically, an Argus Unit was made up of 20 officers and 178 men.

Arisaka—Japanese bolt-action rifle.

ASC- Army Service Corps (NZ).

A/T—Antitank.

Atk By—Antitank battery.

Avenger TBF—U.S. single-engined aircraft made by Grumman and used primarily for torpedo and bombing operations. Used by USN and RNZAF.

Avgas—Aviation fuel.

B-24 Liberator—USAAF strategic heavy bomber produced by Consolidated. One of the most successful American bombers of World War II because of its long range and good payload.

B-25 Mitchell—USAAF twin-engine medium bomber produced by North American—used extensively for bombing. A variant was used for strafing to good effect against naval vessels.

Bandit—Enemy aircraft.

BAR—Browning Automatic Rifle (U.S. machine gun).

Barrage Balloons—Balloons with special steel cables designed to ensnare any unwary aircraft that flew into them. Their main purpose was to deter the enemy planes from bombing targets.

Barrowclough's Charter—The instructions given by the NZ government to Major General H.E. Barrowclough for the committal of New Zealand forces to combat. Barrowclough had the power to decline to commit New Zealand forces to high-risk military operations. A certificate was required from Barrowclough to the New Zealand government confirming that the risks were reasonable before 3NZ Division was to be committed to combat.

Bde—Brigade. A unit of roughly 7,000–8,000 troops of various types, usually made up of three infantry battalions or three tank battalions.

Beachhead—A designated area on a hostile shore that is the objective of an amphibious operation. When seized, it allows the attacker to land troops and equipment with the aim of further operations inland.

Beachmaster—An officer (generally naval) tasked with controlling the beaching of landing craft and amphibious vehicles on a beach.

Beach Red—A particular area of the beachhead. It was common for the beach areas to be given a color designation for planning purposes, e.g., Beach Red, Beach Green, Beach Yellow, etc.

Besa—British-made machine gun of Czechoslovak origin used extensively by Commonwealth forces as a mounted machine gun on tanks. Capable of firing 500–800 7.9mm caliber rounds per minute.

Betty—Allied code name for Mitsubishi G4M medium bomber.

BG—Bombardment Group (USAAF).

BGS—Brigadier, General Staff (chief staff officer at corps or army level).

Binary Division—2-brigade division, cf. the usual three brigades.

Black Cats—A specialized American Catalina Flying Boat squadron used for night operations.

BLO—Bombardment Liaison Officer.

Bloke—Male person (NZ).

Blower—Radio telephone (NZ).

Blue—Color used in U.S. planning to designate U.S. forces.

Blue Beach—Pokonian Plantation.

Bn/Btn/Batt—Battalion—a unit of roughly 700–900 troops, predominantly infantry, commanded by a lieutenant colonel. Contains three to four rifle companies and a company of supporting weapons, or three squadrons of tanks plus HQ (NZ).

Glossary

Boat Pool—Boats used for assault landing from mother ships.
Bofors—A 40mm single-barreled light AA gun of Swedish design.
Bogey—Unidentified aircraft.
BRA—Brigadier Royal Artillery (NZ).
Bren gun—A light machine gun used by Commonwealth forces.
Bren gun carrier—A light, open-topped, tracked vehicle designed to carry a Bren gun but also used for reconnaissance and general transport and haulage work. (See Universal Carrier.)
Brigade—A formation usually consisting of three battalions plus command and supporting elements (NZ).
Brigade group—A flexible formation. Generally these were brigades supplemented by additional support elements (NZ).
B.S.I.—British Solomon Islands.
Bty—Battery, a tactical and administrative unit of artillery roughly corresponding to a company in other branches of the army.
Butai—Japanese unit or detachment.
CA—Heavy cruiser; also Coastal Artillery.
Cactus—Allied code name for Guadalcanal.
Call sign—Code identification of a sender or receiver of a W/T or R/T message.
The Canal—Guadalcanal.
CAP—Combat Air Patrol; a protective aerial umbrella usually provided over a specified area by fighter aircraft.
Capt.—Captain.
Cargo cult—A group of socio-religious movements that began in Melanesia in the 19th century with the basic idea that industrialized goods were created by the spirits of Melanesian people and Europeans had diverted them away from Melanesia. Participants sought to redirect these goods back to themselves.
Carrier—Bren gun carrier.
Carrier Platoon—Platoon normally equipped with universal or Bren gun carriers. On the Treasury Islands, the carrier platoons quite often acted as infantry.
Cartwheel—The Allied code name for the two-pronged drive up the coast of New Guinea (by MacArthur's forces) and the Solomon Islands (by Nimitz's forces) designed to isolate and neutralize the main Japanese base in the South Pacific at Rabaul. Operations began on 31 June 1943, and were completed by 1 March 1944, leaving the 98,000-man garrison bypassed and ineffective.
CASU—Carrier Air Service Unit.

Glossary

Casualty clearing station—First aid post.

Catalina—PBY5A U.S. twin-engined flying boat manufactured by Consolidated. Extensively used by U.S. in patrol, air-sea rescue and anti-submarine work. Also referred to affectionately as "Dumbo" after Walt Disney's flying elephant.

CB—Construction Battalion. Also "Seabee," a USN term for naval construction units which performed prodigious feats of engineering, particularly airfield and base construction. These units were integrated into 3NZ Division operations. Alternatively, confined to barracks.

CBMU—Construction Battalion Maintenance Unit.

CCS—Anglo-American Combined Chiefs of Staff; also Casualty Clearing Station, a medical unit sited between a medical dressing station and a field hospital.

Cdr—Commander.

CE—Chief engineer.

CG—Commanding general.

CGS—Chief of the General Staff.

CinC—Commander in Chief.

CINCPAC—U.S. Commander in Chief U.S. Pacific Fleet (Admiral Nimitz).

CL—Light cruiser.

CNO—Chief of Naval Operations.

Coast watcher—Allied personnel deployed on various Pacific islands with the purpose of covertly observing and reporting on Japanese aerial and naval movement. The Japanese also deployed coast watchers.

"Coconut bombers"—A term used to describe New Zealand soldiers who served in the South Pacific. The term is probably derived from the shortage of weaponry in the early stages of World War II. Instead of grenades, all the soldiers could do in training was to lob wooden imitations. Some soldiers viewed the term self-deprecatingly, whilst others regarded it as a form of abuse. The term "pineapple pickers" was also used by members of the New Zealand public.

COMAIRNORSOLS—Commander Aircraft Northern Solomons (Nov. 43–Jan. 44).

COMAIRSOLS—Commander Aircraft Solomons (TF33). Established on Guadalcanal on 15 February 1943 to control all USMC, USN, USAAF, RNZAF and RAAF units based in the Solomons. The main combat command for ComAirSoPac controlling air activities in the Solomons in New Britain areas.

COMAIRSOPAC—Commander Aircraft South Pacific, commander of all

Glossary

land-based aircraft in the South Pacific command area. Responsible to Admiral Halsey and SOPAC.

COMAMPHIBFORSOPAC—Commander, Amphibious Force, South Pacific Force.

Combat loading—The loading of transport and cargo ships in such a way that items needed for combat could be easily accessed and unloaded first. Not as efficient as "commercial loading," but essential for the success of an amphibious operation.

COMGENFMAC—Commanding General First Marine Amphibious Corps.

COMGENSOPAC—Commanding General South Pacific.

COMLCIFLOT5—Commander, Landing Craft Infantry, Flotilla Five.

COMINCH—Commander in Chief (U.S. Admiral Ernest King).

Commando—British special operations forces which specialized in raiding German-occupied Europe. Because of their elite nature, commando units attracted a certain amount of glamor.

COMSOPAC—Commander South Pacific Area, initially Admiral R.L. Ghormley, then Admiral W. Halsey and finally Admiral Carney.

Condition Black—Invasion imminent.

Condition Green—All clear.

Condition Red—Air raid warning status, air raid imminent. Usually warning was given by three blasts on a siren.

Condition Yellow—Air raid probable.

Copra—The dried kernel of the coconut.

Corps—Military unit composed of two or more divisions.

COS—Chiefs of Staff. Term used to describe either British or NZ heads of service of the Army, Air Force and Navy.

C.O.—Commanding officer.

Coy/Co—Company—Three platoons of infantry.

C.P.—Command post.

Cpl.—Corporal.

CRA—Commander Royal Artillery (NZ) (of Division).

CRE—Commander Royal Engineers (NZ) (of Division).

CREME—Commander Royal Electrical & Mechanical Engineers.

CTF—Commander, Task Force.

CTG—Commander, Task Group.

CTF31—Combined Task Force 31. A USN naval force active in the Solomon Islands commanded by Admiral Theodore Wilkinson. This force provided transport and naval gunfire support to 3 NZ Division.

DADME—Deputy Assistant Director Mechanical Engineers.

DADOS—Deputy Assistant Director Ordnance Services.

Glossary

Daihatsu—Japanese barges used primarily for supply. The smaller variety were forty-eight feet long and eleven feet wide with diesel engines providing a speed of about eight knots. They were capable of carrying twelve tons of cargo. A larger type was sixty feet long and twelve feet wide and capable of a speed of ten knots. These could carry sixteen tons of cargo. Often they were heavily armed.

DCGS—Deputy Chief of General Staff (NZ).

DCM—Distinguished Conduct Medal (NZ).

DD—USN acronym for destroyer.

D-Day—Designated day on which an operation is to commence. When a plus symbol is used it signifies days after D-Day, and when a minus symbol is used it signifies days before D-Day; e.g., D+5 refers to 5 days after the invasion, D–5 refers to 5 days prior to invasion

DDMS—Deputy Director Medical Services.

DE—USN acronym for destroyer escort.

DEME—Director of Electrical & Mechanical Engineering.

Div—Division—a unit of 12000 to 14000 soldiers.

Div A & QMG—Divisional Adjutant and Quarter Master General.

Div Arty—Divisional artillery.

Div G—Divisional General Staff Branch.

Div HQ—Divisional headquarters.

Div Tps—Divisional Troops.

Div Workshops—Ordnance unit responsible for the maintenance of weapons and equipment.

DOD—Died of disease. Alternatively, Department of Defense.

Dog Day—D-Day or invasion day. "Dog" refers to "D" in the U.S. phonetic alphabet, e.g., "Plan Dog."

DSO—Distinguished Service Order; British medal.

Ech—Echelon: a movement of troops in a group. Implies a portion of a unit separated from a parent unit. See also "Flight."

Engr—Engineer.

Exec—Executive officer (USN).

F4U—Corsair, American gull-winged fighter aircraft.

FD—Fighter director.

Fd—Field.

Fd Arty—Field artillery.

Fd Am—Field ambulance.

Fd Coy—Field company of engineers.

Fd Hyg Sc—Field hygiene section.

FDO—Fighter director officer.

Fd Regt—Field regiment of artillery.
Fifth Air Force—The USAAF air unit operating in the southwest Pacific. In June 1944, it combined with the 13th USAAF to become the Far Eastern Air Force.
Flight—An army expression meaning a movement of troops from one area to another, usually by sea.
FM—Fleet Marine Force, Pacific. Also, field manual (U.S.).
FMAC—First Marine Amphibious Corps; also "IMAC."
FMC—Field Maintenance Centre (NZ).
FO—Forward observer, an artillery spotter usually deployed close to the front to observe the fall of artillery shells and report suitable targets for artillery.
Forearm—Allied code name for the invasion of Kavieng.
Foxhole—A hole dug in the ground to provide cover for usually one or two soldiers.
FS—Field security (military police).
G Branch—Staff of division involved with operational matters.
Gen.—General.
General quarters—The quarters or positions manned at action (naval term).
GHQ—General Headquarters.
Gnr—Gunner.
GOC—General Officer Commanding.
Goodtime—Allied code name for the invasion of the Treasury Islands, 27 October 1943–6 November 1943. A diversionary operation involving the invasion of the Treasury Islands by 8 Bde, 3 NZ Division.
GQ—General quarters.
Green Beach—South end Tangalan Plantation.
GS01—General Staff Officer, grade one.
H-Hour—Designated time for commencement of an operation.
HE—High explosive.
Higgins Boat—Landing craft for infantry and light vehicles (LCVP).
HMG—Heavy machine gun.
HMNZS—His Majesty's New Zealand Ship.
HMS—His Majesty's Ship.
HQ—Headquarters.
Hrs—Hours.
Hudson/Ventura—U.S. twin-engined plane made by Lockheed. Frequently used for patrol reconnaissance and anti-submarine work. Used by the U.S. and RNZAF. The Ventura was a development model of the Hudson.

"I" Section—Intelligence Section.
I/C—In command.
IFF or IF—Identification, friend or foe; an electronic device carried on planes emitting a signal identifying the plane as a friendly aircraft.
IGHQ—Imperial General Headquarters (Japanese).
IJA—Imperial Japanese Army (Kogun).
IJAAF—Imperial Japanese Army Air Force.
IJN—Imperial Japanese Navy (Tikoku Kaigun).
IJNAF—Imperial Japanese Naval Air Force (Koku Butai).
Ind Bty—Independent battery.
Inf—Infantry.
Island hopping—An Allied strategy of bypassing strongly fortified Japanese islands and invading where the Japanese were weaker, cutting off lines of supply
JCS—Joint Chiefs of Staff. A committee consisting of U.S. Service Heads, Admiral Ernest King, General George C. Marshall and General Hap Arnold tasked with the coordination of U.S. military strategy.
Juki—Japanese medium machine gun.
Kaigun—Imperial Japanese Navy.
KDOR—Khaki Drill Other Ranks, khaki-colored uniform worn by New Zealand soldiers.
KIA—Killed in action.
Kido Buitai—(Japanese) carrier striking force.
Km—Kilometer.
Kogun—Imperial Japanese Army.
Koku Butai—Imperial Japanese Naval Air Force.
Kokutai—Japanese land-based naval air group.
LAA—Light antiaircraft.
LAD—Light Aid Detachment (NZ). An engineering unit attached to a battalion to assist in repair and maintenance of vehicles and equipment.
LCA—Landing craft, assault.
LCC—Landing craft, control.
LCG (M)—Landing craft, gun (medium).
LCI—Landing craft, infantry. A large landing craft capable of holding 200 men. Of shallow draft, but with seagoing ability. The workhorse of the Pacific War.
LCI (G)—Special landing craft, infantry that had been modified to carry fire support weaponry and whose role it was to suppress Japanese defenses as the vulnerable landing craft approached shore.

Glossary

LCM—Landing craft, mechanized.
LCP—Landing craft, personnel.
LCP (R)—Landing craft personnel, ramp.
LCS—Landing craft, support.
LCT—Landing craft, tank.
LCVP—Landing craft, vehicle personnel, also known as "Higgins boat."
Lewis gun—A light machine gun used by Allied forces.
Liberty ship—Name given to mass-produced, prefabricated merchant vessels built in American shipyards.
LMG—Light machine gun.
LO—Liaison officer.
LSF—Landing ship, fighter direction.
LSI—Landing ship, infantry.
LSM—Landing ship, medium.
LST—Landing ship, tank. A large seagoing landing craft capable of carrying tanks and large numbers of men and supplies. An essential part of amphibious operations in the Pacific.
LtA/A—Light antiaircraft.
Lt. or Lieut.—Lieutenant.
Lt Col—Lieutenant colonel.
Lt Gen—Lieutenant general.
Maj.—Major
Maj. Gen.—Major general.
Marston matting—Prefabricated perforated aluminium plates used by U.S. forces to create airstrips. Named after the North Carolina town where they were first made.
MC—Military Cross.
MDS—Medical dressing station.
MG—Machine gun.
MIA—Missing in action.
mm—Millimeter.
MM—Military Medal (British).
MMG—Medium machine gun.
MO—Medical officer.
MP—Military police.
MT—Motor transport.
MTB—Motor torpedo boat.
NABU—Naval Advance Base Unite (USN). Personnel trair ized to land with the assaulting force and begin functi(base.

Nambu—Japanese 7.7mm light machine gun.

NAS—Naval air station (U.S.).

NatPat—National Patriotic Fund. A New Zealand organization which administered the delivery of personal items such as stationery and creature comforts to New Zealand soldiers. Usually the representatives of the NatPat were YMCA secretaries.

NATS—Naval Air Transport South Pacific. Air transport system operated by U.S. Navy, considered safer than SCATS. Operated by USN in rear areas and flew administrative passenger missions.

NCB—Naval Construction Battalion, i.e., Seabees.

NCO—Noncommissioned officer.

No. 1 Islands Group—The main administrative and command organization of the RNZAF in the South Pacific.

NOAA—National Oceanic and Atmospheric Administration.

NZASC—New Zealand Army Service Corps. Army unit used for supply and support

NZE—New Zealand Engineers.

NZEF—New Zealand Expeditionary Force.

NZEF(IP)—New Zealand Expeditionary Force in the Pacific, i.e., 3NZ Division.

OC—Officer Commanding.

OGPU—The Russian Joint State Political Directorate, or more simply the Russian secret police, from 1922 to 1934.

One day's supply—The quantity of supplies used in estimating the daily expenditure by a unit.

One Mac—1 MAC—First Marine Amphibious Corps.

OP—Observation post or "O Pip."

Operation Kiwi—NZ Code name for deployment of 3NZ Division to New Caledonia and the Solomon Islands.

Operations Order 2-44—USN Operation Order for the invasion of the Green Islands.

Orange—Color used in U.S. planning to designate Japanese forces.

Orders Group Conference, also "O" Group—NZ Army expression; military planning meeting between commanding officers at which orders are given and received.

ORs—Other ranks (i.e., not officers).

PATSU—Patrol service unit.

PBY5A—Catalina, a twin-engine USN Flying Boat.

Pidgin—A simplified language used by two groups that do not have a common language. Pidgin incorporates simple grammar and is con-

structed in an impromptu way by individuals, often primarily as a language of trade. It is not a native language.
POL—Petrol, oil and lubricants.
POW—Prisoner of war; also PW.
Prov—Provisional. A unit formed from assets taken from other units on a temporary basis.
PT boat—Patrol torpedo boat (USN), i.e., motor torpedo boat.
PTO—Pacific Theater of Operations.
Q—Quartermaster.
Quad—Four-wheel-drive truck used for towing British field guns.
RA—Royal Artillery.
RAMC—Royal Army Medical Corps.
RAMSI—Regional Assistance Mission to the Solomon Islands.
RAP—Regimental aid post.
RCT—Regimental combat team.
Recce—Reconnaissance, also "recn."
Red Beach—North end Tangalan Plantation.
Regt—Regiment.
Res—Reserve.
Ret or Retd—Retired.
Rikusentai—Japanese Naval Infantry; see SNLF.
RNZA—Royal New Zealand Artillery.
RNZAF—Royal New Zealand Air Force.
RNZASC—Royal New Zealand Army Service Corps. The organization responsible for the supply of stores to the New Zealand Army and transport services. Stores could range from rations to gasoline and ammunition. Under the Director of Ordnance Stores (DOS). There are Deputy Directors of Ordnance Stores (DDOS), Assistant Directors of Ordnance Stores (ADOS) and at divisional level the Deputy Assistant Director of Ordnance Stores (DADOS).
RNZN—Royal New Zealand Navy.
Ron—Abbreviation of "squadron."
rpm—rounds per minute (i.e., rate of fire of weapons).
RSM—Regimental sergeant major.
RT—Radio telephony; wireless transmission.
SBD—USN single-engine dive bomber; Dauntless.
SCAT—South Pacific Combat Air Transport Command.
Sec—Section. In aviation terms, a unit of 2 to 4 planes; in artillery terms, 2 or 3 guns; in infantry terms, a third of an Infantry Platoon.
Sgt.—Sergeant.

Shackle Code—An alphanumeric message system used with the voice messages over talk between ships. Since voice transmissions could be picked up by the Japanese, it was vital that such things as ships' course changes be encoded.

Sigs or Sigg—Signals, i.e., communications personnel, radio operators, etc.

SMLE—Short magazine Lee Enfield rifle, the standard rifle of Commonwealth forces in World War II.

SNLF—Special Naval Landing Force (Japanese).

SOPAC—South Pacific Area Command. A U.S. area of command that encompassed the Solomon Islands. From October 1942 to late 1944, Admiral Halsey commanded this area. He was, in turn, responsible to the Commander, Pacific Fleet, Admiral Nimitz.

Squarepeg—The Allied code name for the invasion of Green Island, February 1944.

Sqdn—Squadron, in aviation terms, a unit of 18 to 36 planes, or armored vehicles or recce troops.

STAG—Special Task Air Group. An experimental aviation unit that utilized drone strike equipment.

Stonk—Concentrated artillery barrage.

Svy Tp—Survey troop.

SWPA—South West Pacific Area: A U.S. area of command encompassing New Guinea. Commanded by General Douglas MacArthur.

TBF—Grumman Avenger. A single-engine American aircraft used as a torpedo bomber, and for anti-submarine and patrol work.

TBY—U.S. Navy transmitter-receiver.

Territorial—A military unit made up of part-time voluntary soldiers (Commonwealth).

TF—Task force, generally a grouping of naval craft with supporting air and other units for the fulfillment of a particular purpose.

Thirteenth Air Force (13th USAAF)—The USAAF unit that operated in conjunction with the 5th USAAF in the Solomon Islands.

Tin can—Destroyer.

T.O.E—Table of organization and equipment.

Tokyo Ann—A female Japanese propaganda broadcaster. The most famous broadcaster was "Tokyo Rose."

Tokyo Express—Japanese supply operations using warships of the Imperial Japanese Navy.

Tps—Troops; part of a squadron of tanks; part of a battery.

Ultra—Intelligence gained from the interception and decoding of Axis radio communications.

Universal carrier—A tracked vehicle used by British and Commonwealth forces. Also known as a "Bren gun carrier" due to the ability to mount a Bren machine gun in the forward seat next to the driver. Because they were open-topped, they afforded the crew very limited protection. Used mainly for the haulage of ordnance and supplies.

USAAF—United States Army Air Force.

USC & GS—United States Coast and Geodetic Survey.

USMC—United States Marine Corps.

USN—United States Navy.

USNR—United States Naval Reserve.

USS—United States Ship.

VAdm—Vice admiral.

Val—Allied code name for the Japanese Aichi D3A dive bomber.

Valentine—British light tank.

VD-1—U.S. Navy Photoreconnaissance Squadron.

Vickers machine gun—Medium machine gun used by Commonwealth forces.

VJ Day—Victory over Japan Day (2 September 1945).

VLR—Very long range (in reference to aircraft).

VMF—U.S. acronym. "V" signifies fixed-wing aircraft, "M" signifies U.S. Marine Corps, and "F" signifies a fighter unit.

VPB—U.S. acronym for fixed-wing patrol bomber.

Walky-talky or walkie-talkie—Hand-held communication device.

War Plan Orange—U.S. operational plan for the defeat of Japan prepared by the U.S. War Plans Division. It envisaged holding part of the Philippines and advanced bases in the Pacific while a U.S. Naval Force fought its way to the relief of U.S. garrisons. This was going to culminate in a Trafalgar-like battle with Japanese forces.

Wharfie—New Zealand slang expression. A dock worker who loads and unloads ships. The American term is "longshoreman."

WIA—Wounded in action.

WO—Warrant officer.

W/T—Wireless telegraphy.

Yank—A New Zealand expression referring to all Americans, including those from the Southern states!

YM—USN designation for minesweeper.

YMCA—Young Mens Christian Association.

Zeke or Zero—Allied code name for Mitsubishi A6M fighter (IJNAF).

Appendices

I: New Zealand Order of Battle for the "Commando Raid," 30 January 1944

Composition of Force	Officers	Warrant Officers	Sergeants	Rank and File	Total
Battalion HQ	7	1	4	24	36
Attached to Battalion HQ	1	—	—	12	13
3 Rifle Companies	15	3	9	228	255
1 Platoon Rifle Company	1	—	1	23	25
Technicians, etc.	5	—	—	15	20
Divisional Reconnaissance Group	11	—	—		11
Total	40	4	14	302	360

Source: Archives NZ, WAII, DAZ 156/15/1, 30 Bn 00, 22/1/1944.

II: New Zealand Order of Battle, Operation Squarepeg, 15 February 1944

Divisional Commander (Major General H.E. Barrowclough)
GSO 1 (Col. J.I. Brooke)
AA & QMG (Lt-Col. P.L. Bennett, MC)
3 Defence and Employment Platoon (Capt. W.G. Rutherford)
4 Field Security Section (Capt. D. Lawford)

Divisional Signals (Lt-Col. D. McN. Burns)
Headquarters Company (Maj. G.W. Heatherwick)
No 1 Company (Maj. J.K.H. Clark, who succeeded Maj. K.H. Wilson, MC, in December)
No 2 Company (Capt. T.C. Eady)
No 3 Company (Capt. G.M. Parkhouse)

Divisional Artillery (Brig. C.S.J. Duff, DSO)
17 Field Regiment (Lt-Col. B. Wicksteed)
29 Light Anti-Aircraft Regiment, two batteries (Lt-Col. W.S. McKinnon)

144 Independent Battery (Maj. G.R. Powles)
53 Anti-Tank Battery, two troops (Maj. L.J. Fahey)
4 Survey Troop (Capt. N.R. Sanderson)

Tank Squadron (Maj. R.J. Rutherford)

Divisional Engineers (Lt-Col. A. Murray)
20 Field Company (Maj. W.G. McKay)
26 Field Company (Maj. W.L. Mynott)
Detachment 37 Field Park (Lt. L.G. Taylor-Cannon)

Army Service Corps (Lt-Col. C.A. Blazey)
16 MT Company (Maj. C. McL. Brown)
Detachment 10 MT Company (Maj. N.C. Moon)

Medical Services (Col. N.C. Speight)
22 Field Ambulance (Lt-Col. F.G. Barrowclough)
24 Field Ambulance (Lt-Col. W.R. Fea)
No 1 Field Surgical Unit (Maj. P.C.E. Brunette)
Malaria Control Section (Maj. R.G.S. Ferguson)
6 Field Hygiene Section (Maj. R.M. Irwin)
10 Mobile Dental Section (Capt. J.B. Muir)

14 Brigade Headquarters (Brigadier L. Potter)
Brigade Major (Major L.E. Pithie)
Staff Captain (Captain G.C. Sandston)
Brigade Carrier Platoon (Captain J.F.B. Stronach)
Brigade Machine Gun Company (Major L.A. Ross)
30 Battalion (Lt. Colonel F.C. Cornwall)
35 Battalion (Lt. Colonel J.R. Moffatt)
37 Battalion (Lt. Colonel A.H. Sugden)

(Source: Oliver Gillespie, *The Pacific, pp. 179–80*)

III: New Zealand and American Units Involved in Operation Squarepeg, 15 February 1944

New Zealand Units	Total Strength		Total Strength
HQ 3NZ Div	65	HQ 3NZ Divisional Engineers	15
Defence & Employment Platoon	41	20 Field Company	140
4 Field Security Section	15	26 Field Company	70
5 Provost Company	18	37 Field Park Company	7
3NZ Division Tank Squadron	87	HQ 3NZ Divisional Signals	150
HQ 3NZ Division Artillery	27	HQ 3NZ Division Army Service Corps	10
Survey Troop	14	16 Motor Transport Company	150
HQ 17 Field Regiment	28	10 Motor Transport Company	100
"E" Section Signals	20	Ammunition Section NZ Ordnance Company	7

APPENDICES

New Zealand Units	Total Strength		Total Strength
20 Light Aid Detachment	11	HQ 14 NZ Infantry Brigade	44
12 Field Battery	11	"K" Section Signals	56
35 Field Battery	19	Defence Platoon	39
37 Field Battery	177	Brigade Machine Gun Company	116
144 Independent Battery	174	30 Battalion	612
HQ 29 Light Anti-Aircraft Regiment	44	35 Battalion	612
Workshop Section	6	37 Battalion	612
207 Battery	220	Carrier Platoon	30
209 Battery	220	24 Field Ambulance	207
53 Anti-Tank Battery	30	1 Field Surgical Unit	11
		Divisional Malaria Control	3
		Total	**4218**
United States Units			
Comair Squarepeg	100	HQ Construction Battalion Regiment	10
Argus 7	168	33 Naval Construction Battalion	240
Naval Adv Base Unit 11 Base 4P	50	37 Naval Construction Battalion	250
Comm Unit 39	102	93 Naval Construction Battalion	250
PT Base 7	17	967 Army AA Battalion	300
Boat Pool 12	20	Bty A 283 Coast Artillery	6
Hydrographic Survey Unit	15	Naval Fire Control	36
		Total	**1564**
Total New Zealand and United States Personnel			**5782**

Source: Archives NZ WA11, 1, DAZ 121.1/1/13 Appendix 1

IV: U.S. Naval Forces Involved with Operation Squarepeg, 15 February 1944

USS Halford (DD)
USS St Louis (CL)
USS Menominee (AT-73)
USS Sioux (AT-75)
USS Eaton (DD)
USS Conway (DD)
USS Pringle (DD)
USS Sigourney (DD)
USS Philip (DD)
USS Waller (DD)

USS Renshaw (DD)
USS Saufley (DD)
LSTs: 70, 207, 220, 354, 446 and 472 (first echelon)
LSTs: 39, 71, 117, 118, 123, 166, 247, 269, 334, 353 and 390 (second echelon)

LSTs: 40, 70, 120, 220, 339, 341, 354, 446, 447, 460 and 472 (third echelon)
LCTs: 134, 139, 146, 318, 574 and 915
LCIs: 357, 358, 360, 433, 436, 444, 445, 446

V: U.S. Navy Task Organization for Squarepeg

Commander in Chief, U.S. Fleet—Admiral Ernest J. King
Commander in Chief, U.S. Pacific Fleet—Admiral Chester W. Nimitz
Commander Third Fleet—Admiral William F. Halsey
Commander Amphibious Force, Third Fleet (Commander Task Force 31)—Rear Admiral T.S. Wilkinson
Commander Landing Craft Flotillas Third Fleet (Commander Task Group 31.1)—Rear Admiral G.H. Fort
Commander L.S.T. Flotilla Five—Captain G.B. Carter

VI: Specifications of the Valentine Tanks of 3NZ Division Tank Squadron

Valentine Mark III Infantry Tank
Crew: 3-Driver, Commander, Gunner
Combat Weight: 16 tons
Length: 17 feet, 9 inches
Width: 8 feet, 7.5 inches
Armament: 2 pounder (40mm) and one Besa .92mm MG mounted co-axially in turret. One Bren .303 in machine gun on collapsible mounting on turret roof.
Engine: AEC Diesel
Performance: Maximum road speed 15mph

VII: Echelons to the Green Islands

Echelons	Personnel	Supplies and Equipment
1st Echelon—8APD, 13LCI, 7LST, 6LCT	5,806	4,344 tons
2nd Echelon—8APD, 11LST, 2LCI	4,715	6,315 tons
3rd Echelon, 10LST, 3LCI	2,577	6,668 tons
4th Echelon, 10LST, 1LCI	1,048	5,477 tons
5th Echelon, 10LST, 1AK	1,127	9,147 tons
6th and 7th Echelon, 5LST, 3AK	1,175	11,137 tons
Totals	**16,440**	**43,088 tons**

Source: Wilkinson Report, p. 11

Chapter Notes

Introduction

1. It was later speculated that the origin of the codename derived from the shape of Nissan Island and its oval-shaped coral lagoon. In theory, codenames were not supposed to have any relationship to the projected operation. Third Division Histories Committee, *Pacific Pioneers: The Story of the Engineers of the New Zealand Expeditionary Force in the Pacific* (Wellington: A.H. & A.W. Reed, 1947), p. 98.

Chapter One

1. Archives NZ, Series 9, S14, Operations, Halsey to Nimitz/King, 29 April 1944.
2. J.M.S. Ross, *Royal New Zealand Airforce* (Wellington: Department of Internal Affairs, 1955), p. 236.
3. William D. Halsey and J. Bryan III, *Admiral Halsey's Story* (New York: McGraw-Hill, 1947), p. 188.
4. Edwin P. Hoyt, *Nimitz and His Admirals: How They Won the War in the Pacific* (Guildford, CT: Lyons Press, 2002), pp. 327–328.
5. National Archives and Records Administration (NARA), U.S., FE25/A16-3(3), Commander Third Amphibious Force to Commander in Chief, U.S. Pacific Fleet Seizure and Occupation of Green Islands 15 February to 15 March 1944, 24 March 1944 (hereinafter "Wilkinson Report").
6. "In reviewing the troops available for the operation it appeared that those most readily available, and of undoubted competence, were the 14th New Zealand Brigade (the equivalent of a combat team) then on duty in Vella Lavella...." Wilkinson Report, p. 4.
7. John Rentz, *Bougainville and the Northern Solomons* (Washington, DC: Historical Section, Headquarters USMC, 1948), p. 116.
8. Archives NZ, WAII, DAZ 121/1/1/11, Appendix IV & XI.
9. War Diary, Major General Harold Barrowclough, GOC 3NZ Division 31 December 1943, p. 38.
10. To add to the confusion, once the Green Islands were taken by the Allies, both the atoll and the main island, Nissan, were collectively known as "Green Island." Gordon Rottman, *World War II Pacific Island Guide: A Geo-Military Study* (Westport, CT: Greenwood Press, 2002), p. 175.
11. Wilkinson Report, p. 4. A PT boat reconnaissance on 10 January established the navigability of two channels.
12. Archives NZ, WA11, 1,DAZ, 113/1/12HQNZEFIP, Special War Information Summary, no. 4, 16 February 1944.
13. Army Board, *Guadalcanal to Nissan* (Wellington: Army Board, 1945), p. 39.
14. Intelligence Report, 20 January 1944. Author's collection.
15. *Ibid.*

Chapter Two

1. "The Advance Base Assembly," a restricted pamphlet published September 1943 by Commander Air Force, Pacific Fleet, p. 1.
2. Interview with author, 15 July 2007.
3. Barrowclough War Diary. Entry 24 January to 27 January 1944. See Jeffrey Plowman, *Rampant Dragons: New Zealanders in Armour in World War II* (Christchurch: Kiwi Armour, 2002).
4. Archives NZ, WAII, 1 DAZ Narrative History 3NZ Division, p. 233.
5. Gary Nila and Robert Rolfe, *Japanese Special Naval Landing Forces* (Oxford: Osprey, 2006), p. 5.
6. *Ibid.*, p. 10.

Chapter Three

1. Carl von Clausewitz, *On War* (New York: Alfred A. Knopf, 1993), p. 117.
2. Donald Denoon, ed., *The Cambridge History of the Pacific Islands* (Cambridge: Cambridge University Press, 1997), pp. 308–311.
3. Archives NZ, WAII, 1, 1551 DAZ 155/9/1 30 Bn "Commando" Force 00 No. 1, 22 January 1944.
4. Archives NZ, WAII, 1, DAZ 149/1/5–6 Extract from reports of W/O E. Robson, RAAF, January 1944.
5. Joseph H. Alexander. *Utmost Savagery: The Three Days of Tarawa* (Annapolis: Naval Institute Press, 1995), pp. 73, 76–78.
6. William H. Bartsch, "Operation Dovetail: Bungled Guadalcanal Rehearsal, July 1942," *Journal of Military History* 66, No. 2 (April 2002): pp. 443–476.
7. The submarine USS *Gato*, on its seventh war patrol in January 1944, reported chart discrepancies as it traveled through the waters of the Green Islands en route to the shipping lanes of Rabaul. USS *Gato* Seventh War Patrol Report, 01-05-08 1944. SS212/A16-3. The Green Islands–Buki-Feni area was a popular route for U.S. submarines heading to the target-rich area around the Japanese base at Rabaul. There were concerns expressed by the skippers as to the reliability of the charts they were given. As a PT boat commander trenchantly commented of the state of maps in the Solomons, "The charts of these islands are not what you'd call up-to-date. Probably because nobody was interested in them but a few traders…. You're sure you've hit a reef, which is the surest way of finding it." Captain Robert J. Bulkey, Jr., *At Close Quarters: PT Boats in the United States Navy* (Washington, DC: Naval History Division, 1962), p. 156.
8. Robert F. Dorr, *B-24 Liberator Units of the Pacific War* (Oxford: Osprey, 2014), p. 43.
9. Archives NZ, WAII, 1, 1512 Photo Intelligence Unit 12th AAF Photo Intelligence Detachment, 20 December. Commander McElroy of VD-1 flew several photo reconnaissance missions in plane No. 74 at low altitude. He would play an interesting role on 15 February 1944, piloting an observation plane over the landings.
10. These barge-busting operations played a significant role in isolating Japanese garrisons in the South Pacific and rendering Japanese garrisons impotent. See Frank Johnson, *United States PT-Boats of World War II In Action* (Poole, Dorset: Blandford Press, 1983), pp. 82–113, 124–137.
11. Interestingly, the War Diary of Commander Naval Advanced Base Torokina simply notes, "PT Patrols had no enemy contacts. Two PT's departed on a secret mission in addition to the other patrols." Entry 30 January 1944.
12. Bulkey, pp. 147–148.
13. Archives NZ, WAII, 1, 1512, DAZ 121/9/A50/4/2 Brig. Dove, 11 January 1944.
14. Brooke to Potter, 11 January 1944.
15. Henry I. Shaw and Douglas T. Kane, *Isolation of Rabaul: History of U.S. Marine Corps Operations in World War II*, vol. 2 (Washington, DC: Historical Branch USMC, 1963), p. 508.
16. Archives NZ, DAZ 121/1/1/15, Appendix 1.
17. Barrowclough War Diary, entry 31 December 1943.
18. Archives NZ, Puttick 5 W1427/5.
19. NZ Defence Base Records: Trentham. Personnel File F.C. Cornwall.
20. Each platoon was thinned down to 25 men so that some soldiers had to be left behind. Third Division Histories Committee, *Pacific Kiwis; Being the Story of the Service in the Pacific of the 30th Battalion, Third Division, Second New Zealand Expeditionary Force* (Wellington: A.W. & A.H. Reed, 1947), pp. 88, 89.
21. The choice of 30 Battalion was made by Potter and Barrowclough. The battalion had acted as a reserve battalion during the struggle for Vella Lavella and had not experienced combat against the Japanese. Barrowclough thought that the raid would allow it to gain experience. Barrowclough War Diary, entry 1 January 1944.
22. *Ibid.*
23. The troops themselves referred to it as a "Commando Raid." Army Board, *Guadalcanal to Nissan*, p. 40.
24. *Ibid.*
25. Wilkinson Report, p. 4. The principle generally was that the naval commander remained in command until the land forces had beached and then a transfer of command to the land force commander occurred.
26. Recollections of Captain Junius T. Jarman USC & GS, NOAA History. http://www.history.noaa.gov/stories_tales/pathfinder7.html.
27. Contemporary documents often referred to the "Higgins Boat" or landing craft as "barges."
28. Operations Order No. 1, 22 January 1944.
29. *Ibid.*
30. Commando Force, Operations Order 1.

31. *Pacific Pioneers*, p. 99.
32. *Pacific Kiwis*, p. 88.
33. *Ibid.*
34. "Narrative of APD activities during raid and reconnaissance in force—Green Islands, B.S.I." The Commander Transport Division Twelve to the Commander South Pacific Area and Force, 4 February 1944, Cmdr J.D. Sweeney (hereinafter Sweeney Report).
35. *Ibid.*
36. Oliver Gillespie, *The Pacific* (Wellington: War History Branch, 1952), p. 174.
37. For examples of the problems with landing troops on Vella Lavella, see Reg Newell, *The Battle for Vella Lavella: The Allied Recapture of Solomon Islands Territory, August 15–September 9, 1943* (Jefferson, NC: McFarland, 2016), pp. 158, 227.
38. USS *Talbot*, USS *Waters* and USS *Dickerson*.
39. *Pacific Kiwis*, p. 90.
40. Sweeney Report.
41. Samuel Eliot Morison, *History of United States Naval Operations in World War II*, vol. 6, *Breaking the Bismarcks Barrier, 22 July 1942–1 May 1944* (Edison, NJ: Castle Books), p. 414.
42. Bulkey, p. 148.
43. Frank Rennie, *Regular Soldier: A Life in the New Zealand Army* (Auckland: Endeavour Press, 1986), p. 50.
44. *Ibid.*
45. War Diary USS *Dickerson* (157), Entry 30 January 1944.
46. Sweeney Report. Attachment J.R. Cain.
47. War Diary USS *Dickerson*, Entry 31 January 1944.
48. *Pacific Kiwis*, p. 90
49. Harry Bioletti interview 2006.
50. Archives NZ DA 428/3/2 "Past a Joke," Official War Correspondent NZEF, 6 February 1944.
51. HQ NZEFIP, Special War Information Summary no. 44, p. 3.
52. Recollections of Captain Junius Jarman.
53. *Pacific Kiwis*, pp. 92–93.
54. See "Guide to Vern Haughland Papers." http://nwda.orbiscascade.org/ark:/80444/xv58484, Biographical note.
55. *Kansas Star*, 31 January 1944, 17 February 1944, p. 4.
56. Sweeney Report.
57. Mitsubishi Zero-Sen A6M2 Fighters were equipped with two 20 mm cannon and a 13.2 mm machine gun and were capable of carrying two 60-kilogram bombs. Against troops packed into thinly protected landing craft, this firepower was potentially very lethal. The Wilkinson Report refers to seven Zeros, p. 5.

58. Rennie, p. 54.
59. *Pacific Kiwis*, p. 95.
60. Harry Bioletti interview 2006.
61. Rennie, p. 55.
62. Sweeney Report, Attachment J.R. Cain.
63. *Pacific Kiwis*, p. 98.
64. *Headquarters*, p. 241.
65. Rottman, p. 177.
66. *Ibid.*
67. Third Division Histories Committee, *Headquarters: A Brief Outline of the Activities of the Headquarters of the Third Division and the 8th and 14th Brigades During Their Service in the Pacific* [incorporating *Communications: The Unofficial History of the New Zealand Corps of Signals with B Force and the Third Division in Fiji, with the New Zealand Expeditionary Force in the Pacific and the Third New Zealand Division in New Caledonia and the Solomon Islands*] (Wellington: A.H. & A.W. Reed, 1945), pp. 241–2.
68. War Diary USS *Dickerson*, entry 1 February 1944.
69. Rennie describes an American officer being badly injured by being crushed between barge and ship.
70. The details are sketchy. It may be significant that a maintenance order was issued for repair of the davits and tackle after reaching base. This suggests that it was equipment failure that caused the crush injury. I am indebted to R. Robert Palmer for his research.
71. Archives NZ, WAII, DAZ 156/1/40, Appendix, 30 NZ Battalion Commando Raid.
72. Harry Bioletti interview 2006.
73. Sweeney Report.
74. One of the wounded sailors was Vernon S. Cunningham, who had been born in Canada of American parents. On the outbreak of war he enlisted in the Royal Canadian Navy, but after the attack on Pearl Harbor he switched to the U.S. Navy. He suffered the loss of an eye and the use of his left hand in the Commando Raid. *Tacoma Times*, 7 November 1944, Tacoma Public Library Records.
75. *Ibid.*
76. Gillespie, p. 176.
77. *Ibid.*
78. *Pacific Pioneers*, p. 99.
79. *Ibid.*
80. Archives NZ, WAII, 1, DAZ 122/1/20–31, Arty Recce Report, Pokonian Plantation, 31 January 1943.
81. Archives NZ, WAII, 1, 1553 DAZ 156/15/1–3, 30 NZ Bn Commando Force 0.0. No. 9. 1, 22 January 1944.
82. Archives NZ, WAII, 1, DAZ 158/1/26, p. 13.
83. *Pacific Pioneers*, pp. 99–100.
84. The operations order provided for sup-

port from "Black Cats for the approach and retirement of the Transport Unit." Archives U.S. FE25/A16-3(1) Task Force Thirty One Operation Order No 1-44 Rear Admiral T.S. Wilkinson, 25 January 1944. Author's Collection. The "Black Cats" were a specialized PBY 5A Catalina flying boat squadron involved with night maritime attack operations.

85. For Squarepeg, the South Pacific Air Force was directed to provide aerial reconnaissance and "to provide maximum practicable air coverage and support during the operation." Wilkinson Report, p. 5.
86. *Pacific Kiwis*, p. 96.
87. Gillespie, Footnote, p. 178.
88. See Reg Newell, *Operation Goodtime and the Battle of The Treasury Islands, 1943* (Jefferson, NC: McFarland, 2012), pp. 9–12.
89. See Reg Newell, *The Battle for Vella Lavella*, pp. 50–51.
90. Bulkley, p. 153.
91. Bruce F. Meyers, *Swift, Silent and Deadly: Marine Amphibious Reconnaissance in the Pacific 1942–45* (Annapolis: Naval Institute Press, 2004).
92. Gillespie, p. 171.
93. Wilkinson Report, p. 3.
94. Barrowclough War Diary, entry 31 January to 2 February 1944.
95. Gillespie, p. 177.
96. *Ibid.*
97. Archives NZ, WAII, Series 1, DA 438.3/3, "The Japanese View."
98. *Ibid.*
99. *Pacific Kiwis*, p. 98.
100. Barrowclough War Diary, 31 January to 2 February 1944.
101. Morison, p. 414.
102. HQ NZEFIP, Special War Information Summary, No. 44, p. 2.

Chapter Four

1. Army Board, p. 42.
2. Archives NZ Puttick Papers, 1, 5 Barrowclough to Puttick, 2 February 1944.
3. Archives NZ, WAII, DAZ 121/9/ASO/4/2 Brooke to Potter, 11 January 1944.
4. Army Board, *Guadalcanal to Nissan*, p. 40.
5. Gillespie, p. 171.
6. Archives NZ, WAII, 1, AD12 28/15/1.
7. Brooke to Potter, 11 January 1944.
8. Archives NZ, WAII, 1, 1512 DAZ 121/9/A50/4/2 Brig. Dove, 11 January 1944.
9. Army Board, p. 40.
10. Brooke to Potter, 11 January 1944.

11. Archives NZ, WAII, 1, 1512 DAZ 121/9/A50/4.
12. Administrative Order No. 1.
13. War Diary of Captain G.B. Carter, USN, Commander LST Flotilla Five, A12-1 Serial 0062, 1 March 1944 Entry for 10 February 1944.
14. *Ibid.* Entry 12 February 1944.
15. *Ibid.* Entry 15 February 1944.
16. Army Board, p. 42.
17. Alexander, *Utmost Savagery*, p. 62.
18. Alexander, p. xvi.
19. *Headquarters*, pp. 242–243.
20. *Guadalcanal to Nissan*, p. 43.
21. *Headquarters*, p. 243.
22. Archives NZ, WAII, 1, DAZ 122/1/20–31, Operation Squarepeg, Artillery Operations Order no 101, 5 February 1944
23. Archives NZ, WAII, 1, DAZ 155/1/26 War Diary of Headquarters, 14 NZ Brigade, 1–29 February 1944.
24. Admin Order No. 5, 9 February 1944.
25. Archives NZ, WAII, 1, DAZ 121/9/A50/4/2, Headquarters 3NZ Division Special Intelligence Summary, Nissan Island, 9 February 1944.
26. Archives NZ, WAII, 1, DAZ 158/1/26, War Diary 37 Battalion.
27. *Ibid.*
28. *Headquarters*, p. 250.
29. Jeffrey Plowman, *Rampant Dragons: New Zealanders in Armour in World War II* (Christchurch: Kiwi Armour, 2002), pp. 43–44.
30. http://kiwisinarmour.hobbyvista.com History of the 3rd NZ Division Tank Squadron.
31. Gillespie, p. 191.
32. Barrowclough to Puttick, 6 January 1944. Author's collection.
33. Newell, *Operation Goodtime*, p. 178.
34. *Pacific Kiwis*, p. 104.
35. See Archival Footage, LSTs leave Kukum Beach, Guadalcanal, 1944. https://archive.org/details/NPC-1527.
36. See James R. Shock, *The U.S. Army Barrage Balloon Program*, 5th ed. (Bennington, VT: Merriam Press, 2012), p. 44–45. From the number of Axis planes downed by barrage balloons over Britain (24) as compared to the number of British planes lost (38) during the period September 1939 to March 1941, it seems that barrage balloons had pronounced drawbacks, being more lethal to the defenders than the attackers.
37. War Diary, Commander LST Flotilla Five, entry 22 February 1944.
38. Reg Newell, *Operation Goodtime*, pp. 22, 133.

Chapter Five

1. *St. Louis* was part of Task Force 38. She was accompanied by the cruiser USS *Honolulu*, and the destroyers *Farenholt, Buchanan, Woodworth, Lansdowne* and *Lardner* as per Com3rdFlt Operation Order, pp. 58–44. See Report of the Commanding Officer USS *St. Louis* to Commander in Chief, U.S. Fleet Action Report, Anti-Aircraft, on 14–15 February 1944, CL 49/A16-3, Serial (008) 9 March 1944. Also War Diary USS *St. Louis*, entry 14 February 1944.
2. Gillespie, p. 180.
3. The interesting thing was that smoke was used at night. In an official report, the comment was made, "For the first time at night this force employed smoke to great advantage in thwarting attempts of enemy planes to attack. The enemy showed no inclination to enter smoke and press home the attack." Activities of Task Forces under the Command of Rear Admiral Walden L. Ainsworth, U.S. Navy, Solomon Islands Campaigns, 10 December 1942 to 4 June 1944, p. 27.
4. 16 September 1945.
5. www.ussstlouis.com/green_island_operation.htm.
6. Transcript USS *St. Louis* (CL-49) You Tube Video.
7. YouTube Video, https://www.youtube.com/watch?v=qGo7BbegZgM.
8. USS *St. Louis* War Diary, entry 15 February 1944.
9. *Dictionary of American Naval Fighting Ships* (DANFS).
10. Gillespie, p. 181.

Chapter Six

1. *Headquarters*, p. 244.
2. LST Flotilla Five War Diary, p. 4, entry for 15 February 1944. Since her commissioning in September 1942, *Constant* had been heavily involved in convoy escorts and minesweeping. It is noteworthy that she had to travel to Auckland in May 1944 for an overhaul. *Dictionary of American Naval Fighting Ships*, http://www.hazegray.org/danfs/mine/am86.htm.
3. LST Flotilla Five War Diary, p. 4.
4. War Diary, USS *Waller*, Action Report for 15 February 1944, during First Echelon to Green Island, 16 February 1944.
5. Report of Operations 12–17 February 1944, Commander LCI (L) Flotilla Five, 17 February 1944.
6. *Ibid.*
7. A photo was taken by Captain Barchman, AAF staff correspondent and used in a press release, "Airpower meets Seapower." Unfortunately the photo is not of publishable quality. It features in "Solomon Islands Vets," *WWII Newsletter* (Fall 2000): p. 1.
8. *The Coast Guard at War*, VI: The Pacific. https://www.ibiblio.org/hyperwar/USCG/VI-Pacific/USCG-VI 26.html, p. 72.
9. War Diary LST Flotilla Five, entry 15 February 1944.
10. Wilkinson Report, p. 8.
11. Gillespie, p. 180.
12. NARA, Record Group 38, Box 126, Serial 00177 Records of the Office of the Chief of Naval Activity during WWII, WWII Action & Operational Reports, TF30.8.1 to TF31, Action Reports covering Operations of Task Force 31, January 28 to February 17, 1944. Enclosure G, Commanding Officer to Commander Task Force 31, February 19, 1944, Minesweeping Operation.
13. Gordon Rottman, *Landing Craft, Infantry Support and Fire Support* (Oxford: Osprey, 2009), pp. 22–23.
14. Bulkey, p. 148.
15. Milton Bush's website, www.seabees93.net.
16. Joseph Alexander, "Across the Reef, Amphibious Warfare in the Pacific," Chapter 11 in *The Pacific War Companion*, ed. Daniel Marston (Oxford: Osprey, 2005), pp. 196–197.
17. *Headquarters*, p. 245.
18. War Diary, Major General H.E. Barrowclough, entry 15 February 1944.
19. Archives NZ, WAII, 1 DAZ 156/15/1 Historical record of 30 Bn, entry 15 February 1944.
20. Alan Henderson, David Green and Peter Cooke, *The Gunners: A History of New Zealand Artillery* (Auckland: Penguin Group NZ, 2008), p. 350.
21. Interview 2001.
22. *The Tanks*, p. 123.
23. Doug Ross Narrative.
24. *Pacific Saga*, p. 86.
25. Gillespie, p. 181.
26. Wilkinson Report, p. 8.
27. Affidavit of Harland D. Warren, 3 May 2000.
28. Interview, William Laurence. Author's collection.
29. Plowman, *Rampant Dragons*, p. 44.
30. "Problem solved," Frank Cox, correspondence with author, 20 April 2000.
31. Gillespie, p. 181.
32. In the postwar years Guy Powles became New Zealand's first ombudsman.
33. Army Board, pp. 44–45.

34. Gillespie, p. 182.
35. Wilkinson report, p. 10.
36. Skow (1910–1994) was a civil engineer by profession and was awarded the Bronze Star in August 1944 for his achievements in the intelligence field against the Japanese in the Northern Solomons. He became the Chief of Intelligence Section on the staff of Vice Admiral T.S. Wilkinson, and Commander of 3rd Amphibious Force. Skow took part in the landings at Leyte and Lingayen Gulf in the Philippines in 1944. *Ames Daily Tribune*, 2 March 1945.
37. *Ibid.*
38. Vern Haughland, "Allies Take Japs' Green Islands The Easy Way," *Knickerbocker News*, Albany, NY, February 16, 1944.
39. *Ibid.*
40. *Ibid.*
41. Gillespie, p. 181.
42. Ross Templeton, interview with the author, July 2012.
43. George C. Kenney, *General Kenney Reports: A Personal History of the Pacific War* (New York: Duell, Sloan and Pearce, 1949), p. 356.
44. Ross, p. 243.
45. Archives NZ, AIR118, 110, History of Naval Fighter Direction.
46. Barrett Tillman, *U.S. Marine Corps Fighter Squadrons of World War II* (Oxford: Osprey, 2014), pp. 144–145.
47. Henry Sakaida, *The Siege of Rabaul* (St. Paul, MN: Phalanx, 1996), p. 39.
48. Ross, p. 244.
49. *Pacific Pioneers*, p. 101.
50. *Ibid.*, pp. 102–3.
51. Gillespie, p. 182.
52. *Headquarters*, p. 247.
53. *Pacific Saga*, p. 88.
54. "Solomon Islands Vets," *WWII Newsletter* (Fall 2000): pp. 2–3.
55. *Headquarters*, p. 250.
56. *Pacific Saga*, pp. 87–88.
57. *Pacific Saga*, p. 88.
58. Archives NZ, WAII, 1, DAZ 155/1/16 Appendix 2.
59. Naval Photographic Centre Film #1527, National Archives Identifier 76049. https://archive.org/details/npc1527
60. Gillespie, p. 181.
61. Report of Operations 12–17 February 1944, From: Commander LCI(L) Flotilla 5 To: Com Des Ron 22 (Com. Task Unit 31.4.2) LCI (L) Flotilla Five, Third Amphibious Force, South Pacific Force.
62. Gillespie, p. 182.
63. War Diary, USS *Waller* for month of February 1944, entries 15 February to 17 February 1944.
64. Archives NZ, WAII, 1, DAZ, Unit History 30 Battalion, NZEFIP 3rd Division, entry Tuesday 15 February 1944.
65. Archives NZ, WAII, 1, DAZ 121.1/1/13 Appendix XV11.
66. *Pacific Saga*, p. 88.
67. *Headquarters*, p. 250.
68. *The Tanks*, p. 126.
69. Gillespie, p. 182.
70. Archives NZ, WAII, 1, Barrowclough to PMNZ, 5 August 1944.
71. Barrowclough to PMNZ, 5 August 1944.

Chapter Seven

1. 30 Battalion history, entry February 1944.
2. *Pacific Kiwis*, p. 106.
3. *Pacific Saga*, p. 89.
4. *Pacific Kiwis*, p. 106.
5. Plowman, *Rampant Dragons*, p. 48.
6. *Pacific Saga*, p. 89.
7. *Pacific Saga*, p. 90.
8. Archives NZ, WAII, 1, DAZ, Unit History of 30 Battalion, NZEFIP, 3rd Division, Entry 20 February 1944.
9. Barrowclough War Diary, entry 16 February to 19 February 1944.
10. *Headquarters*, p. 251.
11. *Pacific Kiwis*, p. 106.
12. *Pacific Saga*, p. 89.
13. *Pacific Kiwis*, p. 106.
14. 30th Battalion History, entry 17 February 1944.

Chapter Eight

1. Wilkinson Report, p. 9.
2. Gillespie, p. 184.
3. *The Tanks*, p. 124.
4. Barrowclough War Diary, entry 16 February to 19 February 1944.
5. Gillespie, p. 184.
6. 30th Battalion History, entry Friday 18 February 1944.
7. Gillespie, p. 184.
8. Gillespie, p. 185.

Chapter Nine

1. "Jungle Battle," *New Zealand Herald*, 13 March 1944.
2. *The Tanks*, p. 124.
3. Plowman, *History of 3rd NZ Division Tank Squadron*.
4. Archives NZ, WAII, 1, DAZ 149/1/5–

6 Special Tank Squadron, "Report on Tank Action," Tanaheran area–Green Island, Sunday 20 February 1944, Lt. C.A.L. De Vere. (hereafter "De Vere Report").
 5. "Jungle Battle," *New Zealand Herald*, 13 March 1944.
 6. Plowman, *Rampant Dragons*, p. 50.
 7. The Operational History of 3rd NZ Division Tank Squadron, http:kiwisinarmour.hobby.vista.com.
 8. "Jungle Battle," *New Zealand Herald*, 13 March 1944.
 9. *The Tanks, MMGs & Ordnance*, pp. 48–49.
 10. Archives NZ, WAII, 1, DAZ 155/1/26 Appendix VI (b).
 11. Plowman, *Rampant Dragons*, p. 52.
 12. De Vere Report.
 13. "Jungle Battle," *New Zealand Herald*, 13 March 1944.
 14. De Vere Report, p. 2.
 15. Archives NZ, WAII, 1, DAZ 149/1/5– 6 Special Tank Squadron. Report on Tank Action.
 16. Archives NZ, WAII, 1, DAZ 157/1/26, Appendix D, p. 4.
 17. Barrowclough War Diary, entry 20 February 1944.
 18. *Ibid.*
 19. *Ibid.*
 20. Doug Ross Interview, 8 November 2006.
 21. Archives NZ, WAII, 1, DAZ 158/1/26 Appendix, p. 109.
 22. Historical Record of the 37th Bn by Corporal G.A. James, entry 3 April 1943.
 23. *Pacific Saga*, pp. 90–92.

Chapter Ten

 1. *Coast Guard at War: Final Japanese Resistance.*
 2. War Diary, Commander LST Flotilla Five, entry 20 February 1944.
 3. *Headquarters*, p. 254.
 4. Barrowclough War Diary, 26 February 1944.
 5. Bob Conner Diary, entry 3 March 1944.
 6. *Ibid.*, entry 4 March 1944.
 7. *The Tanks*, p. 220.
 8. Archives NZ, WAII, 1, 158/15/1 Historical Record of the 37th Battalion, entry March 4–5, 1944.
 9. *Headquarters*, p. 260.
 10. Historical Record of the 37th Battalion for the month of March 1944, recorded by Corporal G.A. James, entry 8 March 1944.
 11. Archives NZ, WAII, 1, DAZ 155/1/26, Appendix V (g).

 12. Historical Record of 37th Battalion, entry 3 March 1944.
 13. Archives NZ, WAII, 1, DAZ 155/1/26, entries 1 and 29 February.
 14. War Diary, Commander LST Flotilla Five, entries 24–25 February 1944.
 15. Barrowclough War Diary, 21–22 February 1944.
 16. *Shovel, Sword and Scalpel*, p. 79.
 17. *Ibid.*
 18. Barrowclough War Diary, entry 1 March 1944.
 19. General Report, Argus Unit Seven, 25 March 1944, Archives NZ, Air 128, II General Report on Green Island Hereinafter Argus 7 Report.
 20. Argus 7 Report, p. 28.
 21. Argus 7 Report, pp. 36–37.
 22. *The Tanks*, p. 220.
 23. Gillespie, p. 163.
 24. Gillespie, p. 221.
 25. *Shovel, Sword & Scapel*, p. 79.
 26. *The Tanks*, p. 222.
 27. See Newell, *Operation Goodtime*, pp. 170–1.
 28. Ross, p. 247.
 29. 37th Bn Historical Record, entry 6 March 1944.
 30. William Wolf, *13th Fighter Command in World War II: Air Combat over Guadalcanal and the Solomons* (Atglen, PA: Schiffer Military History, 2004), p. 252.
 31. Bruce Gamble, *Target Rabaul* (Minneapolis, MN: Zenith Press, 2013), p. 329.
 32. Barrowclough to NZ Prime Minister, 5 August 1944.
 33. *Headquarters*, p. 257.
 34. Historical Record of 37th Battalion, entry March 7, 1944.
 35. Johnson, p. 109. Torpedoes were sometimes ineffective against the shallow-draft Daihatsus, and PT-boat crews installed heavy guns in order to sink the barges.
 36. Louis B. Dorny, *U.S. Navy PBY Catalina Units of the Pacific War* (Oxford: Osprey, 2007), p. 81.
 37. Recollections of Captain Junius Jarman.
 38. Archives NZ, WAII, 1, DAZ 121.1/1/15 Appendix 1, p. 9.
 39. Archives NZ, EA1, 87/19/7 COMSOPAC to Commander in Chief U.S. Fleet, 19 May 1944.
 40. John Crawford, "Major General Sir Harold Barrowclough: Leadership and Command in Two World Wars," in Glyn Harper and Joel Hayward, *Born to Lead? Portraits of New Zealand Commanders* (Auckland: Exisle, 2003), p. 160.
 41. Interview Ron Tucker, January 2001.

42. Ross Templeton Narrative. Author's collection.
43. Interview with the author, 5 July 2007.
44. Archives NZ, WAII, 1, DAZ 121.4/1/26.
45. Interview with the author, 15 July 2007.
46. *Pacific Service*.
47. Robert W. Conner, 93rd Seabees, diary entry, 27 March 1944. http://www.seabees.93.netdiary. Souvenirs such as samurai swords, some manufactured, were sold by the New Zealanders to the Americans. There was also a ready market for illicitly brewed alcohol.
48. Interview with the author, 15 July 2007.
49. Ross Templeton Interview.
50. Gillespie, p. 189.
51. Historical Record of 37th Battalion, entry 12–14 March 1944.
52. Bob Connor Diary, entry 15 July 1944.
53. *Pacific Pioneers*, p. 63.
54. *Pacific Saga*, p. 90.
55. *Pacific Pioneers*, p. 63.
56. *Pacific Saga*, p. 90.
57. Doug Ross interview, 8 November 2006.
58. Doug Ross Narrative.
59. *Pacific Pioneers*, p. 63.
60. *Pacific Pioneers*, p. 61.
61. *The Tanks*, pp. 63–4.
62. *The MMGs*, p. 128.
63. *Pacific Kiwis*, p. 121.
64. David Williams interview, 2007.
65. *Pacific Saga*, p. 93.
66. Interview with the author, 15 July 2007.
67. Williams interview.
68. Archives NZ, WAII, 1, DAZ 142/15/1, The Unofficial History of the 5NZ Provost Coy, 3NZ Division, Nissan Island.
69. Conversation with Joan Clouston, General Barrowclough's daughter, 29 November 2012.
70. According to Barrowclough's daughter, Joan Clouston, he had a marked reluctance to fly on SCAT aircraft because of their unenviable record. Conversation with the author, 29 November 2012.
71. Hove, p. 122.
72. Hove, p. 124.
73. Archives NZ, WAII, 1, DAZ 1231.2/1/16, 140/1/27.
74. Colonel Charles MacDonald, "Lindbergh in Battle," *Colliers* (February 16, 1946).
75. Hove, p. 124.
76. Nixon/Gannon Interviews, UGA Libraries, Day 1, Tape 4.
77. Nixon/Gannon Interviews, Day 1, Tape 3.
78. Nixon/Gannon Interviews, Day 1, Tape 3.
79. http://www.loc.gov/exhibits/bobhope/uso.html.
80. www.seabees93.net.
81. Paul Fattig, "The Marines Sank My Boat," 23 August 2009, *Mail Tribune*, http://www.mailtribune.com/article/20090823/NEWS/908230325/0/SEARCH.
82. www.seabees93.net.
83. Argus 7 Report, p. 45.
84. Ross Templeton Narrative.
85. War Diary, Commander LST Flotilla Five, entry 21 February 1944.
86. Gillespie, p. 190.
87. Archives NZ, WAII, 1, DAZ 121/1/1/15 Appendix 1.
88. Archives NZ, WAII, 1, DAZ 156/151/1 Historical Record of the 37th Bn for the month of April 1944, entry 3 April 1944.
89. M. Stout and T. Duncan, *Medical Services in New Zealand and the Pacific* (Wellington: War History Branch, Department of Internal Affairs, 1958), p. 60.
90. Archives NZ, WAII, 7, Photo Albums related to 3NZ Division in the Pacific, Green Island, Photo 59.
91. Larry Katz—Dialogues with Susan Conner and Milton Bush 2003; 93rd Seabees Battalion, www.seabees93.net.
92. Stout and Duncan, *Medical Services*, p. 61.
93. Archives NZ, WAII, 1, DAZ 22/1/20–31, Brigadier Duff, Artillery Operations Order no. 101, 5 February 1944.
94. David Williams Interview.
95. *Pacific Pioneers*, p. 32.
96. *Pacific Pioneers*, p. 33.
97. Argus 7 Report, p. 39.
98. Archives NZ, WAII, 1, DAZ 157/1/26 Appendix D, p. 4.
99. *Pacific Pioneers*, p. 43.
100. *Pacific Pioneers*, p. 68.
101. *Pacific Pioneers*, p. 77.
102. Bob Conner Diary, entry 10 June 1943.
103. Archives NZ, WAII, 1, DAZ 156/151/1 Historical Record of the 37th Bn for the month of April 1944, entry 10 April 1944.
104. Barrowclough to NZ Prime Minister, Report on Operations 3NZ Division, 5 August 1944.
105. Personnel File, NZ Defence Force, Base Records, Trentham, F.C. Cornwall.
106. Archives NZ, HQ 3NZ Div Admin order No. 8, 25 February 1944.
107. Archives NZ, CAJM W5726 22899 Box 4 Sickness in the Solomons, 18 April 1944, RMO 29 NZ Lt AA Regt.
108. Argus 7, Report, p. 46.
109. *Headquarters*, p. 261.
110. *The Tanks*, p. 211.

111. Interview Ross Templeton, Authors Collection.
112. *Pacific Kiwis*, p. 122.
113. George Laing, 3NZ Division Newsletter, p. 14.
114. Interview with the author, 15 July 2007.
115. Stout and Duncan, *Medical Services*, p. 101.
116. Albert E. Cowdrey, *Fighting for Life: American Military Medicine in World War II* (New York: The Free Press, 1994), p. 63.
117. Interview with the author, 15 July 2007.
118. Routine order, no 47, 3NZ Divisional Artillery, 28 February 1944.
119. Archives NZ, CAJM W5276 22899 Box 4 Personal file of Col. O.K. Speight, ADMS 3NZ Div. Map Unit Malaria Control Areas.
120. Gillespie, p. 192.
121. *Pacific Saga*, p. 92
122. *Pacific Kiwis*, p. 124.
123. Interview with the author, 15 July 2007.
124. Doug Ross Narrative. Author's collection.
125. Archives NZ WAII, 1, DAZ, 22/1/20–30 Routine Order no 45, 7 February 1944.
126. *Ibid.*, Routine Order no. 46, 26 February 1944.
127. *Headquarters*, p. 261.
128. *Ibid.*, p. 261.
129. *The Tanks*, pp. 53–58.
130. *The Tanks*, p. 129.
131. Ross, p. 268.
132. Ross, p. 270.
133. For a full account of the disaster, see Bryan Cox, *Too Young to Die: The Story of a New Zealand Fighter Pilot in the Pacific War* (Auckland: Century Hutchinson, 1987), pp. 123–132.
134. Sakaida, p. 58.
135. Bruce Gamble, *Target: Rabaul* (Minneapolis: Zenith Press, 2013), p. 350.
136. Cited in Sakaida, p. 60.
137. Archives NZ, Puttick 5, W1427/5 Barrowclough to Puttick, 2 February 1944.
138. Archives NZ, AD12, 28/5 Major General A.J. Barnett, HQUSAFISP to COMSOPAC, 19 March 1944.
139. *The Tanks*, p. 60.
140. Historical Record of 37th Bn for the month of April 1944, entry 7 April 1944.
141. Corporal James, entry 16–30 April.
142. *The Tanks*, pp. 131–2.
143. *Headquarters*, p. 263.
144. Gavin Long, *The Final Campaigns* (Canberra: Australian War Memorial, 1963), p. 22.
145. Karl James, *The Hard Slog: Australians in the Bougainville Campaign 1944–45* (New York: Cambridge University Press, 2012), p. 43.
146. James, pp. 73–75.
147. Long, *The Final Campaigns*, p. 201.

Chapter Eleven

1. *Coast Guard at War*, p. 72.
2. Hiroyuki Shindo, "Holding on to the Finish: The Japanese Army in the South and Southwest Pacific, 1944–45," in *Australia 1944–45: Victory in the Pacific*, ed. Peter Dean (Port Melbourne, Victoria: Cambridge University Press, 2016), p. 62.
3. *Ibid.*
4. Gillespie, p. 193.
5. Stephen R. Taafe, *MacArthur's Jungle War: The 1944 New Guinea Campaign* (Lawrence: Kansas University Press, 1998), p. 75.

Bibliography

Books

Alexander, Joseph H. *Storm Landings: Epic Amphibious Battles in the Central Pacific.* Annapolis: Naval Institute, 1997.

_____. *Utmost Savagery: The Three Days of Tarawa.* Annapolis: Naval Institute, 1995.

Army Board. *Guadalcanal to Nissan: With the Third New Zealand Division through the Solomons.* Wellington: Army Board, 1945.

Bergerud, Eric. *Fire in the Sky: The Air War in the South Pacific.* Boulder, CO: Westview Press, 2000.

_____. *Touched by Fire: The Land War in the South Pacific.* New York: Penguin, 1996.

Bulkley, Robert J., Jr. *At Close Quarters: PT Boats in the United States Navy.* Washington, D.C.: Naval History Division, 1962.

Clausewitz, Carl von. *On War.* New York: Alfred A. Knopf, 1993.

Cowdrey, Albert E. *Fighting for Life: American Military Medicine in World War II.* New York: The Free Press, 1994.

Cox, Bryan. *Too Young to Die. The Story of a New Zealand Fighter Pilot in the Pacific War.* Auckland: Century Hutchinson, 1987.

Crawford, John. "Major General Sir Harold Barrowclough: Leadership and Command in Two World Wars," in *Born to Lead: Portraits of New Zealand Commanders.* Ed. Glyn Harper and Joel Hayward. Auckland: Exisle Press, 2003, pp. 144–163.

Dean, Peter J., ed. *Australia 1944–45: Victory in the Pacific.* POA Melbourne, Victoria, Australia: Cambridge University Press, 2016.

Denoon, Donald, ed. *The Cambridge History of the Pacific Islands.* Cambridge: Cambridge University Press, 1997.

Dorny, Louis B. *US Navy PBY Catalina Units of the Pacific War.* Oxford: Osprey, 2007.

Dorr, Robert F. *B-24 Liberator Units of the Pacific War.* Oxford: Osprey, 1999.

Drea, Edward L. *Japan's Imperial Army: Its Rise and Fall, 1853–1945.* Lawrence: University of Kansas Press, 2009.

Ewing, Steve. *American Cruisers of World War II.* Missoula, MT: Pictorial Histories, 1997.

Gillespie, Oliver. *The Pacific.* Wellington: War History Branch, 1952.

Harper, Glyn, and Joel Hayward, eds. *Born to Lead? Portraits of New Zealand Commanders.* Auckland: Exisle Press, 2003.

Henderson, Alan, David Green, and Peter Cooke. *The Gunners: A History of New Zealand Artillery.* Auckland: Penguin Group NZ, 2008.

Hove, Duane T. *American Warriors: Five Presidents in the Pacific Theater of World War II.* Shippensburg, PA: Burd Street Press, 2003.

Hoyt, Edwin P. *Nimitz and His Admirals: How They Won the War in the Pacific.* Guildford, CT: Lyons Press, 2002.

James, Karl. *The Hard Slog: Australians in the Bougainville Campaign, 1944–45.* New York: Cambridge University Press, 2012.

Johnson, Frank D. *United States PT-Boats of World War II in Action.* Poole, Dorset: Blandford Press, 1983.

Kenney, George C. *General Kenney Reports: A Personal History of the Pacific War*. New York: Duell, Sloane and Pearce, 1949.

Long, Gavin. *The Final Campaigns*. Canberra: Australian War Memorial, 1963.

Lorelli, John. *To Foreign Shores: US Amphibious Operations in World War II*. Annapolis: Naval Institute Press, 1995.

Meyers, Bruce F. *Swift, Silent and Deadly: Marine Amphibious Reconnaissance in the Pacific, 1942–45*. Annapolis: Naval Institute Press, 2004.

Miller, John. *Cartwheel: The Reduction of Rabaul*. Washington, D.C.: Center of Military History, United States Army, 1990.

Morison, Samuel Eliot. *History of United States Naval Operations in World War II*, vol. 6: *Breaking the Bismarcks Barrier, 22 July 1942–1 May 1944*. Edison, NJ: Castle Books, 2001.

Newell, Reg. *The Battle for Vella Lavella: The Allied Recapture of Solomon Islands Territory, August 15–September 9, 1943*. Jefferson, NC: McFarland, 2016.

———. *Operation Goodtime and the Battle of the Treasury Islands, 1943*. Jefferson, NC: McFarland, 2012.

———. *Pacific Star: 3NZ Division in the South Pacific in World War 2*. Auckland: Exisle Press, 2015.

Newsome, Bruce Oliver. *Valentine Infantry Tank, 1938–45*. Oxford: Osprey, 2016.

Nila, Gary, and Robert Rolfe A. *Japanese Special Naval Landing Forces*. Oxford: Osprey, 2006.

Plowman, Jeffrey. *Rampant Dragons: New Zealanders in Armour in World War II*. Christchurch: Kiwi Armour, 2002.

Plowman, Jeffrey, and Malcolm Thomas. *New Zealand Armour in the Pacific, 1939–45*. Christchurch: Kiwi Armour, 2001.

Prados, John. *Islands of Destiny: The Solomon Islands Campaign and the Eclipse of the Rising Sun*. New York: New American Library, 2012.

Rennie, Frank. *Regular Soldier: A Life in the New Zealand Army*. Auckland: Endeavour Press, 1986.

Rentz, John. *Bougainville and the Northern Solomons*. Washington, D.C.: Historical Section, Headquarters USMC, 1948.

Ross, J.M.S. *Royal New Zealand Air Force*. Wellington: Department of Internal Affairs, 1955.

Rottman, Gordon. *Pacific Island Guide: A Geo-Military Study*. Westport, CT: Greenwood Press, 2002.

———. *US World War II Amphibious Tactics: Army & Marine Corps, Pacific Theatre*. Oxford: Osprey, 2004.

Sakaida, Henry. *The Siege of Rabaul*. St. Paul, MN: Phalanx, 1996.

Shaw, Henry I., and Douglas T. Kane. *Isolation of Rabaul: History of US Marine Corps Operations in World War II*, vol. 2. Washington, D.C.: Historical Branch, Headquarters, USMC, 1963.

Shindu, Hiroyuki. "Holding on to the Finish: The Japanese Army in the South and Southwest Pacific, 1944–1945," in *Australia 1944–45: Victory in the Pacific*. Ed. Peter Dean. Port Melbourne: Victoria, 2016, pp. 51–76.

Shock, James R. *The US Army Barrage Balloon Program*, 5th ed. Bennington, VT: Merriam Press, 2012.

Stout, T., and M. Duncan. *Medical Services in New Zealand and the Pacific*. Wellington: War History Branch, Department of Internal Affairs, 1958.

Taafe, Stephen R. *MacArthur's Jungle War: The 1944 New Guinea Campaign*. Lawrence: University of Kansas Press, 1997.

Third Division Histories Committee. *The Gunners: An Intimate Record of Units of the 3rd New Zealand Divisional Artillery in the Pacific from 1940 until 1945*. Wellington: A.H. & A.W. Reed, 1948.

———. *Headquarters: A Brief Outline of the Activities of Headquarters of the Third Division and the 8th and 14th Brigades During their Service in the Pacific*. Wellington: A.H. & A.W. Reed, 1947.

———. *Pacific Kiwis: Being the Story of the Service in the Pacific of the 30th Battalion, Third Division, Second New Zealand Expeditionary Force*. Wellington: A.H. & A.W. Reed, 1947.

_____. *Pacific Pioneers: The Story of the Engineers of the New Zealand Expeditionary Force in the Pacific.* Wellington: A.H. & A.W. Reed, 1947.

_____. *Pacific Saga: The Personal Chronicle of the 37th Battalion and Its Part in the Third Division's Campaign in the Pacific.* Wellington: A.H. & A.W. Reed, 1947.

_____. *Pacific Service: The Story of the New Zealand Army Service Units with the Third Division in the Pacific.* Wellington: A.H. & A.W. Reed, 1948.

_____. *Shovel, Sword and Scalpel: A Record of Service of Medical Units in the Second New Zealand Expeditionary Force in the Pacific.* Wellington: A.H. & A.W. Reed, 1945.

_____. *Tanks: An Unofficial History of the Activities of the Third New Zealand Division Tank Squadron in the Pacific* [*Incorporates MMG and Ordnance*]. Wellington: A.H. & A.W. Reed, 1947.

_____. *The 35th Battalion: A Record of Service of the 35th Battalion with the Third Division in the Pacific,* Wellington: A.H. & A.W. Reed, 1947.

Tillman, Barrett. *US Marine Corps Fighter Squadrons of World War II,* Oxford: Osprey Publishing, 2014.

Waters, S.D. *Royal New Zealand Navy.* Wellington: Government Printer, 1956.

White, B.T. (*AFV 6) Valentine Infantry Tank Mark III.* Windsor, Berkshire, England: Profile Publications, 1969.

Wolf, William. *13th Fighter Command in World War II: Air Combat over Guadalcanal and the Solomons.* Atglen, PA: Schiffer Military History, 2004.

Theses

Mawdsley, Shaun. "'With the Utmost Precision and Team Play': The 3rd New Zealand Division and Operation Squarepeg." Master's thesis, Massey University, 2013.

Newell, Reginald Hedley. "New Zealand's Forgotten Warriors: 3NZ Division in the South Pacific in World War II." Ph.D. diss., Massey University, 2008.

Interviews and Correspondence with the Author

Bioletti, Harry
Rose, John
Ross, Doug
Templeton, Ross
Tucker, Ron
Williams, David

Archival Material

Alexander Turnbull Library, Wellington, New Zealand.
Archives New Zealand, Wellington, New Zealand.
Australian National Archives, Canberra, Australia.
Australian War Memorial, Canberra, Australia.
National Archives and Record Administration, Washington, United States.

Diaries

Barrowclough, Harold Eric, GOC, 3NZ Division.
Conner, Robert (Bob), C Company, 93 NCB.

Magazine Articles

"Jungle Battle—Japanese Routed." *New Zealand Herald,* March 13, 1944.
MacDonald, Charles. "Lindbergh in Battle." *Colliers,* February 16, 1946; February 23, 1946.
Plowman, Jeffrey. "Pacific Dragons Into the Solomons with the NZ Valentines." *Military Modelcraft International* 17, Number 4 (February 2013): pp. 33–41.

Websites

Australian Official War Histories: www.awm.gov.au/collection/awmohww2/.
Bob Hope USO Shows: http://www.loc.gov/exhibits/bobhope/uso.html.
Bulkley, Robert J., Jr. *At Close Quarters: PT Boats in the United States Navy.*

Washington, D.C.: Naval History Division, 1962. https://www.ibiblio.org/hyperwar/USN/CloseQuarters/PT-2.html.

"Charles Lindbergh in Combat, 1944." Eyewitness to History: http://www.eyewitnesstohistory.com/lindbergh2.htm.

Diary of Robert W. Conner, 93rd NCB: http://www.seabees93.net.

Dictionary of American Naval Fighting Ships: www.hazegray.org/danfs/.

Hyperwar: *The Coast Guard at War, VI: The Pacific.* https://www.ibiblio.org/hyperwar/USCG/VI-Pacific/USCG-VI-6.html.

Milton Bush's Website on the Green Islands: www.seabees93.net/GI%20Green%20Island%206th%20ED.htm. Milton Bush served as a Seabee with the 93rd Naval Construction Battalion. His website is a mine of information on the Green Islands.

NARA Argus Unit 7 leaves Guadalcanal lands on Green Island 25 February 1944. ARC Identifier 76244, Local Identifier 428-NPC 1890. Color footage.

NARA Identifier 76245 Local Identifier 428-NPC-1891. Color footage of the offloading of troops and supplies and Argus setup.

NARA—Naval Photographic Centre Film, No. 1527, NARA Identifier 76049: https://research.archives.gov/id/76049. This shows the invasion craft, planes overhead, tanks being unloaded etc.

NARA—Naval Photographic Centre Film, No.15649 NARA Identifier 76053: https://research.archives.gov/id/76053. Aerial views of Invasion Task Force entering Green Island Lagoon, 2/15/44. This shows views from a plane circling above the invasion convoy and captures the landing craft entering the lagoon.

NZ Official War Histories: http://nzetc.victoria.ac.nz//tm/scholarly/tei-corpus-WH2.html.

The Operational History of the 3rd New Zealand Tank Squadron: http://www.kiwisinarmour.hobbyvista.com/.

Recollections of Captain Junius T. Jarman, USC & GS: www.history.noaa.gov/stories_tales/pathfinder7.html.

USS *St. Louis* Association: www.ussstlouis.com/green_island_operation.htm.

United States Navy Argus Unit Historical Group: https://argusunits.wordpress.com.

Video of USS *St. Louis* crew veterans: http//www.youtube.com/wasth?V=PTXBSOxIZ4.

Index

Acorn Units 11
Adams, Capt. P.R. (NZ) 117
Ainsworth, Rear Adm. W.L. (USN) 67
air raids 38, 39, 128, 137, 149, 174, 67–71, 73, 75, 99, 105
airfield construction 130–132
alcohol, beer 136, 155; illicit stills 136
Aldis Lamp 32
Alexander, Joseph (historian) 57, 79
amphibious warfare 3, 11, 15, 56, 57
ANGAU 23
Archer, Lt. F.P. (ANGAU) 23, 34, 150
Argus, Unit 7, 13, 127, 11
Australian troops on the Green Islands 170–171

Barahun 8, 9, 29, 24–25, 28, 29, 32, 41, 46, 47, 60, 103
Barnett, General (U.S. Army) 168
barrage balloons 55, 64–65, 75, 76, 125
Barrowclough, H.E. 6, 12–14, 21–22, 49, 52–53, 63, 80, 102, 105, 117, 118, 134, 156, 173
Bartos, Lieutenant (NZ) 62
battalion combat teams 63–64
Beach Red, Green, Blue 44, 56, 78, 79, 85
Beban, Pat (NZ) 111
Beetham, Sgt. R.H. (NZ) 111, 114
Bennett (U.S. Navy ship) 26
Bennett, Lt. Col. P.L. 52, 144–145
Benny, Jack (U.S. entertainer) 147
Bioletti, Harry (NZ) 31–32, 31, 39, 42, 50, 64, 160,
Bishop, Pvt. L.J. (NZ) 37
Bougainville 4, 6, 7, 8, 9, 18, 27, 29, 45, 63, 67, 91, 105, 125, 142, 164, 171, 172
Brickhouse, Walter 69
Brooker, Capt. L.F. (NZ) 62
Bruton, James Clement (USN) 39
Bryant, A.E. (USN) 37
Bulkey, Robert (historian) 20
Bull, John (NZ) 161–163
Bullen, Maj. A.B. (NZ) 38, 114
Burk, Lt. James (USN) 148

Burnie, Sgt. J.W. (NZ) 92
Bush, Milton 149
Busk, Commander V.K. (USN) 55

Cain, Capt. J.R. (USN) 30, 39
cargo cult 45
Carter, Capt. G.B. (USN) 55, 76
Chew, William C. 70
command arrangements 141
commando raid on the Green Islands 18–51; attack by Japanese Zero fighters 38–39; casualties 37, 39; Japanese reaction 49–50; withdrawal 40–42
Conner, Seabee Bob 122, 125, 155
Constant (U.S. Navy ship) 72
Cornwall, Lt. Col. Frederick C. 22–23, 26, 37
Corsairs, F 4U, 143, 164, 165, 166, 167
Cox, Troop Commander Frank (NZ) 85
Cunningham, Vernon Michael (USN) 39
Cutler, R.W. (USNR) 55

Daihatus 17, 48
Davidson, Cpl. P.A. (NZ) 107, 108
Dement, Pvt. F.W. (NZ) 48
de Vere, Lt. C.A.L. (NZ) 111, 113
Dickerson (U.S. Navy ship) 26, 28, 30, 42
drones 167
Duff, Brigadier (NZRA) 84, 152
Dumas, Brigadier General (USA) 73
Dunlea, Corp. L.N. (NZ) 123

Evans, Lt. T.K. (NZ) 111, 112

field cookers 95, 105
Fifth Echelon 132
First Echelon 72–87
Flint, Maj. Arthur (British Army) 62–63, 85, 113–114
Forward, Lt. Jack (NZ) 120
Fourth Echelon 126–127
Fullam (U.S. Navy ship) 26, 42

Gamble, W.A. (NZ Army) 105
garbage and sanitation 152

212 INDEX

Gillespie, Oliver (historian) (NZ) 83, 95, 101
Green Combat Paint 64
Green Islands: Barahun 9, 25, 32, 47; Hon 7; Nissan 7, 8, 9, 109; North Channel 8; Pinipel 7 8, 9, 119; Pokonian Plantation 7, 29, 43, 44, 46, 47, 49, 60, 93, 105, 125; Sirot 107, 108; South Channel 8; Tanaheran 7, 110–118; Tangalan Plantation 7, 9, 60, 96, 101; Tapangat Inlet 32; Torahatup 7, 108; Yotchibal Village 9
Greenlees, R.M. (USN) 37
Guadalcanal 3, 14, 21, 63, 64, 72, 85, 135, 149; Kukum Beach 53, 63
Guest (U.S. Navy ship) 26
gunboats, fire support 77

Hallright, Major (NZ) 150–151
Halsey, Adm. William (USN) 4–5, 54, 118, 134
Hardy Lieutenant (USN) 78
Harghbergher, Lt. Col. John (USMC) 91
Harrall, William F. 69
Haughland, Vern (U.S. reporter) 36, 37, 95
health 156–160
Hickey, Pvt. J.E. 41
Hinds, John 69
Holden, Lt. D. (NZT) 114
Honolulu (U.S. Navy ship) 68
Hope, Bob 146–147
Hosking, Pvt E.L. (NZ) 30
Hudson (U.S. Navy ship) 26

Imperial Japanese Navy 3, 17; Special Naval Landing Force 15–16
Irwin, Maj. R.M. (NZ) 129
islanders 44, 45, 149–152; Allies intel gathering 18, 103–104; attitude to Allies 50–51; attitude to Japanese 17, 18, 50–51; health 149–152; population 8–9

James, Corporal (NZ) 122, 155, 169
Japanese weapons, capture 109, 129–130
Jarman, Junius T. 23–24, 133–134
Jensen, Arthur Rolland (USNR) 39
Johns, Corp. H. (NZ) 114

Katz, Larry (U.S.) 151
Keefe, Flt. Lt. Francis G. (NZ) 166–167
Keith, Capt. Ron (NZ) 120
Kenney (USAAF) 89
King, Commander in Chief Ernest (USN) 5
Konam (Solomon Islands constabulary) 37
Koontz, Ralph 70

Langford, Frances 147
Laurence, Sgt. William 84
Liberator, B-25 19, 161, 162, 163
Liberty ships 155
Lightning P-38 45
Lindbergh, Charles A. (U.S.) 143–4

MacArthur, Gen. Douglas (U.S. Army) 4, 124, 125, 173
Maita (Solomon Islands constabulary) 37
malaria 158–160
Marley, C.F. (USN) 94
Marston, Matting 98
McIlroy, John H. (USN) 87
Menominee (U.S. Navy ship) 66
Merrill, Rear Adm. A.S. (USN) 67
Miller, E.E. (USN) 37
minesweepers 77
Mitchell, B-25 74
Montevideo Maru 9
Morrison, Samuel Eliot (historian) 51
Murphy, Bill (USN) 69
Murray, Lt. Col. A. (NZ) 61, 195
Myers, Wayne B. (USNR) 77

Nimitz, Adm. Chester (USN) 5
Nisei 119
Nixon, Lt. R.M. (U.S.) 141–146
NZ Units; 3 NZ Division 14 Brigade 6, 13, 52 63, 72, 93, 107, 110, 124, 158, 168, 173;3 NZ Division 8 Brigade 13, 52, 63, 113, 168; 3Z Division Tank Squadron 85, 100; 4 Field Security 123, 150; 17 NZ Field Regiment 60; 20 Field Company 154, 155; 22 Field Ambulance 125, 126; 24 Field Ambulance 150; 29 Lt AA 196; 30 Battalion 21, 23, 31, 27, 81, 102, 103, 107, 108; 35 Battalion 104; 37 Battalion 95, 103, 104, 105, 109; 38th Field Park Company 25; 144 Battery 60, 107; HQ Division Engineers 91; Machine Gun Co. 82, 101, 120; NZ Engineers 91–92; NZ Signal Corps 93–94; NZASC—4 MT Co. 89, 181

O'Dowd, Lt. Peter (NZ) 37, 50
Ogpu 140–141
Operation Cartwheel 4–6
Operation Goodtime 13, 46, 134
Operation Squarepeg, Planning 52–66

Pathfinder (U.S. Navy ship) 24
Philip (U.S. Navy ship) 74
Plunket, Flt. Lt. Jack M. (USMC) 91
Potter, Leslie 13, 14, 42, 141
Powles, Maj. Guy R. (NZ) 86
Pringle (U.S. Navy ship) 74
provosts 141
PT boats 5, 19, 20, 28, 29, 46, 47, 77, 78, 98–99, 147–149
Purvis Bay, Florida Island 70, 71
Puttick, Lt. Gen. Edward (NZ) 21, 168

Rabaul 4, 5, 6, 7, 9, 45, 49, 125, 164–5, 172, 173
radars 60, 127–128
radios 25, 41, 93
Ratcliffe, Corp. L.G. (NZ) 115

rations 15, 106
Reid, Lance Corp. C. (NZ) 107
Rennie, Lt. Frank (NZ) 29, 39
Renshaw (U.S. Navy ship) 73, 74
RNZAF 54, 89–91, 164–167, 172; *Ventura* 32–33, 40, 165, 166
Robertson, Chaplain (NZ) 111
Robinson, Lt. E.C. (NZ) 123
Robson, Flight Lieutenant (RAAF) 9
Rose, John (NZ) 12, 140, 158
Ross, Doug (NZ) 83, 119
Rutherford, Maj. Jim (NZ) 62, 63, 111, 114

St. Louis (U.S. Navy ship) 67–71
Saufley (U.S. Navy ship) 74
Sawyer, Dorothy (U.S. nurse) 144–145
Schwable, Col. Frank (USMC) 91
Second Echelon 65, 121
Seventh Echelon 137
shipping 156
Sigourney (U.S. Navy ship) 74, 90
Sioux (U.S. Navy ship) 66
Skow, Lt. Col. Floyd (U.S. Army) 88
Smith, Cmdr. J. MacDonald (USN) 31, 34, 35, 37, 96, 97, 98
South Pacific Combat Air Transport Command (SCAT) 141–143
Stannard, Corp. Roy (NZ) 111, 116
stevedoring 137
strategic landscape, January 1944, 3–6
Stronach, Capt. J.F.B. (NZ) 110, 111
Sugden, Lieutenant Colonel (NZ) 62, 169
Sweeney, Cmdr. J.D. (USN) 26, 28, 30

Talbot (U.S. Navy ship) 26, 27, 28, 37
Tally, Ollie J. (USN) 148–149

tanks, *Valentine* 62–63, 78, 85, 100, 103, 110–117
Taylor, Lt. E.G. (NZ) 107, 108
tea 140
Templeton, Driver Ross (NZ) 89, 136, 149, 157
theaters 155
Theobold, W. (USN) 88
Third Echelon 125
Tolich, Pvt. I.N. (NZ) 108
Trimble, Lt. M.S. (USNR) 78
Tucker, Ron (NZ) 75, 82

U.S. Coast and Geodetic Survey 24
USMC 11, 16, 21; night fighters 91

Val (Aichi D3A) 67, 68, 69, 75
Van Deusen, H.P. (USN) 37
Varnham, Sgt. L.R. (NZ) 139
Vella Lavella 6, 46, 58, 59, 63, 134

Waller (U.S. Navy ship) 73, 74
Warnock, E.B. (USNR) 78
Warren Harland D. (USNR) 83
water 101, 138–140; coconut milk 79, 138; desalinization 138–140; divining 139
Waters (U.S. Navy ship) 26, 27, 28, 42
Wilkinson, Adm. Theodore Stark (USN) 6, 19, 23, 53, 83, 134
Williams, David (NZ) 141, 158
Wolf, William (aviation historian) 131

Zero 3, 38, 39